THE EXTRAORDINARY LIFE OF THE

WILDLIFE MAN

David Ireland was once a boy weakened by severe asthma attacks. He was given a speech impediment by a negligent doctor, was bullied at school and was made an example of by teachers who predicted he would never achieve anything. Those teachers could not have been more wrong, because now David's Wildlife Man films are seen by millions of people around the globe and his dream to highlight the plight of wild animals fighting to survive in the modern world is a reality.

www.davidireland.com

THE EXTRAORDINARY LIFE OF THE

WILDLIFE MAN

Death-defying encounters with crocs, sharks and wild animals

DAVID IRELAND

with Tom Trumble

MICHAEL JOSEPH
an imprint of
PENGUIN BOOKS

MICHAEL JOSEPH

UK | USA | Canada | Ireland | Australia
India | New Zealand | South Africa | China

Penguin Books is part of the Penguin Random House group of companies
whose addresses can be found at global.penguinrandomhouse.com.

Penguin
Random House
Australia

First published by Penguin Australia Pty Ltd, 2016

10 9 8 7 6 5 4 3 2 1

Cover design by Alex Ross © Penguin Australia Pty Ltd
Text design by Samantha Jayaweera © Penguin Australia Pty Ltd
Front cover photograph by Sam Ruttyn, back cover Shutterstock
Typeset in Sabon 11pt/17pt by Samantha Jayaweera, Penguin Australia Pty Ltd
Colour separation by Splitting Image Colour Studio, Clayton, Victoria

Printed and bound in Australia by Griffin Press, an accredited ISO AS/NZS
14001 Environmental Management Systems printer.

National Library of Australia
Cataloguing-in-Publication data:

Ireland, David, author.
The extraordinary life of the Wildlife Man / David Ireland with Tom Trumble
9780143797036 (paperback)
Ireland, David.
Wildlife conservationists--Australia--Biography.
Zoologists--Australia--Biography.
Motion picture producers and
directors--Australia--Biography.
Other Creators/Contributors: Trumble, Tom, author.

597.9092

penguin.com.au

Contents

This book is a work of non-fiction. I have tried to recreate events and conversations from my memories of them. In some instances, names and identifying details have been changed to protect the privacy of individuals.

Prologue

I can tell you a lot about fear.

In my line of work as a wildlife filmmaker, being able to control fear is critical. I'm not saying I've conquered it. Even if that were possible, I'm not sure I'd want to be truly fearless. After all, fear can be useful – giving you strength and speed you never knew existed or warning of unseen threats. What I'm talking about is the mastery of fear. In this game, knowing when to obey fear and when to ignore it is often the difference between life and death.

Of course, there's more to pulling together a film than keeping your emotions in check. Subject knowledge, soundtrack, cinematography and editing are all important. The job even requires some flair and theatricality to win over viewers, as well as a natural instinct for storytelling. But I'm under no illusions: people watch my films because they expect to see me risk life and limb. If I didn't know how to control my fear I'd almost certainly be dead by now. Because make no mistake, what I do for a living is extremely dangerous.

In 2006, Steve 'Crocodile Hunter' Irwin died when a bull ray's barb pierced his heart during a film shoot off Port Douglas. Three years earlier, Timothy 'Grizzly Man' Treadwell, the naturalist, documentary maker and bear enthusiast, was mauled to death while filming brown bears in Alaska. And in 2010, Malcolm Douglas – an adventurer and pioneering filmmaker the Indigenous communities of the Great Sandy Desert referred to as the 'white-fella bushman' – died in a freak car accident on his wildlife park in Broome. These guys were at the top of their game. They'd wracked up hundreds of hours filming in perilous situations. They were pros.

They also knew the risks involved. Does that mean they had a death wish? I can't speak for the dead, but I doubt it. I certainly don't. I love life and I'm passionate about nature and wildlife.

The risks I take are, in some ways, driven out of a desire to bring nature into people's living rooms. But there's more to it than entertaining and informing people. Those things alone won't sustain you in this business. Nor will the money. Financially, I've lost as much as I've made and, at times, the time spent away from home has put incredible pressure on my family, nearly costing me the things I hold most precious. I won't pretend that, despite the difficulties I've endured, I've loved every minute of it. No man loves having double pneumonia and dengue fever or having his back broken by a whale or ribs shattered by a wild boar. And selling my house to repay debts and being dragged through the courts when business deals went south were not pleasant experiences.

So why do I do it? I'll admit I'm a sucker for adventure. When I read about Special Forces soldiers going into battle, mountaineers summiting the highest peaks or solo sailors attempting to circumnavigate the globe, I understand what they mean when they describe feeling most alive when they're near death. I've had that feeling while handfeeding bull sharks, filming inside the jaws of a saltwater crocodile, looking into the black eyes of a great white shark or feeling the breath of a lion as he devours a wildebeest. But I'm driven by something more complex than simply thrillseeking.

My life story has been one of continual self-discovery. I've made plenty of mistakes and probably failed more times than I've succeeded. But years of working with the most dangerous animals on the planet has taught me more about human nature, human capability and human fallibility than any psychology degree could have. Of all the things I've learnt, two things stand out.

First, that fear in all its forms – fear of failure, fear of humiliation, fear of pain, fear of loneliness, fear of destitution, fear of death – holds us back. Second, that we all have the courage and power within us to overcome fear. I am living proof of the truth of these statements. The story of how I became the Wildlife Man is really a story about how I learnt to master fear.

To understand these things I need to take you back to where it began for me. So clear your head of any preconceived ideas of what you think I was like as a young person and instead envisage an abnormally skinny boy of five. I want you to picture that kid lying in bed, his feet twisted in the sheets, his hands clawing at the mattress, his eyes bulging from his head, his face turning blue. Terrified.

Part One

HEROES AND VILLAINS

The Young Boy and the Sea Monster

The black clouds always came at night, sweeping into my dreams like a thunderstorm. They'd come in so quickly there was never hope of outrunning them. In the mass of swirling sulfurous smoke, wispy tendrils would reach out towards me, as if death itself was extending its fingers around my throat.

My eyes would snap open in the pitch black. My blankets felt like they were lead-lined, squeezing me under their weight. I couldn't breathe! With every ounce of strength, I'd kick them off. But it made no difference. It felt like the air had been sucked out of my bedroom. My chest was going to explode.

Images would float across my field of vision – light spilling into the room from the hallway; my parents pushing open the bedroom door; Dad hopping into my bed. He'd lift me into his arms, placing me gently on his lap. With one hand resting on my chest and the other on my shoulder, Dad would begin drawing exaggerated breaths, whispering instructions in my ear to breathe slowly. The rhythm of his rising and falling chest gave me something to anchor my own breathing to. Eventually, I'd be matching my father, breath for breath. If I was lucky, the ball of tension would ease after a few minutes. During a particularly severe attack, it'd take much longer.

The trauma of those asthma attacks stains my earliest memories of life. I grew up with a sense that death stalked my every move. The only positive thing to come of my asthma was that it brought me closer to my old man.

Dad was the classic strong, silent type. He was a powerfully built man, with a round chest and thick arms. He grew up in Lismore, in northern New South Wales, and worked as a timber cutter, lopping down massive cedar trees with an axe and loading them onto bullock trains. When the First World War broke out, he enlisted in the Australian Imperial Force. Dad was a stretcher-bearer, lifting the wounded out of no-man's-land. He also saw plenty of action, one time finding himself in close-quarter combat after a German charge breached his trench. I heard that he bayoneted a soldier to death, but I don't know for certain. Dad never spoke about the war.

The Western Front changed him. Devoutly Christian before the war, Dad returned home an atheist who drank and gambled more than was good for him. His first marriage failed, but not before it produced two children – my half siblings, Dusty and Joan. He lived as a bachelor for some time, until he met my mother, Lotus.

A different war touched my mother. Her first husband, Colin Twist, a wireless air gunner in the RAAF who crewed B-24 Liberators in the Second World War, was brought down over New Guinea. Colin and two other airmen survived the crash but were captured by the Japanese and beheaded. Colin left behind a five-year-old son, Michael.

There were very few working options for widowed mothers in those days. In that sense, marrying a man like my father, who had established a promising career selling insurance in the interwar period for the AMP Society, was fortunate. But it was far from one-way. Mum brought stability to Dad's life and probably helped keep traumatic memories of the trenches at bay.

But she never managed to cure his gambling addiction. Dad's big wins were matched by even bigger losses. Sometimes, they happened on the same night. Dad once caught a string of golden cards in poker, winning an entire block of terrace homes in the now highly prized Sydney suburb of Paddington before losing it all on the next hand. If he'd quit while he was ahead, my family would be millionaires! But that's the story of all gamblers. They don't know how to stop.

For all his faults, Dad was a good man. His relationship with the children of his first marriage was nevertheless strained. Dusty and Joan were largely absent from my early adolescence. In some ways, I think he regarded his second marriage as a second chance at family. He was a strong figure in my half brother Michael's formative years and when I came along in 1947, Dad doted on me. Still, I learnt very early not to make him angry. When the old man's blood was up it was a truly terrifying thing to behold.

I grew up in Lindfield in the northern suburbs of Sydney. It was an idyllic home surrounded by bush and teeming with wildlife. The one problem was our next-door neighbour. He was a mean-spirited loner whose favourite pastime was taking potshots at native birds with his air rifle. It seemed like every morning we'd wake up to find dead cockatoos and kookaburras strewn across our backyard.

I was obsessed with animals. I also felt a protective instinct towards them. Perhaps this stemmed from being saved at a very young age by an animal. It happened one winter's day at a place we called the Blue Pools. They were crystal clear rock pools in a nearby creek Michael and I often visited to fish for eels. Our family dog – a totally devoted and extremely intelligent border collie cross we named Skipper – always tagged along.

Michael and I had fished one large pool for over an hour without any success. So Michael went and fished further down the creek. It wasn't the most responsible thing for a brother to do, leave a younger sibling who couldn't swim near water. In fairness, Michael was only about twelve.

Soon after Michael left, I noticed a large eel snaking its way around the base of the rock pool. This was fantastic! I was desperate to catch him and impress my older brother and parents. I gently lowered the fishing line into the hole so as not to disturb the eel. But the current kept knocking the line against the walls of the rock pool, where the sinker and hook became stuck. I shimmied closer to the edge to bring the line clear of the walls. I took a seat on the moss-covered rocks that lined the edge of the pool, and slipped . . .

Childhood trauma has a way of remaining vivid in the mind for life. Whenever I recall that event, the memory of the shockingly icy water still makes my body seize up involuntarily. It was so cold, I couldn't scream. My arms were flailing about as I desperately reached out for the edge. But I'd fallen beyond reach. Water started pouring into my mouth. I disappeared beneath the surface. I was drowning.

Next thing I remember was a terrible pain in my shoulder. Skipper had jumped in and sunk his teeth under my collarbone and was dragging me. Michael heard the splashing and arrived just as Skipper was pulling me up the sandy flat bank on the opposite side of the pool. I'd always loved our dog. Now I felt bonded to him. He'd saved my life.

My love of animals was forged at that moment. I grew up from then with a soft spot for all creatures, particularly those most vulnerable. In my mind, there could be nothing more vicious than shooting harmless native birds. Dad had often visited our neighbour's house and threatened to call the police. He was probably worried that the idiot would miss the mark and hit one of us. It didn't have the desired effect. The neighbour simply made sure he did his shooting when Dad was at work. So Michael and I took matters into our own hands.

In those days, fireworks could be legally bought across the counter. Dad always had a ready supply to set off on New Year's Day. Michael was adept at converting a firework into a homemade 'bunger cannon', a tube that shot missiles. The trick was to cut the firework in half and empty the gunpowder into a water pipe that had been stopped at one end with clay. You'd then pack the other end with clay, using a candlewick as a fuse. Once lit, the flame made its way to the gunpowder, the explosive force catapulting anything else stuffed into the pipe with tremendous velocity. On a test model, Michael and I shot a ball bearing into a gum tree from about twenty yards away. The ball bearing buried itself into the trunk, never to be seen again. It was lethal but small, and the size of the projectile was limited to the diameter of the plastic tube. We wanted to make a statement. So we built something bigger. Much bigger . . .

Michael managed to source a disused downpipe big enough to hold a rock the size of a man's fist. He cut the pipe to size and filled it up with a huge quantity of gunpowder. Michael started looking around for a rock large enough to break the window before I struck on a better idea. In our backyard we had a chicken pen that we'd surrounded with rat-traps. That day one of the traps had snagged a particularly fat and juicy specimen. The dead rat fitted perfectly inside the pipe. To compensate for the extra weight of the rat, Michael loaded an especially large amount of gunpowder into the cannon. We aimed the cannon at the side of our neighbour's white weatherboard house.

Michael lit the fuse and we both stood back as the flame inched its way towards the clay. The tension was incredible. We knew it was rough justice. But if this guy felt it was okay to murder native animals and leave them in our yard, then we'd give him a taste of his own medicine. His howls of outrage would be as sweet as Dad's proud look as he admired our ingenuity. This was probably the greatest thing I'd ever done in my life!

When the cannon fired, the shockwave put us on our arses. It was deafening. The explosion was evidently powerful enough to shift the cannon on detonation. Because instead of smashing against the outside of the neighbour's house where we'd aimed it, the rat streaked across our yard like a furry missile, blasting through the window and exploding in our neighbour's hallway. It looked like someone had hurled a bucket of red paint at the hallway wall.

Dad came home breathing fire. He clipped Michael across the ears and smacked me hard on the bum. We were both sent to our bedroom. Michael and I stayed up all night talking about the day's event. We knew we were in massive trouble, but we didn't care. We thought it was fantastic!

Throughout the evening, we heard raised voices next door as Dad had it out with our neighbour. Whatever Dad said or did seemed to do the trick. Our neighbour never again shot at birds with his air rifle.

Those were carefree days in Lindfield. I spent most of my time outside exploring the national parks around our home. Even school was fun. Lindfield Primary was my sort of place, where outdoor activity was encouraged and students were permitted to attend class barefooted.

But the asthma never went away. In fact, the attacks became more frequent. This was before the days of ventolin inhalers. When the asthma attacks came, all I could do was ride them out. One theory kicking around at the time was that penicillin might cure an asthmatic. So, after every attack, my parents would take me to our local doctor to get a jab of penicillin. The injections did nothing but cause me pain. I began to hate them nearly as much as I hated the attacks.

The doctor eventually came up with a bogus theory that if my tonsils were removed I'd stand a better chance of making a recovery. How he arrived at this conclusion is a mystery. Maybe he thought that with my tonsils removed, a greater volume of air could reach my lungs. He assured us that it wasn't a radical procedure. But surgery, no matter how minor, has its risks. My parents went along with it all the same, probably concerned that if they didn't, my next asthma attack would be my last.

I don't remember much of what happened before the operation. But when I woke up, I couldn't speak. Whatever muscles the throat and mouth use to manipulate air into words were completely useless. The best I could manage was a wheezy moan that sounded like I was talking through my nose. The surgeon had inadvertently paralysed the palate in my mouth.

I had to learn how to speak from scratch. My father paid for a nurse to come around to our house on a weekly basis to conduct speech therapy. She'd get me to breathe bubbles through a straw into a glass of water. The only way I could redirect the air was to hold my nose. This was fine for blowing bubbles but I could hardly get around holding my nose every time I wanted to speak.

My doctor advised enrolling me in a school for the dumb. Mum and Dad wouldn't have a bar of it. They were worried that placing me in a school full of kids whose chances of gaining normal speech were unlikely would hinder my recovery. Instead, I was enrolled at Sydney Grammar, one of the most elite private schools in the country.

I was presented with a very smart school uniform, a pair of shiny black shoes and a boater hat. This was a far cry from the barefoot dress code of Lindfield Primary. I felt grown up. I saddled up for my first class, eager to make new friends. Everything changed the moment I opened my mouth to speak. Instead of reading the roll call, the teacher had each of us stand and say our name out loud.

Imagine saying your own name through your nose and you'll get a sense of the sound I produced. The whole class erupted into laughter. I sat down, humiliated.

I lived in a state of constant fear, literally afraid of my own voice. If a teacher selected me to summarise the lesson, my peers would spin around and face me with wide grins, eager to listen to the class freak stammer incomprehensibly through his nose. In no time, the bullies were onto me.

I copped my first hiding at recess towards the end of week one. I was walking through the playground and the next thing I knew I was flat on my face. I turned around to see a big, redheaded brute named Eddie Edwards standing over me. A few of his mates were laughing behind him. When I stood up, Edwards punched me in the face. The blood flowed from my nose and into my mouth, leaving a salty taste.

Edwards and his cronies made it their mission to make my life a misery. I had no older brothers to protect me – Michael was enrolled at the local secondary school – and no friends to rally behind me. The teachers were worse than useless. Sometimes, I got the feeling they even bullied me to win favour with the rest of the class. I spent my days at school hiding in the shadows, sick, weak and afraid.

I learnt that trying to outrun my tormentors was no good. Turning my back and running seemed only to stir their bloodlust. Later I'd learn the same rule applies in the wild. On the days when Edwards beat me up, I could do little but protect my head and fantasise about knocking the daylights out of him. Physically, I was no match for the bullies. The asthma had reduced my lung capacity, leaving me gasping for air after the slightest exertion.

Growing up, I longed to have the strength and physical presence of men like my father. I found a new set of heroes the moment I saw the film adaptation of *Moby Dick*. It was my kind of story: a mad sea captain hunting a giant white whale across the seven seas.

These days, I regard the hunting of whales a despicable act. As a youngster, I found the idea of men in open boats in a showdown with the largest creatures in the world the ultimate demonstration of bravery.

I used to play the scenes of *Moby Dick* out in my head, painting everything with vivid detail. This was the fantasy world into which I'd journey to escape my tormentors. My favourite scene was about halfway through the film where Queequeg – the muscular and tattooed son of a South Sea chieftain – stands at the prow of an open boat and hurls a harpoon into a whale.

I used to imagine myself into Queequeg's whaleboat. I could see the flukes of the whale and its tail crashing into the sea, the salty water splashing across the crew's jubilant faces. I'd throw the harpoon and cheer triumphantly as it plunged deep into the whale's blubber. The rope, fixed at one end to the harpoon and tied off to the boat's bollard, would go taut as the whale pulled us along. It was an exhilarating thought. But the dream was not enough. I wanted to experience the real thing and I knew just the place to do it.

By now, the family had moved to a house in St Ives, very close to the school campus. Home was only a short walk from Cowan Creek, a tidal catchment of the Hawkesbury River. I used to spend hours in my canoe, exploring the riverbanks and staring at the marine life swimming in the clear waters. Fish gathered in great abundance in the shallows beyond a bank of sand flats, drawing in massive bull rays. I discovered that if I paddled slowly and quietly, I could take the canoe right over the top of them.

Measuring nearly ten feet from head to tail, with a wingspan of up to six feet and weighing nearly 300 pounds, a mature bull ray is very powerful and can be extremely dangerous. At the base of its whip-like tail are venomous barbs that the bull ray uses like a dagger when scared. To my young mind, it seemed the perfect substitute for the White Whale.

I began to imagine sending a harpoon into a bull ray's wing and being pulled along in my canoe. I had no intention of killing the animal, so I asked an old man who fished the creek what would happen if a bull ray was harpooned in the wing. He told me that it wouldn't kill it. But he added that the bull ray would retaliate and harpoon me with its barbed tail. He warned me against being so bloody crazy. I ignored the old man and set about finding a harpoon.

Dad kept a set of old curtain rods in the garage. The rods were made from copper that had large spearhead points at each end. I sawed a rod in half and sharpened up the spearhead on a grindstone. I found a length of rope and attached one end to the harpoon and tied the other end to the bottom of my canoe. I pushed off the bank of the river with my paddle and went searching for a giant bull ray, my sea monster!

I found the bull rays schooled beyond the sand flats. I glided above them, setting my sights on an enormous bull ray hovering at the edge of the group. I manoeuvred the canoe over the top of him, stowing the paddle in the bottom of the canoe and then retrieving the harpoon. I pulled myself up onto my knees, raising the harpoon above my head, and aimed for the fleshiest part of the bull ray's wing. Then I launched it into the water with all my strength.

The moment the harpoon lodged itself into his wing, the ray's barbed tail smashed into the hull of my canoe, coming within inches of my foot. Had the barbs driven into me, the combination of blood loss, shock and venom could've killed me in minutes. The ray retracted the barbs and shot off towards the middle of the creek. The rope went taut, hurling me backwards as the canoe was dragged along leaving a frothy wake. I couldn't believe it. It was happening exactly how I'd imagined! I was Queequeg, the hero harpooner of the *Pequod*!

Within seconds, disaster struck. The enraged bull ray came to the end of the sand flats and dived for the safety of deeper water.

The sudden downward pressure of the rope snapped the bow off the canoe. I was now treading blood-filled water amid plywood debris in a strong outgoing tide. A horrible thought entered my mind: blood attracts sharks! Bull sharks were known to enter Cowan Creek to feed on mullet. If a bull shark caught me floundering about in bull ray blood, I'd be ripped to pieces.

Luckily an old oyster farmer had seen the whole event unfold from his clinker dinghy. He paddled over and dragged me on board. I looked up and saw little sympathy in his crinkled old face.

'What the fuck did you do, boy?' he roared.

Shivering under his blanket, I couldn't help but smile. For the first time in my life, I had done something that in my mind was courageous. Sure, I'd been bloody crazy, but name me a kid who'd harpooned a sea monster? I had discovered something within me. It was something I never knew existed. Courage.

2

The Circus
Strongman

I told Dad that the canoe had sprung a leak and sunk to the bottom of the creek. Had I told him the truth, he might not have bought me a new one! I kept the story to myself, using the memory of my giant bull ray encounter to get me through the toughest days of school. Whenever I copped abuse or caught a hiding, I'd remind myself that none of my bullies had ever harpooned a 300 pound bull ray.

There was one day where my life became so unbearable that escaping reality by daydreaming wasn't an option. It happened during maths. Our teacher, an ex-Army martinet who'd lost his hand while throwing a grenade at Royal Military College Duntroon, was taking us through basic arithmetic. Everyone was bored senseless and the kids were getting restless.

Edwards thought it'd be funny to mimic my voice in class when the teacher's back was turned. To give Edwards credit, the bastard did a good job of taking me off. The teacher, who absolutely forbade any talking during class, swung around and stared daggers at me.

'Any more out of you, Ireland,' he shouted, 'and I'll give you six of the finest.'

The threat spurred Edwards on. The moment the teacher returned to the blackboard, Edwards resumed his mimicking. The teacher lost it. He told me that I was to see him at lunch. When I tried to speak in my defence, the teacher shot me down. Edwards and his mates were elated.

I dutifully reported to the teacher's office at lunch. His hair was matted to his forehead and his face was beaded with sweat. I remember the metallic glint of his claw when it caught the ceiling light and the emptiness in his eyes.

'Put your hands out,' he said, the words dripping with hatred. I tentatively presented him my hands. He raised the cane and I quickly retracted them.

'You put your hands out, son,' he hissed. 'Pull them away again, and I'll give you twelve.'

The teacher brought the cane down hard. It felt like someone was pouring boiling water over my palms. I bit down on my lip, counting each strike as it came down across my hands. By the time he got to six, my hands had gone numb. The ends of the thumbs had opened up and blood was dripping onto the floor.

The punishment wasn't over. The teacher started to hit me again. He was striking me with such force that his breathing was becoming raspy. His eyes were glazed over, like he was possessed. I must have entered a state of shock, because I lost count of the number of strikes that landed across my hands. I just remember being pushed out of his office and into the hall and looking straight at Edwards and his mates clutching at their sides with laughter.

I brushed past Edwards' gang and headed for the exit. Once outside, I jogged across the cricket oval, leaving behind a trail of blood and tears. Once I made it to the edge of the school grounds I climbed over the fence and sat under a large gum tree. I'd often come here to escape the bullies. I found the rustle of the wind through the surrounding bush calming. It was under this tree that I'd first imagined canoeing up Cowan Creek and harpooning the bull ray. But on the day I was caned, I couldn't put myself in that canoe. There was no way of escaping the pain and humiliation.

I sat there for hours, skipping the classes after lunch. When the bell rang signalling the end of school, I waited until all the students had cleared off before leaving. When I got to our house, I went straight to my room and closed the door. I felt ashamed, convinced that I'd brought the punishment on myself. Eventually, Mum came into my room.

'What's wrong?' she asked.

I held my hands behind my back and told her I was fine. Mum wasn't that easily fooled. She reached around and took hold of my arms, gasping in horror at the sight of my bloodied hands. I was bundled into the car and driven to the hospital where my cuts were cleaned and stitched up. Our family doctor met us in the hospital and was furious at what he saw. After I was dropped at home, he took Mum to the school to report what happened. The teacher was sacked and the incident hushed up.

Mum kept me at home for a few days to let my wounds heal. Missing school was fine by me. Dad was away at the time selling insurance in outback New South Wales. Mum told me years later that if she'd told Dad, he would've killed that teacher. The injuries he'd inflicted on my palms were painful but would heal. The mental scars were devastating. My self-belief was destroyed.

Any hope I had that the incident would bring an end to the bullying was quickly dashed. Edwards beat me up the first day I got back. I felt more alone than ever. Compounding my desperate sadness, the asthma attacks became more severe. I began to think that nothing could break the miserable routine of my daily existence. That was before a hero entered my life.

—

Don Athaldo was a circus strongman and body builder who'd enjoyed a stellar career in the interwar period. By the 1950s, Athaldo was running muscle-building courses by correspondence, which he used to advertise in local newspapers. The advertisements made reference to some of Don Athaldo's ludicrous demonstrations of strength. One line screamed, 'The man who carried a horse up a ladder!' Another passage claimed Don Athaldo had pulled a touring car loaded with six passengers from William Street in Leichhardt to King's Cross. That's a five-mile journey, mostly uphill!

But it was Athaldo's claim that he'd once been a sickly child who'd overcome asthma through natural remedies and strengthening exercises that caught Mum's attention. Mum and Dad showed me the advertisement. The pictures of Don Athaldo said it all. He was dressed in leopard-patterned tights and leather ankle boots and was striking a classic muscle-man pose. I had a new hero to replace Queequeg the harpooner. Dad asked if I wanted him to pay the five pounds to do the course. Did I ever!

Mum helped me fill out the forms provided in the advertisement and encouraged me to write a letter to Don Athaldo. I wrote about the bullying, the savage caning and how I couldn't play sport with the other schoolkids without bringing on an asthma attack.

Mum sent off the letter with the completed form and the money. In the subsequent days, I'd walk home from school so fast I'd be panting for air when I arrived at the letterbox. Nothing arrived for three weeks. I was beginning to think that the whole thing was a scam. Mum told me to be patient. Sure enough, a couple of days later a huge parcel was delivered to the house. It was addressed to Master David Ireland.

I picked up the parcel and took it straight to my room, carefully pulling off the string and unwrapping the packaging. I pulled out an enormous wall chart that unfolded to reveal detailed images of Don Athaldo performing various muscle-building exercises and calisthenics routines. There was also a personalised letter from Don Athaldo himself. The letter began –

Dear David,

You can be what you want to be! I will change your life!

You will find and believe in the courage that I know is

within you, mate!

They were the sweetest words I'd ever read. I felt a surge of excitement that rivalled the day I harpooned the bull ray. In addition to that inspiring message, Don Athaldo had mapped out a daily routine that involved eight exercises that he'd circled on the wall chart. I was to perform these exercises with my chest smeared in Vicks VapoRub while concentrating on my breathing. Dad bought me a wall mirror so that I could maintain proper posture and technique.

The first few weeks were incredibly difficult. The exercises initially brought on mild asthma attacks. But I persisted. Within a couple of months, my breathing became easier and the asthma abated. After a year, my voice began to improve. My body had totally changed. Although I was still small, I was far stronger than most kids my age: certainly strong enough to join the school's boxing team.

Mum didn't like the idea of me boxing one bit. Dad thought it was a great idea. My old man had been an amateur boxer before the war. He knew how to fight. I heard that he knocked out two thugs who'd tried to rob him after a big win at the dogs. But rather than throw me into the ring untrained, he bought me a punching bag on a large steel stick to teach me the basics. I very quickly discovered just how unready I was to start boxing. When I punched the bag, the spring on the base of the stick retracted, sending it back into my face. My first ever punch left me with a bloody nose and a loose tooth. Dad gave his first instruction: 'Move your bloody head!'

I hit the bag and dodged out of the way before it flung back at me. The harder I hit the bag, the faster it came back, sometimes hitting me before I had time to move. It would take a few black eyes and several blood noses before I learnt that dodging a blow was just as important as dishing one out.

After I'd developed my skills at evasion and improved my balance, Dad demonstrated a jab to help me improve the power of my punch.

'Tuck your elbow into your body,' he said, 'then drive forward with your back leg towards the target and then – *jab*!'

The bag flew backwards, smacking the floor hard before rocketing back. Dad caught the bag with one and then repeated the jab. Once I was consistently getting the bag to hit the ground he'd let me join the school's boxing club. It took a week of hard training before I had the bag hitting the ground every punch. After a fifteen-minute demonstration in front of Dad, he told me that I was ready.

I walked into the school gymnasium the afternoon the boxing team trained. The eyes of all the young boxers turned towards me. Some started snickering. I felt my face redden. I looked back at the door and thought about leaving, until I heard a voice in my head. It was Don Athaldo telling me that I could be whatever I wanted to be. I took a deep breath and walked towards the ring.

The boxing coach – one of our regular teachers – told me to get dressed. When I returned, I was pulled up in front of the group. The coach explained that all new boxers were initiated into the club with a bout. He asked for volunteers to face me in my first fight. The first person to step forward was Edwards.

Since the day I first crossed paths with Edwards, I'd dreamt of this moment. I won't pretend I wasn't nervous. But as I stepped into that ring, I knew I was ready. Edwards' posse thought otherwise. They were sneering and laughing, expecting an absolute walkover. I had nobody in my corner, so the coach helped me with my gloves before reading out the rules – no punching below the waist and no biting. Edwards and I nodded, touched gloves and squared off.

Back then, when boxing in primary school was permitted, a bout lasted two rounds. I had resolved to not throw a punch in the first round, certain that Edwards would come out swinging. I was right. He practically ran at me, throwing haymakers that would have knocked me out if they'd connected. The lessons learnt with the boxing stick served me well. I dodged and weaved, running him around the ring. I could see his frustration building. By the end of the round neither of us had landed a punch. The difference was that Edwards was gasping for air and I was completely relaxed.

When the coach signalled the beginning of round two, Edwards rushed me again. His gloves were drawn back, preparing to launch another punch. I saw my chance. I planted my feet, drove forward with my right leg just as Dad had taught me, and landed the perfect jab on his mouth. The force of the punch caused Edwards' head to snap back and his knees to buckle. He landed on the seat of his pants. A trickle of blood made its way from the corner of his mouth and down to his chin, and he had a look of astonishment on his face. I looked down at him and smiled, and saw fear in his eyes. Edwards could have stood up and kept fighting, but he was scared stiff. I was almost disappointed.

You'd think that Edwards and his bullies would've got the message that I was no longer a weakling that they could torment. But it seemed they were as stupid as they were cruel. Not long after I walloped Edwards, one of his goons, a big brute named Glenn, decided to try his luck. I was told to be ready to fight him out by the back gates after school. Word got round quickly. I turned up at the designated time and found a large group of kids gathered for the fight. Glenn was waiting in the middle.

I put my bag down, rolled up my sleeves and squared off. Just like Edwards, Glenn ran at me. I didn't bother evading. I stood my ground, waited until he was within striking distance, drove forward with my front leg and punched him in the mouth with everything I had. I caught him right in the mouth with a sublime jab, sending a tooth flying into the air. He went to the ground clutching his mouth and bawling his eyes out. I turned around, picked up my bag and pushed past the kids. I walked all the way home with a grin.

That night an urgent knocking came from the front door. It was Glenn's father. He looked every bit like his son – overweight and brutish. He was full of bluster, accusing Dad of having raised a thug who punched up his defenceless son. I was sent to my room while Dad talked things through with Glenn's dad. The injustice of it all was infuriating. For three years, I'd been the victim of vicious bullying. Despite regularly coming home with blood on my collar and fresh bruises, I never once snitched to my parents. The moment I'd turned the tables on one of my tormentors, he squealed like a baby.

I seethed in my room and waited to be summoned. Outside, I could hear raised voices. Glenn's dad was getting worked up. The voices dropped and I heard a sudden scuffle of feet before the door slammed. I walked over to the window and looked outside, catching sight of Glenn's father shuffling towards the front gate clutching his face. Clearly Dad had not taken kindly to being accused of raising a thug and had given him one in the chops.

There was never any discussion about what had happened between me and Glenn. Dad was old-fashioned in his belief that a man has to learn to stand up for himself. He'd known that I'd been bullied and he probably figured I was learning to take care of my own problems. Dad was not one for overt displays of affection, but I detected a hint of pride in the way he looked at me after that week.

The day after Dad sorted out the bully's father, more violence came to our home. Yet again, Dad had gone on an insurance-selling expedition into the outback. I went back to school and Mum was alone in the house.

It was the height of the post-war European migration. An influx of Greek and Italian migrants entered the suburbs of the major cities. Many were unemployed. It wasn't uncommon to get a knock on the door from a new arrival. It's fair to say that the migrant influx awoke racial tensions in the local community. In those days, people would call them 'wogs' or 'Ities' and nobody would bat an eyelid.

On this day, a man in his mid-thirties arrived at the house asking for work. Mum has a soft spot for hard luck cases and is the sort that always likes to help out those who show initiative. Notwithstanding her charitable nature, she shouldn't have let the man inside the house or showed him around the backyard. She was young, very attractive and vulnerable, and she was letting into our home a desperate man. And desperate men are capable of heinous acts.

While Mum listed the things she wanted done, the man grabbed her by the throat and tore her shirt and bra down off her shoulder. When she screamed, the man produced a knife, slashing her across the shoulder and cutting her chin and cheek. Mum was shocked into silence. The man pushed her against the wall and tried to tear off her skirt.

That bastard had come prepared. He was armed and he knew that there was no man in the house. The one thing he hadn't counted on was Skipper. Our trusted collie was over ten years old by then, and not nearly as strong as the day he saved me from the rock pool. But when he saw Mum being attacked, his protective instincts kicked into top gear.

Mum would later say that Skipper jumped down a full flight of stairs, burst through the back door and bit that cowardly bastard in the backside. Mum's attacker screamed in terror and took off running for the back fence. Skipper wasn't done. He ran after the man, and they both disappeared over the fence.

Mum ran inside. I arrived home to find my shaken-up mother

screaming down the phone to the police. The cops and I then took off after Skipper and the man. It wasn't hard tracking them. There was blood all down the pathway to our fence and even over the back wall. We walked over a mile through heavy bushland, occasionally finding evidence of a struggle – a broken branch, scuffed-up ground and blood on leaves.

Eventually Skipper burst through the bush covered in blood. He lay down at my feet, panting heavily. I slowly walked him home and gave him a good bath to properly inspect his wounds. It quickly became apparent that none of the blood belonged to Skipper. That rotten prick might've gotten away, but at least he'd been savagely mauled for his trouble.

The school year ended without any more bullying incidents. The kids knew that you messed with David Ireland at your peril. Life suddenly got much better. Dad announced that we were moving from St Ives into a house in Avalon, a beachside suburb in northern Sydney. To spare me a lengthy commute, I was taken out of Sydney Grammar and enrolled in the local government school.

Avalon presented me with a chance to completely reinvent myself. With my newfound physical strength and confidence in speaking to people, I had no trouble making friends. After each school day, my mates and I headed down to the beach to surf. I'd come home at night completely exhausted. After dinner I'd fall into bed and wake up the next morning, eagerly anticipating another day of school.

Suddenly I was living the sort of adolescence that every child should have. I hadn't realised until then how fun life could be. Looking back, I'm glad for the lessons I learnt at Sydney Grammar. I learnt to fight for myself and I discovered a reserve of courage I never knew existed.

Towards the end of that school year in Avalon, I mapped out the summer holidays with my mates. It was going to be jam packed with swimming, canoeing and surfing. I could hardly wait. But Mum had something else in mind for my summer break. She was about to send me on my first real adventure.

3

The Great Adventurer

I hardly knew my maternal grandparents. They lived in Adelaide, a five-day train trip from Sydney in those days. Given their advanced years, there was unlikely to be another visit from them in the offing. When Mum broke the news that I'd be spending the first three weeks of the holidays with them, I was furious. I'd prepared a summer with my mates to last the ages. But no amount of whining would change her mind.

Mum drove me down to the station on the day school broke up and bought a return ticket to Adelaide. She helped me aboard with an oversized suitcase and a small bag holding fifty pounds that fitted inside my coat. A huge amount of money for a ten-year-old to carry, the fifty pounds was to be spent in the dining carriage for the trip. Once I was settled into my seat, she planted a big kiss on my cheek and left. I saw her waving from the platform as the train pulled clear of the station.

You wouldn't dream of sending a ten-year-old on such a long train journey these days. Even then, it was a big deal and Mum was clearly anxious. She rang every station between Sydney and Adelaide, asking someone to check up on me and pass on a message.

Every stop, a grizzly old stationmaster clambered aboard calling out my name and telling me to behave or to eat something.

The train was an old steam locomotive. I'd been warned against putting my head out the window. The train conductor had told me that the steam was hot enough to burn my face off. I was starting to develop a habit of doing precisely what I was told not to do. When the train gathered speed and ribbons of grey steam whistled past my window, I gave in to temptation and curiosity. I leapt up onto my seat, squeezed my head through the window and opened my eyes. The blast of hot air sent me toppling backwards into my chair. For the next few hours, it felt as though my face had been sunburnt. I was lucky the sooty steam hadn't brought on an asthma attack.

That was the only setback on what was a glorious trip. The view from my seat was the most awe-inspiring and beautiful spectacle I'd ever seen. From the towering green summits of the Great Dividing Range to the sunbaked ochre soil of the outback, the dramatic contrast of the scenery was intoxicating. Kangaroos and emus were everywhere, taking fright as the train rattled through their habitat. I spent the entire trip staring in wonder out the window. I had fallen in love with the Australian outback.

Eventually the train pulled into my destination – Glenelg Train Station. Glenelg is a popular beachside suburb about six miles from Adelaide. I lugged my massive suitcase off the train and dumped it on the platform. A small, thin man with kind eyes was waiting for me at the foot of the carriage. Here was my grandfather Arthur.

He shook my hand, patted me on the head and then helped me with my suitcase. I noticed that Arthur walked with a limp and one of his arms seemed locked upwards, as if it had been broken and then incorrectly set. I'd later learn that these afflictions were the consequence of being shot in the foot and the arm in the trenches of the Great War. But they didn't seem to worry him at all. He was beaming with excitement to see me, genuinely enthralled at how much I'd grown since we'd last met. Very soon, it would be me that was in my grandfather's thrall.

Arthur loaded my suitcase into his old car and we drove to his house, which would be my home for the next month. My grandmother, Amah, was waiting at the door. She was a wonderful English grandmother – plump, rosy-cheeked and full of laughter. She hugged me to her enormous bosom and planted a massive kiss on my cheek. The huge amounts of powder she applied to her face nearly brought on an asthma attack!

Over dinner, Arthur entertained me with some of the stories of his life. Of all the tales I'd been told as a kid, nothing mesmerised me like listening to my grandfather talk about his adventures in the South Sea Islands. It was a dangerous time to travel those waters. Although much of the Malay Archipelago – a chain of islands stretching from Sumatra to Melanesia over many thousands of miles – had been under European control for centuries, the practice of head hunting and tribal wars persisted.

My grandfather got to know those islands very well. He had established rubber plantations and we believe he may have been involved in 'blackbirding', a despicable practice that was slave trading in all but name. It essentially entailed the kidnapping of young native men and selling them on to British landowners to work the rubber plantations in Malaya. Although slavery was prohibited throughout the British Empire, the practice was justified on the grounds that the men were paid and that they were being 'liberated' from their savage lives and brought into civilisation.

The length of time my grandfather was involved in this practice is a mystery. All I know is that he spent years sailing the islands of the South West Pacific. He became so familiar with the area that the Dutch colonial authority in Batavia – modern day Jakarta – hired him to search for a group of Dutch explorers missing in the Solomon Islands, an island group at the eastern edge of the Archipelago.

My grandfather accepted the job, setting off in a wooden sloop with a small crew of Javanese sailors and an English adventurer who was Arthur's best friend. They arrived at a large island called New Georgia and laid anchor in a sheltered bay while they decided on where best to begin the search.

During the night, spear-wielding warriors boarded the boat and kidnapped the search party. They were brought ashore and paraded in front of hundreds of chanting tribespeople who wore feather headdresses and covered their faces in paint. The chanting stopped abruptly when an elderly woman was ushered forward. In pidgin English, the woman identified herself as the queen of the tribe and made it clear that the kidnapped party would remain on the island. A group of tribesmen abruptly seized the men, leading them off into separate grass huts.

Arthur was placed in his own hut with guards posted outside the entrance. At daybreak, he stepped outside his hut to find his best friend's head on a stake. He had landed on an island where the local inhabitants practised cannibalism. The Javanese sailors were missing too. Arthur never got to the bottom of their disappearance. In all probability they met the same grisly fate as Arthur's friend.

Arthur guessed that he was spared because he was the group's leader. Either that, or they were saving him for tomorrow's main course. He knew that keeping his head on his shoulders hinged on giving them something, so he offered the one thing he knew nobody else on that island possessed: medical knowledge.

Arthur began to treat tropical ulcers and jungle sores among the children and quickly won the queen's favour. She spared his life and welcomed him into the tribe. As a man of fighting age, however, he was expected to become a warrior. For the next few months, my grandfather would periodically board a fifty-man canoe and travel to surrounding islands to do war with neighbouring tribes. Having had his rifle confiscated, Arthur had to fight with wooden spears. After six months, once he proved himself worthy, the queen released him.

Before leaving, Arthur's rifle was returned and he was presented with two gifts: an intricately designed dagger and another rifle of Dutch design that belonged to one of the explorers he'd been sent to find. After the warriors canoed him out to the sloop, Arthur sailed back to Batavia to report on the grim fate of the explorers and the rest of his crew.

By the time I went to bed, Arthur had become my hero. Every night for the next month, I'd sit at my grandfather's feet in the living room, staring up at him in quiet awe as he recounted his adventures. He told me about encounters with crocodiles and showed me illustrations of the Solomon Islands that are now held in South Australia's state library.

He'd tell me about romancing an English expatriate he met in Penang – my grandmother – and about naming my mother after the beautiful lotus flower that grew in abundance in the high tropics. Then he'd talk about catching sharks and hunting wild boar on the jungle-clad island. He was the greatest storyteller I've ever met.

Maybe the greatest gift Arthur gave me was introducing me to the sport that'd change my life forever. I'd initially been disdainful of Glenelg Beach. There was no surf. To me, beaches were all about surfing. What else could you do? Arthur had an answer. He bought me an old circular mask, a snorkel, a pair of flippers and a three-pronged spearhead attached to a broom handle from a bait and tackle shop. He sent me out spearfishing.

When I slipped beneath the calm, crystal clear waters of Glenelg, it was like opening my eyes for the first time. I'd never seen anything so beautiful. The water teemed with marine life and the seabed was covered in vibrantly coloured sponges. I was so distracted I ended up inhaling a mouthful of seawater through my snorkel. I came to the surface gasping for air, but I wasn't bothered. Once I'd gathered myself, I returned to this remarkable new world.

My first attempts at spearing a fish were hopeless. The fish darted off the moment I came within striking distance. I was out there for hours, desperate to catch a fish for my grandfather. Shortly before giving up, I noticed something scurry across the seabed. It was a large blue swimmer crab. I dived down to the bottom and gave chase. The crab burrowed into the sand leaving an indentation. I lined up the crab with my spear and drove it deep into the sand. I've had many amazing experiences spearfishing in my life, but very few to match the exhilaration at spearing that crab.

I swam to the shore with a huge blue swimmer wriggling at the end of my spear. My grandfather met me at the edge of the water, his eyes welling up with pride. We returned to the house and after crab dinner, I collapsed into bed, dreaming about spearfishing.

Had I spent the rest of the year spearing crab I would've been a happy boy. I became so proficient at finding them that I started selling my daily catch to locals walking along the foreshore. The month spent in Glenelg passed by in flash. Before I knew it, I was heading back to Sydney. My grandparents were devastated to say goodbye and so was I.

After bidding farewell to my grandmother, Arthur took me to the train station telling me one last story en route. Before he left the Solomon Islands, the queen had told him that the skulls of all the chiefs and great warriors that had been slain were taken to a smaller island near New Georgia. He was certain that the heads of the Dutch explorers and the Javanese crew were on that island.

Before I boarded the train back to Sydney, Arthur gave me a gift wrapped in newspaper. He told me to open it once I was on board. We shook hands and went our separate ways. Sadly, I only met him once more in my teenage years before that great adventurer died.

As the train drew out from the station, I opened up my present. My grandfather had given me the long-handled knife that was gifted to him by the queen of New Georgia. Forging metal was beyond the people of the Solomon Islands in the 1920s. My grandfather had told me the patterns and tracery on the handle of the knife called to mind weaponry he'd seen in Manila. The knife had most likely belonged to a Dutch trader or explorer who'd strayed into the queen's domain.

I carefully packed the knife into my suitcase and settled into my seat. The whole way home I dreamt of journeying to the islands my grandfather visited during his days as an adventurer. I vowed that one day I would travel to the Solomon Islands and seek out the island of skulls.

4

The Beautiful
Wide Country

When Dad revealed that we were moving to Gordon, I could have cried. It made no sense to me at the time. Everyone seemed so happy at Avalon. Gordon was not far from St Ives. That meant I'd be heading back to Sydney Grammar.

The moment I put on that school uniform, I felt a familiar dread. But returning to the school wasn't as bad as I expected. I had left Sydney Grammar only a year earlier, having cemented a reputation as a kid who knew how to fight. After a summer of swimming and spear fishing, I was as fit and strong as I'd ever been. The bullies wanted nothing to do with me. The problem was that nobody wanted anything to do with me. I was lonely and mind-numbingly bored.

Dad could see that I was miserable. He bought me a puppy I named Chester. He was a beautiful little dog with a lovely brown and white coat, and he was an absolute barrel of energy alongside our old dog Skipper. The minute I got home from school each day I'd be playing with Chester. We were inseparable. We'd even go billycarting together.

The only thing that could be said of Gordon was that the streets were steep. I'd roll the billycart to the top of the hill, Chester would leap inside and we'd go careening down to the bottom at breakneck speed. Chester would be terrified, barking all the way to the bottom until we came to a stop. The barking became so bad that I decided to blindfold him with Mum's scarf before we set off. We must've made a curious spectacle – an eleven-year-old, grinning ear-to-ear, with a blindfolded dog in a billycart tearing down a suburban street.

In time, Chester and I began to draw a crowd of one person. Her name was Gretchen. She was a blonde-haired, blue-eyed girl who lived up the street. She became my first girlfriend. It was all very innocent. In fact, we were more like best mates who occasionally pecked each other on the cheek. I was not yet at that age where women occupy a man's every waking thought! But she made me feel special all the same and I was certainly the only boy I knew at Sydney Grammar who had a girlfriend at my age. Who would've thought the least popular kid at school was the one to get the girl?

For a while, Gretchen and Chester were a welcome distraction from the tedium of school life. That was until Chester died. One minute he was a happy, healthy dog; the next minute he was lying dead in our backyard. It was inexplicable. Dad investigated and found shards of glass inside Chester's mouth. My dog had been murdered and the number one suspect was the man next door. Once again, we'd landed alongside the neighbour from hell.

He'd been complaining about Chester's barking for months. We'd all done our best to keep Chester quiet, bringing him inside or taking him out on night walks. It really wasn't that bad. Our neighbour saw things differently. He threw a glass bait over the fence and Chester devoured it. The police got involved, but nothing came of it. The culprit denied everything, of course, and the matter remained unsolved.

I was devastated. I'd had some challenges growing up. But I'd never experienced profound loss. Chester's death was a mild taste of the personal trauma to come.

—

Dad delivered the bad news the first week of summer holidays. He'd asked Michael and me to come talk to him in his study. Dad sat on a chair, lifted me onto his knee and told Michael to sit opposite.

'I've got cancer of the throat,' he said. 'They'll operate on me, but it's not good.'

I remember being confused at the meaning of the words. I was old enough to know that cancer was a serious illness. But it was the gravity in Dad's voice that had me worried. Dad went on to explain that he would be undergoing a laryngectomy, an operation that would leave a gaping hole in the middle of his throat. I remember looking at Michael, horrified.

Dad asked Michael to leave the room. He wanted to talk to me in private. Dad explained that the next couple of months would be tough. He would need Mum to take care of him while he recovered. With Mum fully occupied, someone would need to keep an eye on me. So Dad was sending me off to Dusty's farm. I barely knew Dusty. He was nearly twenty years older than me and I regarded him more like a distant uncle who I saw every other Christmas than a half brother.

'What about Michael?' I asked. 'Will he be coming?'

Dad explained that Michael was old enough to take care of himself. It was clear to me that I was being shielded from the horror to come. I didn't like the idea of being sent away when my old man was seriously crook, particularly to the home of a virtual stranger. But Dad's decision was final. Within a couple of days, my bags were packed, and Dad and I were off on the five-hour drive to Dusty's property in our old Chevrolet.

Dusty lived with his wife and four young kids in Rylstone, a small country town in the Central Tablelands of New South Wales. Excluding my train trip to Adelaide, I'd never ventured this far from home. It seemed to take forever to get there. When we arrived at the gate to Dusty's property, Dad stopped the car and told me to get out. The heat was like a hammer blow. Dad opened up the boot of the car, pulling out his Lithgow .22 rifle and three boxes of bullets.

'Here,' he said, handing me the rifle and the cases of bullets. 'In case you want to do some hunting.'

Dad's rifle had always been strictly off limits. He'd never taught us how to shoot or even how to handle a rifle safely. It seems an irresponsible act for a father to gift his twelve-year-old son a rifle in these circumstances. Maybe Dad felt that his end could come at any time and this small gesture was a passing of the baton – a father telling his son that he was now a man.

We got back in the car and drove the rest of the way up to Dusty's homestead. Dusty met us in the drive. He and Dad shook hands and had a cool exchange of pleasantries. Dad told me to behave, patted me on the head and then drove off. I felt far from being a man as I watched his Chev leaving a trail of dust in its wake. As I walked into Dusty's home with my suitcase, it took everything I had to hold back the tears.

Dad was not a good father to Dusty. He never gave Dusty the love and attention that all children need. Dusty was born when Dad was in his early twenties and perhaps he was too young to handle the responsibility of parenting. Instead of patching things up with Dusty, Dad allowed the distance to grow between them. Their relationship contrasted sharply with my relationship with Dad. Relatively speaking, I'd grown up as the golden child and I'd always sensed that Dusty harboured some resentment towards me.

My time at his house was not a holiday; I was well and truly put to work. Although Dusty had sheep on his property, his main source of revenue came from wheat. I'd arrived on the farm on the eve of harvest. Unseasonably dry weather had given rise to a locust plague of biblical proportions. Aside from threatening to decimate the crop, locusts wreaked havoc with the machinery. This was particularly an issue during the harvest, where they became trapped in the tractor engine, causing it to overheat.

My task was to clear the blasted things from the tractor's radiator; the horrible insects would get in my ears, eyes and mouth each time I did the job.

We worked dawn to dusk, returning to the house each night completely exhausted. I hated every minute of it. The thought that this would be life for the next eight weeks was soul-destroying. I went to sleep each night dreaming of locusts crawling over my body.

A few weeks into my stay, I decided to go exploring. Dusty's property was situated at the edge of the Nullo Mountain State Forest at the western edge of the Wollemi National Park. From the homestead, there was a good view of Blackjack, a dramatic-looking mountain with an impressive tabletop summit.

'I'm going to climb Blackjack,' I told Dusty, in a voice that brooked no argument. I was sick of working on the farm and felt that I was due for a day off. Dusty nodded and had his wife prepare a hamper. He told me that the only way to the summit was up the southern side of the mountain. That was on the farthest side of the mountai fn.

'You'd better get a move on if you want to be back before nightfall,' he said.

I filled up a bottle of water and placed it into a backpack with my lunch. I also brought along Dad's .22 on the off-chance I came across any rabbits.

The weather was not ideal for hiking. Morning dew had made it slippery underfoot and a thick fog blanketed the mountain. By mid-morning, I'd made it to Fernside – a valley of plush green paddocks hemmed in between two prominent mountain ranges. Around the base of Blackjack, the bush became thick. I'd spent plenty of time as a kid walking around the natural parks and bushland on the banks of Cowan Creek. But this was altogether different. The fog and the terrain just swallowed me up.

Blackjack is shaped like a truncated pyramid, with steep slopes leading up to a flat summit. Eventually I was above the tree line. The slopes were marked with lichen-covered boulders. I navigated a path between the boulders, kangaroos and wallabies leaping away as I approached. I hauled myself up to what I'd thought was the top of the mountain, only to be disappointed.

After countless let-downs, cresting ridges only to discover another false summit, I came to the top of the mountain. It was now getting late in the afternoon, a little over four hours after I'd set off up the mountain. The fog hadn't lifted. I set down my pack and looked around, completely devastated. After three weeks of blazingly hot weather without so much as a wisp of cloud cover, the fog reduced visibility to thirty yards.

I screamed in frustration and then, as if in response, the wind changed. Within minutes the fog vanished, revealing a spectacular vista. The sunlight turned the sandstorm escarpments a brilliant red. The creek wound through paddocks and towering eucalypts along the valley floor to the limit of the horizon. Just like that first time under the waves in Glenelg, I felt like I was casting my eyes on the Australian bush with new eyes.

I felt rejuvenated. Rather than being afraid and trapped in the landscape, I felt completely at home in it. This was where I belonged. I absolutely loved the wilderness. I wanted to find someone to share this revelation.

First, I had to get back down! The day was marching on and this was a dangerous descent. Shadows were already lengthening across the landscape, concealing crevices, ledges and shale. I gathered up my gear and set off down the mountain.

I learnt a valuable lesson about the Australian bush that day. It looks completely different on the way in compared to how it looks on the way out. I walked around the plateau, desperately trying to retrace my steps. Every path I started down led to a precipitous drop. It was as if the path that I'd taken to get up the mountain had disappeared behind me. Nothing looked the least bit familiar. I could feel myself beginning to panic.

In the end, I was rescued by some sheep I spotted grazing near a cliff edge. They were coated with thick wool and looked as if they hadn't been shorn in years. These sheep must've escaped their paddock and were now living feral. Clearly they didn't live up here permanently. They'd need to go down to the valley floor for water.

I reached into my bag, pulling out the box of bullets and loaded a cartridge into the breech. One shot into the air were enough to get the sheep scurrying away towards the opposite side of the plateau to that which I'd ascended. I shouldered my rifle and chased the flock down a dry creek bed. I nearly lost my balance a couple of times on the mossy ground. But I eventually managed to negotiate my way down to the first ledge.

Halfway down the mountain, I found an old ewe lying on a peculiar angle. She'd fallen and broken her back. The sight hardly filled me with confidence. Perhaps this was not the right way, after all. There was no point dwelling on it. By then, I was too far down the mountain to turn back.

I took the remainder of the descent very slowly. I knew I was close to the bottom when the sheep were no longer anywhere to be seen. Finally, with nightfall fast approaching, I arrived at the tree line. I'd made it!

It'd been a fantastic day. Not only had I controlled my emotions, I'd proven that I had a natural resourcefulness and instinct for getting myself out of a potentially dangerous situation. A thought was beginning to form in my head. I was beginning to understand that I belonged in the beautiful open country rather than in the stuffy confines of a school.

5

The Headmaster

The years of Dad's cancer battle were horrific. When I returned from Dusty's property, the powerfully built father of my youth was already unrecognisable. The once strong man of action was reduced to sitting in his study coughing from the inflamed hole in his throat. He'd forever be wiping the blood and mucus that oozed from the hole with a rag, rotting away before my eyes.

Dad communicated with a 'mechanical larynx', a strange metal contraption that he'd hold to his throat to amplify his words. His voice took on a metallic quality that gave me nightmares. I often didn't understand what he was saying. Not that it mattered. The pain in his expression said it all.

Nights were the worst. I lost count of the number of times I cried myself to sleep at the hideous sound of his coughing. The next morning I'd find the bathroom sink splattered in blood. Sometimes I wondered if it would be kinder to enter his room with my .22 and shoot him.

Dad died not long before my fifteenth birthday. I was at his bed-side when it happened. His final gesture before he slipped away was squeezing my hand. I'd known his life was nearing an end. The doctors had called us into the hospital the previous night. It was time to say our final farewells. I remember entering the hospital room and finding Dad conscious, but fading fast.

'God's not ready to take me,' he rasped, before falling asleep.

For a man whose belief in God was shattered on the Western Front and who'd regularly derided the Church, it was a startling remark. Whether he rekindled his faith at the very end is impossible to know. It was the last thing he ever said.

While Dad had been dying our home had felt like the scene of a drawn-out tragedy. School was only slightly less miserable. Dad had wanted me to follow in his footsteps and had enrolled me at Knox Grammar to complete my mid levels. It was as stifling as Sydney Grammar. The only difference was the size and ferocity of the bullies. I came up against a brute named Ferguson.

Maybe I could've avoided the beatings I'd copped if I'd kept my head down. But that was no longer my style. It seemed every other day, Ferguson and I were duking it out. He usually overpowered me with sheer force. On the good days, I'd land a punch or back him up with a flurry of jabs and hooks. More often, he'd knock me down within seconds. Nobody ever stepped in on my behalf. I was as friendless at Knox as I was at Sydney Grammar.

Just like at my old school, the teachers were useless. In those days, teachers seemed incapable or unwilling to deal with students who were falling behind or struggling to fit in or dealing with a crisis at home. The teachers offered me nothing – no comfort, no solace, no compassion. Instead they shamed me in class for my poor academic performance. I didn't care. I couldn't stomach the idea of doing homework with my old man dying in agony in the next room. I was being eaten up inside.

Relieved though I was when Dad's suffering ended, I was still utterly devastated. His funeral was the worst experience of my life. I remember someone saying a few words before automatic curtains were drawn across his coffin at the crematorium. It was a lousy way to send off my greatest hero.

On my first day back to school after Dad's funeral I was called before the school assembly. I thought the headmaster was preparing to discuss the grief that I was enduring and perhaps read a prayer in Dad's memory. He had something altogether different in mind. He cleared his throat.

'It has been brought to my attention that David Ireland has carved his name on the wall inside the chapel,' he said.

I looked up at him, shocked. I had no idea what he was talking about. The headmaster had produced a cane and was walking towards me with pent-up fury. All the fear that I'd managed to overcome with the help of Don Athaldo came rushing back. My voice betrayed me. I looked around the school hall for help, but all I could see were the sneering faces of teachers and students. I caught sight of Ferguson, beaming in his seat. I knew without doubt that he'd scratched my name into the chapel. He was probably the one to alert the teachers, too.

The headmaster told me to touch my toes. I looked at him, horrified. Did he know what I'd gone through these last four years? Did he know my father had died only days earlier? Could he imagine the sort of treatment I would receive from the bullies after being humiliated in this fashion? My guess is that he knew everything. He was after revenge. The chapel had just been built. He wanted to make an example of anyone who dared deface it. Caning the culprit was not enough. The headmaster planned to publicly shame me.

I lent over and the headmaster delivered six strikes across my backside. With each *thwack* of the cane, I could hear the students tittering. Caning as a form of discipline still prevailed in many Australian schools at that time. But even if I had been guilty of vandalism, how the headmaster of a prestigious school could deem publicly caning a grief-stricken student an appropriate punishment is gobsmacking.

Once the headmaster was finished, I was told to return to my seat. The students jeered as I made my way back. The headmaster looked on as I took my seat, wincing in agony. Then he called for silence.

'David Ireland will never achieve anything in his life,' he said, his words stabbing me like hot daggers. 'As further punishment, he will spend the rest of the school day picking up rubbish.'

All the anger, hurt, grief and betrayal I felt culminated in a moment of clarity. This was not where I belonged. I'd climbed mountains, canoed rivers, surfed waves and spearfished oceans. Dad's death had taught me that life was too precious to waste in a place where kids were viciously caned in public. My life was worth a lot more.

I waited until assembly was over and then I walked to my classroom and gathered my schoolbag. Blood was leaking from the cuts across my bum and seeping down my legs. I paid no attention. I walked calmly out the school gates and found my bike. I couldn't ride home. The wounds inflicted by the headmaster were too painful for a hard seat. So I walked home and never looked back.

My formal education was over. My real education was about to begin.

Part Two

WILD DAYS

6

Factory Kid

If Mum had reservations about my decision to drop out of school, she kept them to herself. We had bigger concerns: Dad had sunk all his savings into a large metal-processing company before he died. It was an investment in his family's future; the annual dividend intended to get me through school and put food on the table. Problem was, the metal company was full of crooks. We never saw a penny. Overnight, we went from a prosperous middle-class family to being penniless.

We were on our own. After Dad's funeral, Michael returned to a sheep station in western New South Wales where he'd been working as a jackaroo for a couple of years. Dusty was busy on his property near Rylstone and Joan kept to herself in country Victoria, showing no interest in me or Mum. Our only option was for both of us to find work.

Mum wrote freelance for magazines and I landed a job as a process worker for a nearby suitcase manufacturer called Stamford's. I was paid eleven pounds a week working an eight-hour day with a half-hour lunch break and a ten-minute smoko. My job was to cut leather from a pattern that would be turned into suitcases.

I hated everything about factory work. It was dirty, smelly and stinking hot in the summer. We worked on eight-foot benches, standing all day on a grimy, sticky floor that clung to your shoes. The foreman – a foul-mouthed, obese Englishman with a vicious temper – made my life a misery. Every day I'd be scolded for something I did wrong or told I was a worthless shit. If I was even a few seconds late to 'bundy on' – slang for punching your card in the time clock – I'd be savagely rebuked. Worst of all, he insisted on calling me 'fifteen' – my employee number. I was deliberately made to feel like a number, as expendable as a faulty machine.

The factory was full of low-skilled migrant workers from Greece, Italy and various Eastern European countries. In this place, English was a foreign language. I was an outsider and inevitably came in for some unwanted attention. Things came to a head early on when I ran out of rivets. When you work on an assembly line, that sort of thing can grind the factory to a halt. The foreman told me to take rivets from Joe's workstation. It was the last thing I wanted to do. The workers regarded their workstation as sacrosanct and Joe was a hot-headed Italian. But I had no choice. I took a handful and got to work. When Joe came back from smoko, he immediately noticed the missing rivets.

'What the fuck do you think you're doing?' he shouted.

'The foreman told me to take them,' I said.

Joe didn't want a bar of it. He told me that he'd fight me on our break. Joe was a skinny bloke, not much taller than me. After four years fighting against much larger opponents at Knox, I was confident I could take him. I shrugged and went back to work.

Nothing happened the rest of the morning. I was happily taking lunch on my own when the foreman rudely interrupted.

'Put your sandwich down, fifteen,' he said. 'Joe wants to fight you for stealing his rivets. We'll see how tough you are.'

I couldn't believe it. Here was the foreman – the person entrusted with the safety of his workers – sanctioning a fight that he'd caused! I was white hot with anger. It was time to send the foreman and the factory a message. *I might look like a private school boy, but I'm tougher than you lot.* I'd soon discover that factory fights don't adhere to the Marquess of Queensberry rules. The second I shaped up, Joe kicked me in the balls. While I writhed in agony on the ground, the bastard kicked me twice in the head. I could barely keep myself upright for the rest of the day.

First law of the jungle: the strong prey on the weak. Suddenly everyone wanted a piece of me. I caught a few terrible hidings. Second law of the jungle: those who adapt, survive. I learnt how to fight like a factory kid: standing side on, headbutting and getting the first one in. These skills would serve me well in the years to come.

I settled into a routine of working full-time at the factory and spearfishing on weekends. I found awesome fishing spots along the surf coast near my old stamping ground at Avalon. I'd thumb a ride to Avalon every Saturday morning, spearfish through the day, crash the night at a mate from primary school's house, then head home Sunday night.

Back then hitchhiking was generally regarded as a safe way to get around for kids. But it wasn't without risk. Once I was picked up by a paedophile. I'd stayed the night at a mate's house in Turramurra near our old place. I left before dawn, walking a fair distance to the Mona Vale Highway where I flagged down a small car. I jumped into the front seat and asked to go to Avalon. The driver – a normal-looking middle-aged man – nodded and we were off.

About two minutes into the drive, the man opened up his glove box and pulled out disgusting illustrations of men sodomising boys. I pushed them away, telling him I wasn't interested. He took us off the road along a dirt track hidden in dense bush. It was still early in the morning. Nobody would be coming along this road, not at this hour. I tried opening the door, but he reached over and pulled it shut.

The man stopped the car and started stroking my leg. Factory fights had taught me the importance of striking first and striking hard. While the creep was salivating in anticipation, I calmly reached into my duffle bag at my feet and felt around for my pranger head. A pranger is a three-pronged, razor-sharp head you fix to the top of the spear. I pulled out the pranger and plunged it into the man's thigh, driving it in as far it would go. The paedophile screamed in agony, clutching at his impaled leg. Here was my chance. I opened the car door, grabbed my bag and ran.

I pulled up quickly about twenty yards from the car. That pranger head had cost me two quid, nearly half my weekly food bill. I sprinted back to the car. The bastard was still screaming, looking at me through weeping eyes. I didn't feel the slightest pang of sympathy. I reached over the passenger seat, took hold of the pranger head and wrenched it out of his leg. A fountain of blood spurted upwards, splattering the roof of the car. I slammed the car door and walked up the dirt track towards the main road. The paedophile's screaming lifted the birds from the treetops. There was no need to run. Judging from the sizeable chunk of thigh skewered on my pranger head, that man was in no condition to give chase.

I often think about my encounter with that scum. I think of the kids they rape and often murder. I'm not a violent man. But if I had my time over, I would've driven that pranger into his crutch rather than his leg. Who knows how many kids I would've saved?

Every morning on my way to work I'd pass the same pretty girl in her uniform heading for school. She looked a few years younger than me and she had the most amazing smile. The sight of her in the morning was the only enjoyable part of my day. I felt something inside me for the first time – something new and exciting. I was head over heels in love and I didn't even know her name!

But I just couldn't stump up the courage to ask her out, or even find out her name. The factory job was robbing me of confidence. Every day I'd hear the voice of my old headmaster telling me I'd amount to nothing. I was beginning to think the prick was right, that I'd spend my life working within the filthy confines of a factory. I felt trapped. So I turned to the old circus strongman who'd saved me once before.

The letter I wrote to Don Athaldo gave a snapshot of all my achievements and setbacks to date – overcoming the asthma; dealing with the bullies; teaching myself how to spearfish; losing my father; and dropping out of Knox Grammar. I wrote about the humiliation of being caned by the headmaster in front of the whole school, and my fear that his prophesy would come true. I posted the letter to Don Athaldo's old address. Two weeks later, I got a reply.

'Dear David,' he wrote. 'I told you long ago that you can be who you want to be.'

He instructed me to get back into the calisthenics routine that he'd devised. He also challenged me to do as many push-ups as possible on a single breath and to report back to him in a month. By month's end, I replied telling him I could manage twenty push-ups. His response was to double that number. We went back-and-forth for several months. Eventually I got the number up to eighty push-ups on one breath, completely surpassing my own expectations.

Don Athaldo's reply was full of praise. He finished his letter with the question, 'How many push-ups do you think that headmaster could do on one breath?' That sweaty old bastard would struggle to do one. My self-doubt and anxiety vanished. What gave a man the right to humiliate me publicly and obliterate my dreams when he couldn't match me physically? Don Athaldo had led me to an important self-discovery: It doesn't matter what people say about you. All that matters is what you think of yourself. Don Athaldo was saying that if I believed in myself, I could do anything.

The ceiling above me was gone. I started acting on dreams and desires, finding courage I never knew existed. I stopped wondering if it were possible to make money from spearfishing, and gave it a crack. After filling a bag with kingfish, black drummer and trevally off Avalon, I walked to the Newport Arms Hotel in Pittwater to sell my catch. I sold the entire bag in about two minutes. A day's spearfishing earned me the equivalent of three days' wages at the factory. I wasn't proficient enough yet to spearfish in bad weather, which meant I couldn't depend exclusively on fishing to make ends meet. But I'd make enough to work fewer shifts at the factory.

The foreman, who couldn't sack me because of staff shortages, didn't like it at all. I think my happier demeanour pissed him off the most. The job was no longer a life sentence. I'd rivet away without a care in the world. When work became tedious, I'd look through the window above my workstation onto Wakehurst Parkway, reminding myself that Avalon beach was at the end of the road.

Sometimes, I'd count the number of cars zipping past. What struck me was the number of motorbikes. The idea of having a bike became intoxicating. I could see myself biking around the country, finding unexplored beaches and unseen hinterlands. Those machines became the ultimate symbol of freedom. I vowed that the moment I had enough money, I'd buy myself a bike.

Breaking Free

Not long after I started making money from spearfishing, I met Ted Harvey. Ted was a rough diamond half-Aboriginal, half-Filipino with fuzzy black hair, a winning smile and a terrific sense of humour who landed a job at the factory. He was treated atrociously when he arrived. I'd never seen racism like it. The fact that the taunts were coming from migrant workers must've made it all the more galling, given Ted's background gave him greater claim to the country than anyone else. He responded with his fists. Violence was the one language everyone in that place understood. Very quickly, nobody was messing with Ted.

I liked him immediately. We'd talk often of quitting Stamford's. Ted made some enquiries at his local pub and got wind of a factory in Willoughby that was looking to hire. Hallstrom Factory – owned and operated by Sir Edward Lees Hallstrom – was a refrigerator manufacturer that turned out 1,200 fridges a week at its peak. Hallstrom wages were the major draw card, an increase of two pounds a week on what we currently earned. Ted and I needed no further convincing. The next day at work, we submitted our resignations to the Stamford's foreman in the form of two-fingered salute.

We should've done more research on the Hallstrom job. The factory was an enormous concrete building with a corrugated iron roof that stood on the site of a disused quarry. Conditions were hotter and more unpleasant than at Stamford's. The foreman – even more of a prick than our former boss – put Ted to work in the spray-painting ovens while I worked on the assembly line.

My job was to cut the pink fibreglass batts and put them on the inside of the fridge door for insulation. There were no gloves or protective clothing issued and the fibreglass would get under your fingernails and into your skin causing incredible irritation. I loathed the job every bit as much as I loathed Stamford's. Lining up in a queue waiting to bundy on each day was degrading. It reminded me of corralling the sheep on Dusty's farm into a chute when we drenched them to get rid of parasites.

The worst part of the job was an Armenian who worked near me on the assembly line. There was some talk that he was an ex-mercenary on the run from the law. It was probably bullshit, but he certainly looked the part. He was a giant of a man whose face was crosshatched with scars. Thick clumps of greasy black hair spilled down over his shoulders, sometimes falling across his permanently scowling face.

The first words he spat in my direction were, 'Slow the fuck down!' He didn't like that I was cutting and installing the batts into the fridge doors so quickly. It made him look bad. I couldn't care less. If a worker exceeded the monthly quota of fibreglass batts, he'd take home a two-pound bonus. I needed the money. Ted and I had moved into a boarding house together in Kirribilli. We were so broke that our weekly wage wasn't enough to cover rent, transport and food. It got so bad we started raiding the fridges of other tenants for lunch and dinner.

I wasn't going to slow down to make the Armenian look good. I was still working at a ferocious pace when I noticed something dark and menacing enter my peripheral vision. I spun around as the Armenian leapt over the assembly line towards me. I'll never forget the look of utter malice on his face or the glint of the trimming knife he held above his head. Those knives were designed to cut through fibreglass.

There was no escape. A brick wall behind me and fridge doors stacked either side of the assembly line hemmed me in. I grabbed a freezer fridge door and held it up as a shield. My attacker drove the knife into the fridge door. I fell onto my back, still holding my make-shift shield. The knife had driven through the fibreglass and stopped inches from my eye.

The Armenian was pulling out the knife when another man entered the fray. It was Ted Harvey. He hurdled the assembly line and delivered an uppercut to the Armenian's jaw. It was a beautiful punch. The Armenian was unconscious before he hit the ground.

The foreman fired the Armenian on the spot. I reckon he got off lightly. He should've been put behind bars. That psychopath was a risk to society.

A motorcycle shop opened up in Willoughby. My desire to buy a bike had never burnt so fiercely. I used to run to the bike shop every day at lunch, eating my sandwich on the way. I'd look around for five minutes before legging it back to work. A few weeks after opening, the owner of the shop, a bald bloke with a huge amount of nose hair, put a 250cc Honda motorcycle in the shop window. It was the mid-sixties. The stranglehold that the old American bike manufacturers had on the market was about to change. The Japanese were coming. This model was at the forefront of a new era of motorcycles and I wanted it bad.

I worked seven days a week, making fridges and spearfishing. Within a couple of months I'd dug myself out of financial destitution.

A few months later, when I'd saved up enough cash, I went down to the bike shop and bought a brand-new 250cc Honda. I went riding up the coast, spearfishing in places that had previously been beyond reach. Before long, I was riding with a crew: not a bikie gang with links to the underworld, but a group of like-minded individuals who loved the open road and 250cc bikes.

Around this time my spearfishing skills reached a higher level. Don Athaldo's single-breath training enabled me to free dive to tremendous depths. I could now enter the domain of the big fish. I found incredible hunting grounds near Little Reef, a rock platform a few hundred yards off the coast of Newport Beach. I'd swim out to the reef with a float and duck dive right down to the seabed, spearing unsuspecting blue morwong and kingfish. I became so proficient that I could spear fish in dirty water or bad weather.

Eventually I was raking in more money spearfishing a single weekend than I'd make in a week at Hallstrom's. The time had come to put my factory days behind me. I decided to move out of the boarding house and into a beach hut in Newport. My office was a one-minute walk out my front door, across the sandy beach and under the waves. I'd spearfish every day, sell my catch to the punters at the Newport Arms Hotel, and then hit the town with Ted. Life was fun. All I was missing was a girl.

There'd been the odd pick-up from a night out with Ted, but nothing serious. Problem was, I'd never got over the infatuation with the pretty girl I'd seen each day walking to Stamford's. With my newfound confidence, I decided to do something about it. I rode my bike from Newport to Chatswood and waited outside her house. I must've been there for hours, because it was late afternoon when she came home in her school uniform.

Her name was Pam O'Neill. It was her last year of school. When she turned the corner, we locked eyes and she broke into a huge grin. I introduced myself and we got talking. When I suggested we go on a date her eyes flashed and she said, 'I was wondering when you'd ask me out.'

I fell for Pam big time. Nothing much happened at first. She agreed to ride on the back of my bike every so often. But she was worried about an ex-boyfriend. She'd all but taken out a restraining order against this guy. He was a real thug. Pam was more worried for my safety than her own.

Word must've got out that Pam had been spotted riding on the back of someone's bike, because Pam's ex tracked me down. I found him waiting for me one day outside my beach hut. He was a barrel-chested bloke and, like most blokes, far bigger than me! He had a black beard, and wore a leather jacket, stone-washed jeans and steel-capped boots. When he saw me, he made a show of pulling the studded belt out of his jeans and wrapping it around his fist.

'I don't want to fight you, mate,' I said, my palms facing up in surrender.

'It's too late for that now.'

I walked towards him slowly, keeping my hands raised. I kept telling him I didn't want to fight. Judging from his smirk, he was thinking I was a chicken-shit upstart who'd be easily scared off. When I was within an arm's length, I balled my right hand into a fist and hit him in the throat with everything I had. He fell to the ground, gasping for air. I stepped over him and walked into my beach hut. I never saw that bloke again.

The following day I rang Pam's home. Her mother picked up the phone and told me that I was forbidden from seeing her daughter. I pressed for an explanation and was told the police had called to advise her to keep her daughter away from me. Turned out, Pam's stalker had filed a complaint with the police, making out like *I* was the aggressor! The bastard had ratted on me.

I asked Pam's mum if I could meet her to put forward my side of the story. She agreed. The one positive that can be said of my time in private schools was that I came out of it speaking like a well-educated young man. Pam's mum was clearly taken aback. She was probably expecting a thug who could barely string a sentence together. I turned on the charm and, after an hour of talking, Pam's mum gave me her blessing to see her daughter. My pulse quickened. I had the dream girl, the dream job and the dream beach lifestyle. Life was amazing!

Being able to live off the money made from spearfishing gave me huge flexibility. I basically picked my own hours. If I found myself running short on cash, I'd string together a few weeks under the waves and I'd be back in the black in no time.

When I wasn't spearfishing or surfing, I was patrolling Sydney's northern beaches on my bike as if I owned the joint. I perfected a way of pulling the bike up on the kerb that used to scare the daylights out of pedestrians. I'd be cruising down a street before turning sharply up onto the kerb and braking hard, killing the engine, parking the bike and dismounting in one move.

I once tried the manoeuvre after passing a group of good-looking young ladies drinking coffee at a table outside a café. Problem was, I cornered too fast. I caught the lip of the kerb, my hand jolting off the brake and sending the bike straight through the window of the café. The bike miraculously remained upright in the shattered windowpane. I turned the engine off, brushed the glass off my jacket and dismounted. I left the bike where it was and took a seat at the table alongside the shocked female onlookers. A waitress came outside, mouth agape.

'Black coffee, please,' I said.

I got a written warning from the cops for that stunt. The café owner agreed not to press charges provided I paid for the damage. I was grateful to get off, but I didn't learn.

No matter how bad things got, I always seemed to land on my feet. I had a young man's sense of invincibility on steroids. I nearly died in a crash that I blame on two leggy blondes in miniskirts I saw while riding the bike at speed. Completely distracted, I didn't notice the traffic stopped ahead at a red light. I hit the rear bumper of a stationary Pontiac at about thirty miles per hour. I flew through his back window, smashing into the seat with enough force to send the driver through the front window.

The next thing I remember was lying in the hospital bed with bandages around my legs. The driver was fine, but understandably pissed off. A cop was outside the hospital room waiting to interview me. Before the nurse let him in, an old bloke in the next bed told me the cops would charge me unless I said I couldn't remember anything. It was damn good advice. The cop spent a long time trying to pin the blame on me. I repeatedly told him that I had no memory of the accident. Frustrated, he eventually slunk off.

I'd escaped a charge, but the injuries were worse than originally thought. A couple of days after being discharged, my right knee had swollen to three times its size. I could hardly walk. My local doctor told me that if the infection didn't clear up soon, the leg could become gangrenous. In that event, my leg could well be amputated. Ted Harvey picked me up from the hospital and I filled him in. I was beside myself with worry. I also thought something was still inside the knee.

When we got home, I hobbled to the bathroom. I told Ted to sterilise my hunting knife over the gas burner. With my leg extended over the bath I stabbed the knife into the wound. A jet of pus and blood shot out into the tub followed by a large sliver of glass.

I returned to the doctor the following day and explained what I'd done. He looked at me like I was some sort of madman. With the help of antibiotics, my self-administered surgery saved my leg.

—

Life only got wilder. I was acting like I had something to prove. When someone dared me to do something, I'd accept without thought. I agreed to represent the Newport Surf Club in a spear-fishing tournament even though the competition went against my principle of only taking what you needed from the sea. I hated that competitors would spear a fish then throw it away if they found a bigger one. But turning down a dare or declining a challenge was, to me, a sign of weakness.

The competitors all looked like seasoned professionals, equipped with the latest gear and flashy aluminum boats with outboard engines. All I had was my spear gun, snorkel, flippers and a large net attached to a float to store my catch. I remember the other competitors pointing and snickering as I swam out to Little Reef. None of them were laughing when I hauled in a catch three times the weight of the second placegetter.

That night, after a hard celebration boasting to other spearos at the Newport Arms Hotel, a punter challenged me to kill a wobbegong shark. The wobbegong is a superbly camouflaged carpet shark that can be found in shallow waters along the New South Wales and Queensland coasts. The name of the species is derived from an Aboriginal word that roughly translates to 'shaggy beard', a reference to the unusual protrusions that grow around the shark's mouth. They are precious animals, harmless if left undisturbed. In later life I would devote much time advocating for the protection of the wobbegong. To my everlasting shame, I accepted the dare.

The terms of the challenge were to kill a 'decent sized' wobbegong shark with a hunting knife and haul it back to the pub before sunset the following day.

'No problem,' I said.

Wobbegong sharks rarely grow longer than four feet. The spotted wobbegong is an exception, growing up to nine feet in length. I'd often encountered them while spearing off Little Reef. They were mysterious creatures, slowly gliding along the seafloor, minding their own business. They seemed not to mind my presence, carrying on as if I wasn't there. But I knew that their unusual appearance and languid demeanour concealed a lethal predatory instinct. I'd seen them gobble up fish with lightning speed.

The next morning, with a small group of onlookers, I swam out to Little Reef with my float and hunting knife. Once in place, I duck dived to a depth of fifty feet. Within a few seconds of surveying the seabed, I found a fully-grown spotted wobbegong swaying backwards and forwards with the current. I surfaced, took an enormous gulp of air, then went back down.

I expended a good amount of air getting to the bottom and approaching the shark slowly so as not to startle it. By the time I was hovering above my catch I'd been under for about a minute. Once the wobbegong was absolutely still, I threw my left arm around its body and thrust the knife down into its head. The knife jarred in my hand when it struck the shark's skull. I stabbed again and again, but my knife bounced off harmlessly as if it were hitting concrete.

The wobbegong went mental. I grimly held on as it twisted its body, desperately trying to bite me. I was running out of air, but if I let go the animal would turn around and grab me with its vice-like jaws equipped with hundreds of back-facing teeth. A wobby this size would drown me. My only option was to continue to attack. I stabbed into its fleshy flanks, working the knife up into its gills. The shark was bucking like a bull as I reached deep into its innards, spilling blood and guts across the seabed. The gill rakers sliced up my right arm quite badly. Soon the water was misted with blood and gore.

I needed air. I released the shark and headed for the surface before being brought to a sudden stop. I looked down to see the wobbegong latched onto my left fin. I kicked hard, but the animal refused to release me. I felt like my head was about to explode.

I reached down and pulled off the fin and kicked hard. It took an eternity to reach the surface, but I made it.

I coughed and spluttered for a few minutes on the surface. Once I'd settled down, I went back under. I found the wobbegong bleeding out on the bottom, still clutching my fin in its jaws. I remained on the surface for about half an hour waiting for it to die. Eventually it stopped moving and I went down and got it. Once I was back on the surface, I tied its tail to the float and started the quarter-of-a-mile swim back to the beach.

I emerged from the sea dragging a nine-foot wobbegong shark to a chorus of cheers. We tied the shark to the bull bar of a Kombi van and drove straight to the pub. I was feted as a great hero and felt good about myself, showing off the gashes the shark's gill rakers left on my arm. It wasn't until later that I realised I'd been a total idiot. I'd atone for my stupidity later in life, producing a film shown worldwide on the Discovery Channel campaigning for the protection of the wobbegong.

8

Going Feral

It was a fantastic time to be alive!

The sixties were swinging and everything was changing, from the clothes people wore to the decimalisation of the currency. Every jukebox in every pub in the country was blaring the music of the Beatles or the Rolling Stones. It seemed like the entire world was shaking off the stifling conservatism of the fifties and going crazy.

It was also the time of Vietnam. Shortly after I turned nineteen, I was called up. This was in the early stages of the war. Nobody seemed to know what was going on over there. None of us were the least bit worried. If anything, those I met who were called up were excited about the prospect of heading to this exotic Asian country. It all seemed like a great adventure.

Every conscript first had to pass a medical. I went along to the physical examination in the city with two mates. There were about forty men crammed into a large room. An officer came out and told us all to strip. To pass the time, men were allowed to smoke. It was a strange sight, forty stark-naked blokes puffing away in an orderly queue. The room was absolutely choking with smoke in minutes. Nothing sets off an asthma attack like a roomful of smokers. By the time I got to the doctor, I was wheezing hard.

'You're no good,' the doctor said. 'Go out that door.'

I was so desperate for fresh air that I pushed through the nearest exit. I ended up on George Street, one of the busiest streets in the city. With a few old ladies screaming in horror, I tried to get back inside. But the door had locked behind me. I rushed around the block to the front entrance to get my gear, pedestrians and passersby copping an eyeful.

My two mates passed the medical and laughed hysterically at my misfortune. I was initially disappointed to have been denied the chance to go to Vietnam. Had the medical been conducted in a non-smoking environment, I'd have been rated the fittest bloke in that room. Thankfully, it wasn't. One of my mates was killed and the other came back completely traumatised. He'd spend the rest of his life in and out of mental health clinics. It's funny to think that cigarettes and asthma probably saved my life.

Pam was busy during the week with university so I was left largely to my own devices. There seemed to be a party every night and Ted and I went to most of them. Otherwise, we went to a pub. We'd find ourselves in some backwater dive filled with wharvies and wannabe underworld types.

We stumbled on a place where the price of admission was entering the one-dollar raffle. First prize in the raffle was a night with the near-naked woman serving behind the bar and second prize was a chicken. Ted won first prize and elected to have the chook rather than the woman. She hurdled the bar wearing nothing but her knickers and punched him in the nose, spraying blood everywhere.

That was a harmless bit of violence. Other nights ended in worse fights. Most of these places had ignored the universal message of the sixties – peace and love to all. Ted was forever the target of racial slurs. Some low-life would point a finger and call him nigger, coon or Abo. Then it'd be on. We'd be up against men who were down on their luck, filled with hate and booze. Some of these guys had done time. The wiser course of action would've been to ignore the taunts and leave. But that wasn't in Ted's nature and nor was it in mine.

I felt a protective instinct towards Ted. He'd saved my life by king-hitting the knife-wielding Armenian back at Hallstrom's, and I hated bullies. Whenever Ted was racially attacked in my presence, I would try to get him out of there, but often we'd end up in a fight we never won. The lack of decency and respect he was shown was amazing. In the eyes of some, Ted's colour made him subhuman.

Ted didn't cop it just in the pubs. Once it happened in his home. Ted and I were listening to music in his Kirribilli flat when we heard a loud thumping on the door. It was the tenant from the flat below, who was irate because we were playing the music so loud. Rather than ask Ted to turn it down, he called him a filthy Abo and punched him in the head. The tenant was a heavy-set builder who, Ted claimed, had made money in property development with the help of his dodgy union mates. The punch left Ted wobbly for days.

I hatched a plan to hit Ted's attacker where it really hurt. The bastard owned a red, twin-cam MG sports car that he kept in mint condition. Under cover of darkness, Ted and I removed the hubcap on the front wheel on the driver's side and shoved a dozen raw prawns inside. We put the hubcap back on the wheel.

After the prawns had spent a day marinating in the Australian heat, you couldn't walk to within twenty feet of the car. With great satisfaction, we watched the builder strip the car, trying to find the source of the putrid smell. He removed the seats and carpet and eventually the dashboard. He never thought to look in the hubcap. The smell ruined the car. He ended up trading it in for parts.

—

My behaviour became even riskier. Ted and I went on a road trip up to Noosa for a music festival. When we arrived, huge breakers were rolling along the coast. A cyclone in the Coral Sea had whipped up waves big enough to close the beach. Ted and I paid no attention. We parked the car, changed into speedos, waited for a lull in the surf, and swam out.

The waves were incredible, upwards of twenty feet. The normally aqua waters had been churned into a murky brown. After a few minutes duck diving under some of the most powerful waves I'd ever experienced, the sea settled into an eerie calm. The water started surging out with the speed of a flooded river. Ted and I were swept out to a sand bar. We dug in our feet and stood up, noticing, with mounting horror, the enormous white crest of a wave across the horizon. It looked like a tsunami.

We were in shallow water, a dangerous place to be if a wave broke. I screamed at Ted to get out to deeper water so that we wouldn't be crushed on the sandbar. We had made it a few strokes when the wave was on us. Rather than take the sensible course and dive under the wave, both Ted and I decided to bodysurf back to the beach.

The wave scooped me up and propelled me shoreward with incredible speed. I managed to stay high on the crest as we passed over the sandbar. The sound was unbelievable, like having a jet engine roaring in my ear. I didn't dare look to see how Ted was getting on. If I turned my head, I'd lose balance and risk being sucked into the broiling mass of water that was carrying me. The wave entered shallow water and formed into a massive crest. Looking down from its apex felt like being two storeys up. It was a huge adrenalin rush.

Then the wave collapsed. I thrust my hands out in front of me to break my fall on the sand. I landed hard, water and foam bearing down on me. The wave tossed me around, thumping me hard into the sandy bottom. Eventually, I surfaced with two badly dislocated thumbs.

Ted had been washed up onto the concrete porch of the Noosa Surf Club, unconscious. We were both taken to Noosa Hospital and kept overnight for observation. The doctors told us that we were lucky to be alive. We thought it was fantastic! Not only had we managed to bodysurf a once-in-lifetime wave, we'd scored a free bed for the night while being waited on by the gorgeous nurses.

But it wasn't a laughing matter. It never occurred to me that I was still grappling with the anguish and hurt from my childhood. The fists of bullies and the canes of teachers had never really left me. Don Athaldo's training had helped me face my fears, but not my feelings of alienation. It would soon become clear that I was trying to prove to the world that I was tougher than the assailants of my past.

I saw Ferguson standing at a bus stop in Kirribilli. I'd just picked up Ted from his unit on my latest Honda sports bike. Both Ted and I had long hair and wore black leather jackets and bike boots. In contrast, Ferguson was dressed in suit and tie: the quintessential Old Knox Grammarian probably working in a bank or a law firm.

Rage welled up inside of me. This prick had made my life hell at school. Putting aside the countless times he beat me up, I held him responsible for my humiliating caning at assembly. It was time to put things right.

I braked hard and pulled the bike up alongside my old enemy. Ted was asking what was going on. I ignored him. I was in a trance. Despite the years that had passed since I last saw him, Ferguson still had that look of smug pomposity. He looked at me in bewilderment as I advanced, and then it dawned on him.

'Ireland,' he said, a mix of fear and astonishment in his voice. I looked more like a biker than the skinny kid he'd once tormented.

I dropped him to the ground with a massive hook. It didn't knock him out and I was very tempted to absolutely give it to him. But the look of sheer terror on his face and the sight of his hands raised feebly above his head was enough to satisfy me. I looked down at him with utter disdain and then I left.

When I explained to Ted what had just happened, he wanted to go back and give Ferguson a proper walloping. But I'd made my point. The roles had been reversed. I'd given him a taste of the fear and anguish I'd experienced through those years at Knox. An old score had been settled.

Not long after the run-in with Ferguson, another ghost from my past swept back into my life. I saw him at the end of the bar in a pub in Chatswood, a miserable old bugger half collapsed into his schooner. What drew my attention was the metal claw he used to prop himself up at the bar. Blood beating in my ears, I walked over and introduced myself.

'My name's David Ireland,' I said. 'You're the teacher who was fired after you caned me at Sydney Grammar.'

The hatred in my old teacher's eyes when he shredded my hands with his bamboo cane was gone. The man who looked back at me was destitute. He apologised, said he was no good, and then burst into tears. He ended up throwing an arm over my shoulder. He was a broken man. The resentment I'd felt for this guy was now pity. I told him not to worry about it and left him to his beer.

These encounters probably should've sorted out my ego problems; made me realise that the shame and humiliation I'd secretly carried all these years was not my fault. But my wild ways weren't over.

My first serious run-in with the police happened on a winter's night after a row with Pam. It was an old argument. Pam still lived with her parents and they forbade me from staying the night. I found the situation infuriating and left in a huff. I leapt onto my bike, kicked the engine into life, and headed home. It was a beautiful night for riding: crisp air, full moon and no traffic. With the argument with Pam swirling around my head, I barely noticed how fast I was going. I'd cannoned over the Roseville Bridge and swung onto Warringah Road when I saw the blue lights in my side mirror.

I took a quick glance behind. A copper on his 650cc Bonneville Triumph with his lights flashing was signalling for me to pull over. I'd recently traded my Honda for a six-speed 250cc Suzuki that was lightning fast. The cop was trailing me by 200 yards, too far to see my registration. So I dropped down a gear and took off.

I led him up Wakehurst Parkway towards Newport. This was my terrain. I'd taken this route more times than I could remember. I knew every bend and dip in the road. The blue lights stayed in my mirrors, but the gap remained. Once we reached Newport, I gunned it through to Avalon, pushing up the peninsula towards Palm Beach.

The houses and bush at the road's edge flashed past. We entered a series of sharp bends. I wound that Suzuki up like never before, not once daring to look back out of fear of crashing. I knew the cop was still tailing me. I could hear that Bonnie humming above the roar of the wind. Crazy as I was, I felt no fear, only pure exhilaration. This was a *race*.

At Palm Beach, the road went into a long corner. Here was my chance. The bend in the road obscured me from view. I braked, planted my foot on the road and spun the Suzuki up a driveway. I lay the bike down and killed the lights. A couple of seconds later, the copper flew past. I waited a few minutes before heading back to Newport, having proven that over a distance of twenty miles, a 250cc Suzuki could outrun a 650cc Triumph. I'd also proven that I had a lot of growing up to do.

The authorities eventually caught up with me, but not for speeding or failing to pull over for a policeman. I was arrested with Ted. It happened the night of a fancy-dress party in Chatswood. I was dressed as Santa Claus and Ted went along as Zorro. Around midnight, having drunk a skinful, Ted and I decided to go for a drive in my newly bought FJ Holden. This was before the days of breathalysers and booze buses. Everyone was drink-driving in those days. Still, it was no excuse.

Ted was really charged up and decided to get on the roof racks with a rope, and 'ride' the car Zorro-style. I took the wheel and drove off towards the shops. We didn't make it far down the main street of Chatswood before we were pulled over. A big fat copper with a red face stepped out of his police car and strode towards us, screaming at Ted to come down from the roof.

'Is there a problem, officer?' I asked through my white beard, absolutely straight faced. He reached in to grab my red Santa suit and pull me from the car. He succeeded only in ripping out the pillow I'd used to plump myself up. Eventually he got me out and threw me onto the road.

'What's your name?' he shouted, as I clambered to my feet.

'Santa Claus,' I said.

Ted leapt down from the top of the car, unsheathing his rubber sword. 'And I'm Zorro!' he shouted, stabbing the policeman with the toy.

We were piled into the police car and taken directly to Chatswood Station. The sergeant took one look at us and burst out laughing, much to the chagrin of the constable who was sent back out on patrol.

The sergeant put us in the holding cell for the night and fed us coffee and biscuits while we sobered up. As it happened, the sergeant was a keen spearfisherman. He'd heard of my exploits when I cleaned up at the fishing competition in Newport. For the rest of the night, he called me 'Dave the Diver', the nickname I went by around Newport. We talked through the night, trading spearfishing stories. The next morning, Ted and I were released without charge.

9

Growing Up

Pam broke up with me. I could hardly believe how much it hurt. It was like someone dying – worse in some ways. When people lose a loved one they are expected to be in mourning. The heartbroken aren't allowed to grieve. They're told to move on, buck up or get over it. Outwardly, I didn't have anything to justify feeling down. I had the dream life – an endless supply of parties, a job I loved and there were good looking ladies all around. There were times I'd succumbed to their advances. By my reckoning, the infidelity was justified by the issues Pam and I were having. I hadn't been a great boyfriend. But God, I loved her.

Pam reasoned that my life was going nowhere. It was a view she'd formed at university. Alongside the smart college boys with their dreams of making it big in the corporate world, I was an uneducated spearo without a plan. It was the first time that I had encountered the intellectual snobbery of so-called 'educated' people from universities. The break-up drew out the insecurities of my youth, and made me feel worthless and empty all over again.

Looking back, it was the best possible thing that could have happened to me. I began to re-evaluate my life. It was time to bring to an end the reckless stupidity of my late teens. I stopped trying to prove myself to others and started turning down the ludicrous challenges that people set me. I also started to think about the direction my life was headed. I felt proud that I was standing on my own two feet, working full-time in a job that I loved. But it wasn't amounting to anything.

Around this time I walked into Surf Dive 'N' Ski in the city. In those days, Surf Dive 'N' Ski was an obscure store known to spearos for the high quality gear they stocked. I'd gone in to buy a new spear gun. I picked one out and took it up to the register. I waited for twenty minutes to be served while the bloke behind the desk prattled away on the phone to a friend. What made the experience more infuriating was the badge on his chest that identified him as the store manager. Eventually, I lay the spear gun next to the register and walked out.

Around the corner from the store, I came to a sign on a door that read 'Surf Dive 'N' Ski Management'. An idea popped into my head and I knocked on the door. A couple of seconds later a man opened up.

'Can I help you?' he asked.

'Are you the owner of Surf Dive 'N' Ski?' I asked.

'Yes.'

'I'm here for the manager's job for your store around the corner.'

'We're not advertising a manager's job.'

'Well, you should be,' I said, 'because I had to wait for fucking twenty minutes for that prick to serve me.'

A smile broke across the owner's face.

'Alright,' he said. 'You're hired.'

The owner, Greg McDonagh, would become a great friend. After working as a store manager for a few months, Greg promoted me to General Manager of the stores. Together, we'd take Surf Dive 'N' Ski out of obscurity and transform it into the number one dive and beach apparel shop in the country.

I was put in charge of opening seven new stores and hiring staff. My policy was simple – hire the hottest chicks around. My experience as a spearfisherman and surfer stood me in good stead with the customers, but managing staff was a completely new experience. I made sure to treat those under me like human beings. Having worked under foremen who treated me like shit, I knew how much that killed an employee's enthusiasm for the job. I'd tell the staff that it didn't matter if they'd worked in the company since it first opened its doors or it was their first day on the job. Everyone was treated with respect.

The hardest part of my job was running staff meetings. My childhood fear of public speaking hadn't left me. I was terrified that at any moment, my voice would betray me and I'd be the scared little schoolboy speaking out of his nose. But I soon discovered everyone had the same fear. Whenever someone was asked to speak, he or she would be a nervous wreck. It led to one of my most important observations – most people lack confidence, are terrified of failure and lack self-belief. So instead of boring the staff with a rundown on new stock or administrative stuff, I approached meetings as if I were delivering a motivational talk.

I taught them the visualisation techniques I'd used to harpoon the bull ray, to Don Athaldo's breathing and strength-building exercises. I'd set the staff personal and team goals rather than goals that were directly related to the business. For instance, I was more interested in shop design or an innovative approach to sales than sales figures and quotas. I welcomed initiative and individual approach to customer service and made sure that each staff member was pursuing an exciting activity out of work. Consequently, every shop was staffed with bubbly people whose exuberance transformed the atmosphere from a potentially dull and dreary retail outlet to an exciting and fun place. Customers *wanted* to be there.

The sales figures went crazy. Greg was delighted. I got a huge raise. I had enough money to rent a nice place closer to the city and even bought a new Chrysler Valiant sports car. Life was great. I became even more confident in myself and more at ease with people. My fear of public speaking was turned on its head. I came to enjoy that part of the job more than anything. The one casualty of my new approach to life was my friendship with Ted Harvey. Ted was still mired in our old ways, drinking and partying hard and getting into fights. It wasn't like we fell out. We just drifted apart.

Pam also became a distant memory. About two years after we broke up, I got an invite to her twenty-first birthday. It was completely out of the blue. I arrived at the party a different man to the one she'd dumped. I dressed smartly and I carried myself with great self-assuredness. Before long, I had a couple of girls flirting with me. I ended up taking one of them home. Before leaving, I caught sight of Pam seething that I'd picked up a stunner at her own birthday. I'd be lying if I said I didn't love every minute of it.

The majority of my spare time was spent surfing and spearfishing. But the bush still held tremendous wonder for me. I'd never forgotten the time at Dusty's farm when I summited Blackjack and the clouds parted revealing the wonder of Fernside Valley. I did my best to rekindle that passion. I'd drive out to Broken Hill, stay the weekend at a friend's property and go bushwalking or pig hunting with my .22 rifle.

Sometimes, I'd stay the weekend with Dusty on his farm near Rylstone, forging a close bond with my half brother. Dusty once told me the story of a local bushranger who roamed the area. 'Lambert', as he was known, most likely operated out of a cave near Fernside at the back of Nullo Mountain during the gold rush years of the 1850s and 1860s. This was a lawless time in New South Wales history that would become known as 'the bushranging epidemic'. Sons of convicts and squatters were choosing the glamour life of bushranging instead of mining, farming or prospecting. Bushrangers were operating with impunity, police resigning in droves in favour of striking it rich in the goldfields. Lambert targeted the gold-laden Cobb and Co stagecoaches that were transporting nuggets from the Central Tablelands to Sydney. Owing to the remote location of his base, Lambert did a roaring trade.

But like so many before him, Lambert's luck ran out. The circumstances of his capture are largely unknown. He was charged, tried and hanged for bushranging in Mudgee. Stories began to circulate through the region of a cave where Lambert had stored his plunder. The exact location of the cave and the amount of gold he stole was a secret Lambert took to the grave. Countless expeditions were mounted and all of them failed to find any trace of the cave or the gold. Soon the facts of the story merged into legend.

I became obsessed with Lambert's gold. Over the course of several years, I'd search for the cave every time I was in the area. Dusty's theory was that the cave was probably at the back of Nullo Mountain somewhere in the Fernside Valley. A hideout situated in that location would've given Lambert an unimpeded view onto the dirt track that served as the main thoroughfare to the goldfields further west. Not only would Lambert have been able to see an approaching stagecoach, he'd also be able to monitor police movements. It was a region covered in dense eucalypt, impenetrable to outsiders. I agreed with Dusty. The back of Nullo Mountain would be the ideal place for a hideout.

Fernside Valley is a place of tremendous beauty. Extinct volcanoes, towering sandstone escarpments and dark caves give it an air of ancient mystery. But it's also a place of hidden danger, full of crevices and false paths leading off cliff edges. After several unsuccessful attempts at locating Lambert's hideout, I set off with a plan to follow the most difficult route. Wherever the mountain seemed to be leading me, I'd go the opposite direction. I worked my way around the mountain, arriving at a small clearing. I looked up and saw, for the first time, a large cave carved into the side of the slope. I couldn't believe I'd never noticed it before.

It took me hours, but eventually I arrived at the mouth of the cave. Before entering, I looked back down the valley and knew instantly that this was Lambert's hideout. The towering trees concealed the cave entrance from the valley floor. They also impeded the view down to the old dirt track, but you only needed to ascend the mountain a few feet to get the perfect lookout above the tree line.

I set down my pack and retrieved my torch. The cave was deceptively large, about the size of large living room. The roof was at least two storeys high. I switched on my torch and lit up a beautiful leather saddle leaning against the cave wall. I could hardly believe what I was seeing. How the man pulled a horse up here was a mystery. I figured there must've been another way down to the valley floor. Underneath the saddle, I found an antique pistol that looked to have been European-made. The only thing missing was the gold.

I searched the cave, lighting up every nook in the wall, finding nothing. It wasn't until I played the torch up and down the walls that I noticed a section of roof had caved in. There was a crack between two enormous boulders several feet above my head. I managed to pull myself up and peer through the gap. With great difficulty, I shone the torch into the next cave. The way the rocks had fallen limited my view so all I could see was the roof. Interestingly, the limestone roof was rendered black. I concluded that I was looking at the scorch marks of the campfires that Lambert lit to cook his food and keep warm.

I climbed down the rock face and switched off the torch. I had to leave Lamber's saddle and pistol where I found them. There'd be no way of getting the saddle down to the valley floor and I knew that if word got out that I'd found an antique pistol in a Fernside cave, Nullo Mountain would be crawling with prospectors trying to strike it rich.

I can't say for certain that Lambert's gold is buried under those boulders. The only way into the other cave would be to scale the boulders, abseil down the other side and plant some explosives to remove the rocks – a seriously dangerous exercise in an unstable cave. It's one mystery that will most likely remain unsolved.

10

The Dive School and the Great Mongrel Dog

The job at Surf Dive 'N' Ski started to wear thin. As General Manager, I was forever driving across Sydney visiting all our shops. The traffic was killing me. It was like being back in the line at Hallstrom's, waiting to bundy on at the start of each shift. My passion for the job had waned, so I left. In the end, my time at Surf Dive 'N' Ski had been incredibly positive. I left on great terms. Not only had I learnt important skills in management and business, I had conquered my fear of public speaking.

I moved back to my beach hut in Newport and started actively pursuing a passion I'd developed outside of work – scuba diving. I was already working weekends as a scuba diving instructor at a dive school in Cremorne. Once I'd built up enough experience, I decided to open my own shop. In my days travelling south to Sutherland Shire to oversee the opening and staffing of our shop in Miranda, I had learnt about the diving off Cronulla.

I began to visualise opening my own dive school in the area. I could see myself taking students out on a motorboat and diving the beautiful coral and sponge gardens of the reef the locals call Jibbon Bombora. The dive school would operate out of a retail shop selling diving gear that I planned to open along the esplanade. It'd become one of the greatest dive schools in the country and a genuine local attraction. I'd call it Cronulla Dive. In the summer of 1970, aged twenty-three, my dream became a reality.

Within a few months of opening, Cronulla Dive was flourishing. Students were put through two weeks of comprehensive training – five nights of theory and seven full days of diving, including six ocean dives. This was fairly standard practice back then. But what set us apart was our focus on overcoming fear.

While working as a diving instructor in Cremorne, I'd learnt that most people are afraid of the ocean. Some were scared of sharks, or water leaking into their mask, or the possibility of running out of air. I'd devote hours to helping the students master their fears, passing on the techniques I'd developed since I was a kid. I'd discuss breathing techniques, visualisation and the importance of self-belief. All the while, I'd drill into them the lesson that Don Athaldo had taught me: that we all have tremendous reserves of courage, we just have to be prepared to dig deep to find it.

In between dives, I'd ask each student what he or she wanted out of life. Everyone had a desire, whether it was quitting smoking, starting a business, travelling around Australia, or resigning from a bad job. I told them that learning how to dive was as much about dismantling the barriers and limitations we imposed on ourselves. The same was true of achieving any dream. I wasn't just teaching these guys how to dive. I was teaching them how to live.

When the students passed their final practical and theoretical exams, we'd make a huge deal of the achievement. I'd present each student with a diving certificate, and then deliver a speech. I ran through what their diving certificate meant, that they could dive to eighty feet, monitor the air, adjust buoyancy and read the currents. 'If you can become a certified scuba diver after applying yourself for two weeks,' I'd say, 'imagine what else you can do!' Many people would be moved to tears and tell me it was the greatest achievement of their lives.

Word got around about the dive school experience I was offering. I never had to put a cent into advertising. Cronulla Dive became one of the biggest dive schools in Australia. I was made an Ambassador for the National Association for Underwater Instructors for teaching the most students in the country.

They were glorious times. The employees of Cronulla Dive became my greatest mates, and there were plenty of perks to being a dive school owner and instructor. I was in the middle of that heady period when women consumed every waking moment of my thoughts. Women *fascinated* me. The way they talked, walked, flicked their hair or smiled was utterly intoxicating. Fifteen thousand people came through the dive school. About a third of them were women. God, they were wonderful times!

Sometimes, in the midst of all the fun and success, I'd catch myself pondering my younger self. Only a few years earlier, I was a tormented asthmatic who was told he'd amount to nothing. Now I was an incredibly fit man running a successful business with a huge circle of friends. I was the prime example of the message that I was preaching at the dive school: if you dream big, work hard and believe in yourself, anything is possible.

I wanted a dog. I'd always had a dog growing up and was now in a position where I could afford one. I came across an advertisement in the classifieds that read 'Dog to a good home'. The advertisement included an address in Frenchs Forest. I was in the car in a flash. Once out front, I rang the bell and a lady opened the door. Behind her was a beautiful golden retriever. I told her I'd be thrilled to own her dog, promising to look after him well.

'Oh no,' she said. 'It's not this dog.'

While she led me through the house, the woman told me that her property backed onto a national park. She'd managed to trap a wild dog that was killing all her chooks. She said the dog was a bit aggressive, but she was certain he had a good heart. I was expecting to find a feral half dingo. He was much worse, a snarling mongrel with scars all over his body and burrs in his coat. He bared his teeth when we approached.

'Do you want to take him?' asked the woman, sounding desperate.

I said yes without hesitation. I've always had a soft spot for dogs and an even softer spot for hard luck stories. The woman beamed and went to fetch a rope. After several attempts, I managed to lasso the dog. He growled and barked as I dragged him to the car. I put his age at eighteen months, probably too old to fully train the feral out of him. I figured if I failed to bring him to heel, I'd give him to the pound.

We hadn't driven to the end of the street before the dog started going crazy. He was barking and jumping about. I reached around to try and calm him down. His jaws clamped down on my hand and drew blood. I pulled over, got out of the car, opened up the back door and whacked the dog hard in the mouth. He yelped and cowered away in the back seat.

'Now we understand each other,' I said.

I named him 'Shek', a Chinese word that means strength (so I'm told). Shek became the most wonderful companion and a crowd favourite at the dive school. He was a real rascal. Often he'd go wandering around Cronulla and return with ice cream on his face. I went investigating one day, following him up the main street of Cronulla to an ice cream shop. I watched him crouch low and snarl at little kids who were coming out of the shop. They would drop their cones and run. Shek would calmly walk over and lick up the ice cream. I smacked him for that.

He was always up to mischief. One memorable occasion, a stranger walked into the shop and told me that Shek was abusing another dog. I ran outside to find Shek on a shop awning, having his way with a Labrador. Shek had obviously chased the poor bitch off the street, through the shop, up the stairs and out the window. A small crowd was gathered, some were laughing. Others were horrified.

'Is that your dog?' someone asked.

'Never seen him before in my life,' I said.

In terms of humiliating his owner, Shek outdid himself during a speech I delivered at Cronulla High School. The school's headmaster had invited me to talk to the school assembly about the marine life off Cronulla. I drove to the school directly from home. There was no time to drop Shek off at the shop, so I left him in the car with the windows down an inch. I raced up to the assembly hall, arriving just as the kids were taking their seats.

Halfway through my speech, I heard a commotion towards the back of the hall. Shek was ambling his way up the aisle towards me. He'd obviously managed to prise open the window and had picked up my scent. He didn't look in great shape. He was making a dreadful coughing sound and his tongue was dangling out of his mouth, lapping up bits of food around his jaw. It looked as if he'd been fossicking in the garbage bins. He leapt up on the stage, wandered over to me and with one final retch, threw up all over my feet. Thanks a lot, Shek!

If ever I got mad at Shek, it was never for long. He was the most loved of all the animals I kept in the shop. Far more popular than Ollie, the octopus who would climb out of his huge fish tank at night and steal Shek's dog food, and Clydie, the seagull who Shek found outside the shop with a broken wing, and Budge, the budgerigar who parked himself on the shop bench.

I used to take Shek out with me on dives. Despite his hard, ragged-looking appearance, the old dog had a calming effect on the students. They just loved him. I'd leave him happily to his own devices on the boat while the rest of us went and explored the world beneath the waves. No matter the size of the swell, Shek was never bothered. It was as if he found the sea air invigorating.

Shek came out with me for the start of an advanced course for four young divers on a summer's day back in the eighties. The weather was breathless and stinking hot. The forecast was for a change to sweep through in the afternoon, nothing out of the ordinary for that time of year. But nobody had predicted just how severe the storm would be.

I anchored my old thirty-foot wooden clinker in about a hundred feet of water half a mile off the coast of Royal National Park. The sea was pancake flat. It took us less than half an hour to get there from Port Hacking. When the dive began, the sky above was cobalt blue. In the far distance, puffy white clouds were coming over the horizon. Otherwise, there was no warning of the mayhem to come.

The diving was brilliant: good visibility and plenty of marine life. Once we got to eighty feet, the fish disappeared. One of two things was happening – either a shark had entered our domain or something major was happening above. It's almost impossible to tell what the weather is doing when you are down at eighty feet. But I sensed a storm had swept in. The atmosphere down deep felt different.

I got the attention of my four students and aborted the dive. At about thirty feet depth, I started to feel the turbulence of the seas rolling us around. The sun had obviously gone behind the clouds too, because it had become noticeably dark.

I surfaced in the trough of a massive wave. I looked up into a wall of water and was abruptly dunked back under. I surfaced for the second time, and gazed across the horizon. The sea was a ruin of rolling waves and white foam. The Beaufort scale – the international measurement relating wind speed to sea conditions – ranges from 0 (calm, less than one knot wind) to 12 (hurricane, greater than 64 knots). The wind blew in excess of 60 knots that day. We were smack bang in the middle of a storm whose wind speed measured a couple of knots below a bloody cyclone!

The waves were so big I couldn't get a visual on my old boat. I'd dived these waters hundreds of times, so I had a good sense of where we were. I inflated my buoyancy vest and screamed above the wind for my divers to do likewise. I pulled them all together, and slowly we made our way over the waves to where I knew I'd anchored the boat.

After a tumultuous few minutes, we made it to the old clinker. Mercifully, she was still afloat, rocking and rolling like a cork in a washing machine. How she didn't capsize in that sea is a miracle. There's no art to getting aboard a boat in that sort of weather. You just have to grab on as best you can and drag yourself in. Luckily for me, my students had mastered the basics of diving. I shudder at the thought of what might have been if I had a group of beginners.

Each of us grabbed hold of the side of the boat as she dipped below the water and pulled ourselves aboard. Once we were all in, I instructed everyone to put on a life jacket. I set about weighing anchor – not the easiest of tasks in the shocking conditions – and then set off for Port Hacking.

It was the most appalling boating experience of my life. Ribbons of white foam streaked across the ocean, spray detonated off the bow of the boat and waves seemed to be building. My divers were bailing water with buckets and bare hands. It was a miracle we didn't capsize. Progress was slow, but we methodically worked our way back along the towering sandstone cliffs towards our destination. The journey back must've taken us five times longer than the journey out.

It wasn't until we'd made it through the mouth of Port Hacking when a dawning realisation ripped me in two – *Where the fuck was Shek?* My beloved dog and best mate had been washed overboard in the worst conditions I'd ever seen. I had no doubt that Shek was dead. Even if he managed to swim to the coast, his body would've been dashed against the rocky cliff face. I cried the rest of the way into port.

It took a week for the storm to clear. The weather morphed into the gorgeous warm conditions of early autumn. Not that the temperate conditions improved my mood. I buried myself in work to put Shek's death out of my mind. When I wasn't working, I was working out in my makeshift gym that I'd set up at the back of the dive shop. I'd put myself through punishing gym sessions, bench pressing and powerlifting weights. The physical pain was a welcome distraction to my internal agony.

Halfway through a set on the bench, I felt something wet touch my leg. I looked down to see Shek nudging me with his nose. It took a few moments for my brain to compute what I was seeing. Two weeks after being washed overboard, the old mongrel was back! He looked terrible. His coat was full of grass seeds, his nose and paws were cracked and bleeding, and one eye was badly inflamed and infected. I cried as I hugged him. All he could manage was a pitiful whimper.

Shek spent five days with a vet mate. I feed him T-bone steaks for a month before he came good. There's no way of knowing for certain how Shek survived. My best guess is that he swam a mile through those horrible seas to Marley Beach. That would've left him a five-mile hike through the dense bush of Royal National Park. Then he'd have been confronted with a half-mile swim across Port Hacking River before making his way through Cronulla. All the while, he'd have survived on whatever scraps he could scavenge. What a dog!

To say I was overjoyed that Shek was back is an understatement. I took extra special care of my mate after that. I fed him whatever he wanted and treated him like a prince. Within a couple of years, he paid back the favour.

The business continued to do extremely well. One of the most pleasing stories to come out of the dive school was Neil Thomas. Neil had come to me as a young schoolteacher keen to fulfil a lifelong ambition to learn how to dive. He was an absolute natural. He progressed through basic training with ease and immediately signed up for the advanced course. He was among the best students I'd ever taught. It came as no surprise that he wanted to make a career out of diving.

Neil's skills as a teacher could easily be applied to becoming a dive instructor. I took him on, coached him on how to coach others and started to groom him as my number one assistant. We became close mates. Neil and I even shared a rented home in Cronulla. But our friendship would be sealed with a near-death experience.

Neil loved the job and his work ethic was phenomenal. He'd happily work the cold winter months, the time when a lot of instructors tend to go missing. It was in the dead of winter one weekend on an exceptionally cold day when Neil and I nearly died. We'd had an arduous session teaching a full class of divers and spending many hours in the water. When we finally got home we tucked into dinner and sat by an open fire, working our way through a carton of beer as we discussed the day.

After polishing off the last of the beers, we turned in. I was excited to get into bed. I'd just bought an electric blanket and couldn't wait to collapse into its warmth. I fell asleep in seconds, not realising the blanket had doubled over itself in one corner and was smouldering. I suppose it's a measure of just how tired (and boozed)

I was, that I slept through a fire in my bed. Had it not been for Shek, I wouldn't have woken up.

My dog leapt onto the bed and bit me hard on the hand. It was like waking into one of my worst nightmares – a smoke-filled room where I couldn't breathe! I looked down to see my mattress aflame. I crawled up the hallway staying as close to the floor as possible, Shek barking like mad. I made it to Neil's room and shouted at him that my bed was on fire.

We scrambled outside with Shek, smoke billowing out of my bedroom window. Once I got my breath back I ran back inside and dragged out the burning mattress. Shek had saved our lives and the house. Damn, I loved that dog!

11

Shipwrecks and a Forbidden Paradise

It was a Saturday and the weather outside was poor. I decided to cancel diving and was spending the day in the shop catching up on bookwork when a lady walked in. She asked about a silver ladle I'd put on display in the front window. I'd found the ladle while spearfishing on my own near a cliff face off Royal National Park. It was half buried in about twenty feet of water along a section of coast not commonly frequented by boats or surfers. When I tried to pull it out, the ladle wouldn't budge. It was as if it had been welded to the seafloor. I returned to the boat, took an exact measurement of my bearings and returned the next day with scuba gear and a chisel. With great effort, I chipped the ladle out from the seabed. It looked impressive, but I'd given it little thought since.

The lady told me she worked at the Mitchell Library and specialised in historical artifacts. I fetched the ladle from the window for her to inspect. She was drawn instantly to the insignia embossed on its head. She explained that it was a hallmark, an official stamp that would help identify where the spoon was manufactured.

'Would you like me to find out the history of this spoon?' she asked.

I handed over the ladle and almost forgot about the whole thing. A few weeks later she rang in a state of great excitement. She explained that a French company had made the ladle for a sloop called the *Success*. The *Success* had sunk without a trace somewhere between Port Phillip Bay in Victoria and Port Jackson in the mid-nineteenth century. And here was the exciting part: according to shipping records kept in the library, the *Success* was carrying a few thousand ounces of gold in the cargo hold.

I closed the shop and headed straight back to the dive site in the boat. I'd built an enormous venturi pump, a simple device consisting of a long pipe into which air is pumped that expands as it rises, creating a vacuum effect. My pump was powerful enough to suck up rocks the size of tennis balls. After nearly filling the boat with sand and kelp from the seabed, the pump started to find man-made objects. I brought up a tantalising assortment of artifacts including knife handles, belt buckles, shards of crystal vases, a pair of sailor's pants, brass pins that held the ship together and solid oak dead-eyes – thick discs with holes through which ropes and rigging were threaded.

I worked the wreck for several days, concluding that the current, weather and tide had strewn artifacts and pieces of ship across a wide area. Much of the ship's booty seemed to have found its way into three large depressions in the seafloor that had been gouged out by waves. Given its weight, the gold was most likely sitting at the bottom of one of those holes. Problem was that several boulders had fallen from the eroding cliff face and also rolled into the depression. There was absolutely no way of prising them away. I returned to port and sought some advice.

My friend Ted Louis was a part-time diver and explosives expert who owned a filling station in Hurstville. He'd recently finished a contract to work the wreck of the HMS *Pandora*, discovered in the outer Great Barrier Reef by two RAAF planes. The *Pandora* was a

24-gun porcupine-class ship of the Royal Navy that was wrecked on its return mission to track down the whereabouts of the mutineers of the *Bounty.*

When I explained the situation to Ted he told me that I needed to blow up the rocks. He supplied explosives and a detonation device and warned me to be well clear when she went up. I went out the next day, diving down and setting the explosives. I returned to the boat and drew her away from the wreck. On detonating, the surface of the water shimmered, the boat shuddered and a huge spout of water shot into the air. The surge of water nearly capsized the boat.

I put the venturi pump back to work and brought up even more ship fragments, articles of clothing, rigging and the odd piece of china and crystal. But there was no gold bullion. After I dived down and inspected the seabed, I determined that there were still several large impediments blocking the largest of the three depressions. This was where I'd find the gold. But I was reluctant to set off another charge. I felt uneasy about the damage I'd done to the wreck and the marine life. I decided to leave the wreck for a few days and stew over the problem.

I returned to the dive shop to discover that the federal police had paid a visit. It wasn't any great secret that I was working a wreck. I was displaying some of the artifacts in the shop window. Had I known I was breaking the law, I would've been far more discreet.

Two federal police came by the next day. The elder of the two, a heavy bloke with a fat neck, started accusing me of being a pirate. I said I didn't know what he was on about. He said that he knew I was working a wreck and that I was therefore in breach of the Historic Shipwrecks Act. Apparently the law prohibits the removal of any artifacts or relics from a shipwreck. It sounded like bullshit to me. I felt like saying that I was invoking the ancient law of finders keepers. The cop started pressing me for details.

'I can't remember where it is,' I said. 'I've forgotten.'

The cop's face turned red. He threatened to charge me if I didn't reveal the information they were after.

'I'm sorry,' I said. 'But I don't have a very good memory.'

There was nothing he could do. Until they determined that the site was an historic wreck, I couldn't be charged. But he didn't give up easily. On diving trips out to Jibbon Bombora, I'd occasionally be followed by the police and watched with binoculars. I had to abandon the wreck.

Somewhere off the coast of Royal National Park, a ship of gold lies wrecked under the waves. But don't think I'm going to tell you exactly where to find it!

I started to expand the business, offering up two-week overseas diving adventures around the islands of the southwest Pacific. I caught the travel bug in a big way and in my own time went looking for the most remote places in the world to dive. The locations that were off limits held the most allure, the danger element heightening the adventure.

One such place was Ouvéa, one of the Loyalty Islands in the archipelago of New Caledonia. I'd heard that the diving off Ouvéa was insanely good. I'd also heard that the local Melanesian population despised French rule and hated anyone with white skin.

My girlfriend Jane spoke fluent French. She was desperate to come along and made the point that her language skills would come in handy in communicating with the locals. If anything, she said, it'd be safer if she came along. I agreed.

We flew into New Caledonia and caught a ferry to our destination. Ouvéa is a crescent-shaped paradise with white sandy beaches and pristine aqua water. We took a room in the island's only resort hotel, which was owned and operated by a big, bald man of Hawaiian and Melanesian descent. He was the funniest man I've ever met, a generous host and a brilliant chef. Jane and I went to bed that night believing that reports of animosity directed towards foreigners were exaggerated.

We had a change of heart the next morning. Large numbers of muscular men roamed around the island in gangs. They leered at us and muttered profanities. It wasn't easy to keep our distance, the island being only twenty miles long. But we did our best. Hard to believe that by lunchtime they'd be looking at me like I was some sort of god!

The incident that changed everything happened at the end of a wharf that stretched 300 yards from the front door of the resort into the ocean. A group of bare-chested young men were at the end of the wharf, jumping around with great excitement. Jane and I went down to inspect.

As we walked along the wharf, I spotted a huge bait ball of trevally about a hundred feet in diameter swirling around the water at the end of the wharf. Barracuda had herded the fish into shallow water and were picking off the trevally one by one. The bait ball was densely packed, allowing the locals to fish with light lines and silver hooks. The trevally were confusing the glint of the silver hooks for glassfish and gobbling them up. Hundreds of fish were being pulled onto the wharf where they'd be clubbed.

The barracuda continued to shepherd the fish closer into shore until they were swirling around the pylons directly below us. Every so often, massive yellowfin tuna measuring over six feet carved straight through the bait ball. I saw one tuna knife through the mass of trevally and cannon into a pylon directly below where I stood. I dived straight into the bait ball without explanation. The fish parted as I entered the water, revealing the tuna convulsing at the bottom. The collision with the pylon had knocked the daylights out of it. The seabed was twenty feet deep. I swam down to the tuna and slipped my right arm up its gills and through its mouth. The fish put up no resistance, but the gill rakers cut up my arm. I surfaced seconds later in the middle of the bait ball with my arm sticking out of the mouth of an enormous tuna.

The young men were all staring at me, mouths agape. An old man who looked to be the chief could see that I was struggling to bring the tuna to the wharf. He ordered a couple of men to jump in and help. In the end, it took ten of us to get the fish up a ladder and onto the wharf. As we lay it on the wooden planks, the tuna suddenly came to its senses, thrashing around madly. The young men grabbed their wooden truncheons and clubbed it to death.

When the fish lay still, the men lowered their clubs and looked at me in awe. None of them – Jane included – had seen the tuna plough headfirst into the pylon. They were all in a state of shock. Who was this white man in speedos who could pull a live tuna out of the sea with his bare hands?

The chief approached and started talking in French. Jane said that he wanted to know how I captured the tuna. I looked the chief squarely in the eyes, and with Jane translating, said, 'It's all about timing.' I explained that I was a professional diver and had captured tuna in this way many times before in Australia.

'I watch the tuna closely,' I said, 'timing the dive so that I fall on top of it when it swims past.'

It was a total lie. But nobody could dispute what I was saying. The stunt proved to be the perfect way of winning over the locals. The chief was incredibly impressed. He invited us to go spearfishing, took us sailing in their outriggers and showed us one of the most beautiful natural wonders of the world – the Turtle Hole.

The Turtle Hole is located in the middle of the island. Just getting there was an exercise, requiring a hike of many hours through thick jungle. It was also a privilege. The local people of Ouvéa protected this site like it was sacred, forbidding foreigners from entering.

The chief told us that nobody knew the actual depth of the Turtle

Hole. He estimated that his boys could swim down to about fifty or sixty feet without fins. Unfortunately, I'd only brought along my snorkel and flippers. Lugging scuba all the way into the jungle was too tiring. But I was in peak physical condition, capable of holding my breath for up to four minutes. With fins I'd be able to make it down much deeper than sixty feet.

We arrived at the Turtle Hole: huge thirty-foot limestone cliffs surrounding a circular pool of crystal clear water around seventy feet in diameter. The local men led the way, swan diving straight into the water from the cliff edge. I followed them in, surprised to discover that I'd dived into salt water. The hole must connect all the way out to sea. Jane threw down my fins and goggles and torch. I got myself ready, taking large sips of air to oxygenate my body. When I was completely calm I inhaled a lungful of air and went under.

The key to free diving great depths is slow, methodical kicking. Overexertion depletes oxygen reserves. I made steady progress through the beautifully clear water. The temperature decreased dramatically the further I descended. Once I reached a depth of around sixty or seventy feet, I started to encounter coconuts in various stages of sinking. Air trapped inside the coconuts obviously prevented them from going straight to the bottom. They were the strangest sight, seemingly motionless as if they were suspended in time.

Eventually, the hole opened into an enormous underwater cave. I played my torch around the cave walls, lighting up enormous stalactites and stalagmites. The cave system must've been formed millions of years ago before disappearing under the rising ocean. I only had a few seconds to look around before I had to begin my ascent. It was a long way back. I estimated that I'd dived to around 150 feet, my absolute limit.

When I broke the surface, I looked up to see Jane in the arms of the chief on the cliff edge. I'd been down for more than four minutes

and they'd obviously thought I'd drowned. The chief was aston-
ished at what I told him about the hidden wonders at the bottom of
the Turtle Hole. He embraced me like a brother and we became the
dearest friends.

A year after the trip to Ouvéa I heard terrible news. French
soldiers had killed the chief after he kidnapped a gendarme. The
kidnapping was a harmless political statement – the local inhabitants wanted independence. The French saw the incident as an act of
violent sedition and deployed soldiers based in New Caledonia. The
chief was killed in a one-sided skirmish. The French soldiers found
the kidnapped gendarme living a life of luxury in a beachside cave.
While he was under local protection, the gendarme was fed fresh
fruit and lobster and given two young women in the cave 'for company'. The whole thing was a reminder that the issue of European
rule in many islands of the South Pacific still rankles with the local
people.

12

A Girl Named Sue

I'll admit it. In the madness of the 1970s, I was a ratbag when it came to women. I've heard it said that women absolutely swoon over ski instructors. Well, I reckon dive instructors give those blokes a run for their money. Let me be clear: I was always courteous and gentle to the ladies. I just had no interest in being in a monogamous relationship. This may sound a little shallow, but look at it this way: if not for my philandering ways I never would've met my wife!

It was the early autumn of 1977. I was out on the prowl with three great mates, Mark Mountain, Neil Thomas and Wayne Elstub. We'd fetched up at Moylan's Hotel, our favourite watering hole to meet ladies. The fellas were sidling up to the girls at the bar, shouting drinks and turning on the charm. I had my eye on the bubbly blonde working behind the bar. Her name was Jill. I got her number and lined up a date.

I went round to Jill's house, rang the buzzer and the door opened revealing the most stunningly gorgeous woman I'd ever seen in my life. Problem was, I wasn't looking at Jill. I was looking at her flatmate, Sue Popplewell. I knew at once that I was with the wrong girl.

Sue was intriguingly beautiful. She had this otherworldly quality – the glow of her long brown hair, the smile from heaven and the
perfect body that seemed to float across the ground. I was head over
heels in love from that moment on.

But what was I supposed to do? Jill was very keen on pursuing a relationship. So I tried to do the right thing and went steady
with Jill. It was torture! Spending time with Jill meant spending time
in her flat. Before I knew it, Sue and I had struck up a friendship.
It was the worst possible outcome. I didn't want to be her friend.
I wanted to be her lover. I seethed with jealousy every time I saw her
with other boyfriends. I guess I should've broken up with Jill. But I
couldn't stand the thought of not seeing Sue.

Six months after first meeting Jill, I was given a reprieve. Jill and
Sue decided to explore Europe together. Although devastated that
Sue would be out of my life for an indefinite period, I'd at least be
able to drop the charade. My relationship with Jill became ambig-
uous – we were sort of still together, but not really. I didn't ask for
clarification. The way I saw it, I was back in the game.

And, God, did I go wild with the girls! I rekindled an old romance
with a tall blonde by the name of Robyn. Robbie was the perfect
antidote to my aching heart: a casual relationship with no strings
attached. All the while, I was having flings with students from the
dive school. The high point was dating two girls named Marie
and Karen simultaneously. It's true that having two girlfriends at
the same time wasn't that unusual for me. The difference was that
Marie and Karen were sisters. What can I say? It was the seventies.
Life was complicated and awesome.

Turned out Sue and Jill were having a ball too. They worked
everywhere from Greece to Austria. But, after eighteen months
travelling Europe, Sue became homesick. She returned to Australia
to see her family and randomly we bumped into each other at a
nightclub in Caringbah. Sue was on a date with a footballer and I

was there, completely drunk, with a diving mate. I couldn't believe my eyes when I saw her.

I muscled my way into her conversation with the footballer and greeted her like a long-lost friend. I bombarded her with questions, asking her about the trip and how Jill was getting on in Europe. All the while, I was desperately trying to think up ways of getting her on her own. An idea popped into my head.

'Do you mind stopping by the dive shop?' I asked. 'I want to talk to you in private so that you can pass on a few messages to Jill.'

Sue arrived at my dive shop for a short meeting a couple of days later. I told her I was far too busy filling up scuba tanks to talk to her. I suggested dinner that night. Sue eyed me suspiciously. She knew I had a reputation as a bit of a pants man. Reluctantly, she agreed.

I made sure I kept things strictly above board and Sue seemed to enjoy herself. It would be the first of several outings. When my birthday came around, she suggested I join her parents for dinner. Mum had moved to Norway a couple of years earlier, where she'd met a nice bloke. I was happy for her, but it meant I had no family close by.

It was incredibly sweet of Sue and clearly indicated that she was developing feelings for me. But I said no. I told her I had to lecture at my dive shop that night and told her I would call her in a few days. It was a lie. I'd actually already lined up a date with one of the sisters. Like I said, I was a ratbag with women.

That night I picked up Marie and went to a local restaurant. We walked inside and sitting at a table near the front door were Sue and her parents. I felt like a criminal. I looked at Sue and she gave me a withering stare as if to say – *well, I don't care!* I was a proper bastard. I left with Marie after entrée, explained to her that I was in love with another girl, and broke it off.

The next day, I went to Sue's house. She'd told me earlier that her family was having a barbeque. I arrived at the front door with a bucket of red morwong I'd speared that morning. Norma, my future mother-in-law, answered the door. She immediately knew who I was. She frostily told me that Sue was asleep and didn't want to see me. Behind Norma, I could see Sue's father George firing up the barbeque.

'No problem, Mrs Popplewell,' I said. 'I'll just drop these fish off to your husband and then leave.'

I squeezed past her, walked through the house and into the backyard.

'What do you want?' George asked. 'Why are you here?'

'Just wanted to give you a bucket of fresh fish I speared this morning,' I said.

George, being a very keen fisherman, took one look at the fish, a smile slowly breaking across his face.

'Do you want a beer, mate?' he said.

I stayed for lunch and Sue came to forgive me.

Next day, Sue agreed to come to the dive shop. She'd revealed over lunch the previous day that she was planning to go back to Europe. I was shattered. But I had one last trick up my sleeve. When she turned up at the shop, I made out like I was in a frantic rush, telling her that there was a problem with the boat that needed fixing before the next day's dive. I took Sue outside, closed the shop for the day and managed to get her into the car and down to the boat.

I parked the car and walked her down to my old boat, a twenty-foot ocean-going catamaran that I used for diving. I fiddled around with the engine, pretending that I was fixing something, before telling her that I needed to take the boat out for a quick run. Before Sue knew it, I'd started up the engine and cast off. A knowing look came across her face. She was smiling with her eyes. I took her up the Port Hacking River and asked her if she was hungry. Sue gave me a questioning look.

'I always keep lunch in the boat,' I said.

I lifted the lid of my esky. It was brimming with chicken and champagne. I'd stocked it up before Sue came down to the shop. She burst out laughing and accepted a glass of bubbly.

Sadly for me, Sue went through with her plan to return to Europe. I was devestated, but that didn't last long: two months later, she returned home to Australia for good and we quickly became an item.

I proposed to Sue in a Chinese restaurant in Cronulla. I told her that I loved her with all my heart, but I also said that I was an adventurer and I'd never be able to change my ways. It was the truth. I remember sweating on her answer. If she said no, I would've died.

I had nothing to worry about. With tears filling her eyes, Sue said yes. We'd been dating for four weeks.

Surrounded by friends and family, Sue and I made our vows in a ceremony in a small Cronulla church. Life was amazing! The dive school was at the peak of its popularity. I was making more than enough to put down a deposit on a beautiful house in Caringbah – about five minutes from the dive shop – and book a honeymoon to the Solomon Islands.

The beautiful atolls of the Solomon Islands draw incredible marine life. The diving was fantastic. The Solomons are also home to a graveyard of Japanese and Allied shipwrecks from the Second World War. Peering through portholes into well-preserved cabins and touching gun turrets and wheelhouses that are now covered in crustaceans is a haunting experience. At the end of a day of diving, Sue and I would walk the pristine beaches at night and fill up on seafood in one of the island's resorts before turning in.

Poverty was endemic in this part of the world. With few avenues for entertainment, young men would band together getting drunk on metho. Unemployment and chronic alcoholism have always been a recipe for violence. In a place as small as Honiara, violence has a way of finding you. Sure enough, Sue and I had some trouble after stocking up on groceries in a Honiara corner shop. Food and provisions in hand, we headed outside to find a group of ten men eyeing off our rented car. I wasn't worried about the car. It was a beat-up Suzuki with no doors and no roof. But it was also our only means of escape.

I told Sue to smile and walk fast towards the Suzuki. These men were in a terrible condition. They were spoiling for a fight. I learnt from school that a sure way to stir up a thug is to run away. So I remained calm, smiling in a sort of deferential way, as if to acknowledge that this was their home. I put the bags of food in the back seat and started up the car. The men drew apart to allow us to pass and I nodded gratefully.

We'd driven a few yards when I heard a loud clink, like metal striking metal. I turned around and saw a machete lying across the back seat. One of the men had hurled his jungle knife at my head. If not for the metal headrest, the knife would have sliced through my skull.

The incident outside the corner shop marked a turning point in the trip. That night, Sue started feeling ill. Her symptoms were ominous – terrible headache, delirium, nausea and cold sweats. Sue had contracted cerebral malaria, the worst form of the disease. We'd been taking anti-malarial tablets but had only started the course a day before we arrived. We should've been on the tablets two weeks earlier.

I pumped her full of Fansidar and chloroquine. But the malaria had taken hold and the drugs were useless. Sue's condition deteriorated through the night. The next day she struggled to hold down fluids and I was worried about dehydration. I didn't want to risk the hospital in Honiara. We needed to get back to Australia.

The last night at Honiara I thought I would lose my new wife. Her temperature was through the roof, her body seemingly on fire. I lay wet towels on her naked body to try and keep her brain from cooking. At first light, I practically carried her onto the plane. The guys at customs looked worried. I knew they wouldn't let us on the plane if they thought she had a disease.

'My wife gets migraines,' I said, in my calmest voice. 'Nothing to worry about.'

We breezed past them. Sue didn't know what was happening. She was starting to hallucinate.

The flight home was a nightmare. Sue was comatose and incapable of drinking water. I lifted her off the plane when we landed in Sydney and took a cab directly to Caringbah hospital. They put her on a drip and gradually her condition improved. A few weeks later, she was discharged.

It would take a year for Sue to shake the headaches. On occasion, she'd wake up screaming from a nightmare, drenched in a cold sweat. But she was incredibly lucky. And so was I. I'd come within days of losing my wife on our honeymoon!

13

The Turning Point

It was the beginning of the roaring eighties. Australians seemed to have entered a new period of confidence. The economy was booming and the dive school was doing fantastic business.

I started delegating responsibilities to my trusted diving instructor, Neil Thomas, which gave me more time to explore Jibbon Bombora. I'd discover underwater nooks and features I never knew existed. I was out there one day in seventy feet of water, following a gutter-like reef formation, when I arrived at the mouth of a cave. The cave was about twenty feet wide with a ceiling about eight feet high. Inside the cave lived seven grey nurse sharks.

Divers generally kept away from this species of shark. Growing up to ten feet in length, they are fearsome-looking animals. The scientific community believed that grey nurse sharks posed no threat to human beings. The 'educated' view was that grey nurse sharks were equipped with 'holding teeth': capable of holding and swallowing small fish but not larger animals. In other words, they were physiologically incapable of harming humans.

Although I found the grey nurse to be docile, I thought the holding teeth theory was bullshit. I'd seen a grey nurse rip a kingfish in half with a forceful shake of its head. But that was a one-off. Grey nurse sharks hunt at night unless food strays into their path. If I wanted to observe them feed, I'd have to take food into their lair.

I speared a bagful of kingfish and dived down to the grey nurses of Jibbon Bombora. When the blood leaked into the cave, the sharks took on a different persona. They darted towards me, jaws snapping. Each shark lined up to take its food, forcefully biting down and chopping the fish in half. So much for the holding teeth concept! A grey nurse had the jaw strength to take a man's leg off.

I spent months feeding the sharks. To my astonishment, I found they could be conditioned. For instance, if I thumped my weight belt with a clenched fist, the sharks would emerge. The vibration the sound produced became synonymous with feeding time. I also noticed a distinct hierarchy within the group. The largest shark, a female that I called Big Shot, would cruise about while the others backed off in deference. Big Shot was also the most curious, venturing closest to me and sometimes circling in a predatory fashion. But she never attacked. It was territorial behaviour. My observations led me to the conclusion that grey nurse sharks are a highly intelligent species.

They are also creatures at risk. During a feed, I noticed fishhooks in their mouths. I'd seen the same thing in grey nurse sharks off Montague Island and South West Rocks on the NSW mid coast. Fishhooks are a diabolical problem for sharks, often leading to infection and death. The main culprits were the wobbegong fishermen with their set lines.

I decided to mount a campaign. I took hundreds of photos and began writing essays about the risks the grey nurse shark faced. Eventually, I was getting invited to speak at fishery conferences and to rooms full of marine biologists. I couldn't believe the snobbery from these university-educated 'experts'. They all seemed uncomfortable with the findings – particularly my theories on feeding, hierarchical structure and territorial behaviour – of a person who had no academic qualifications. They'd counter my theories with stuff they'd learnt in books. I'd let them air their doubts and have them eating their words when I showed them my photographs.

The publicity I generated to save the grey nurse shark began to have a positive impact on the business. People started showing up at the shop asking to be taken out to the grey nurse cave. I happily obliged and accidentally stumbled on my biggest discovery. Big Shot showed clear signs that she recognised me among the group of divers. It didn't seem to matter what wetsuit I was wearing or whether I was holding a fish or not, she'd always come to me. The same thing happened after the sharks returned to Jibbon Bombora following the winter migration. Big Shot and her crew *remembered* me. These creatures were capable of detecting my smell and electrical impulses and had incredible instinctive memory.

I also noticed that, if I remained calm, Big Shot would brush past me. The key was to keep my breathing measured and heartbeat slow. If I remained completely calm, she'd allow me to take hold of her dorsal fin. In front of groups of divers, Big Shot would take me riding through her cave.

In those days, the only people who rode sharks were the crazy islanders of the South Pacific. When word got out that I'd ridden a grey nurse, the publicity went off. Newspapers were queuing up for interviews. Eventually I got a call from Channel Nine. They wanted to do a story for their news bulletin. I agreed on the proviso that the angle of the story was about the plight of the grey nurse. The next day, Channel Nine sent a cameraman and a producer.

We arrived at Jibbon Bombora. The cameraman and I dived down with a bag of kingfish. As we approached the cave, I thumped my weight belt. The sharks shot out at me. The bag of fish was leaching a huge amount of blood and stirring up the sharks. I'd never seen them in such a frenzied state. I kicked and punched them away. I wanted Big Shot.

Eventually, she came out of the cave. Big Shot's first appearance on camera was certainly memorable. With a flick of her tail, she muscled the other sharks out of the way and then sized up the king-fish I dangled in front of her. She put on the afterburners, shooting straight at me, jaws wide open. I dropped the fish into her mouth, which she gratefully demolished.

I turned around to see if the cameraman had got the footage. All I saw was the bottom of his fins as he made his way up to the surface. I was all set to follow when I noticed his camera sinking towards the seabed. I swam down and took hold of the camera. It was a 16mm Bolex movie camera with waterproof housing. I'd never filmed underwater before. The cameraman had given me a crash course that morning in operating the camera.

It was a challenging experience, feeding kingfish to ravenous sharks while trying to film them. But I got four minutes of footage of the sharks bumping up against the camera and tearing the kingfish apart. Once the fish were all gone, I made my way up to the surface. I passed the Bolex to the cameraman and hauled myself into the boat.

'What happened to you?' I asked.

'I had some trouble with my ears,' he said.

Sure you did, I thought. I didn't blame him. It was frightening down there with the sharks going crazy and competing for a feed. I guess he just panicked. Besides, that cameraman did me a huge favour. I'd captured some of the best close-up footage of grey nurse sharks feeding the world had ever seen.

When Channel Nine ran the story, my phone rang off the hook. Everyone wanted my footage. I went out and bought myself a Bolex camera and started filming everything I did underwater. I'd shoot for hours, condensing the footage into three-minute films that I'd sell directly to the networks. I was getting prime-time segments on all the big shows, from Ray Martin and *Good Morning Australia*, to

Quantum and every news bulletin across the country. I even started fielding offers from the Disney Channel. No matter what I shot on camera, there was always someone interested in buying.

My work started to garner international attention. The Maldivian government offered an all-expenses-paid trip to film the diving in the Maldives. Why not? I upgraded my Bolex camera, reading the directions on how to use it on the flight over the Indian Ocean. I flew into the capital, Malé, and was met by a group of government officials on the tarmac. Over lunch, they gave me a rundown of exactly what they were after. Top of their list was shark feeding.

The following day, three Maldivian fishermen took me to a reef a few miles off the coast of Ferrana, a tiny island in the Maldivian group. We motored out in a wooden boat called a *doni*. It was the perfect day for shooting underwater film – blue sky, turquoise sea and barely a breath of wind to stir up a swell. We glided over shallow coral reefs, arriving at a point where the water turned a dramatic blue. The sea colour marked a sheer wall that plunged 400 feet. About eighty feet across, another wall rose up towards the surface, creating a cavern that trapped an abundance of sea life at low tide.

I lowered a fish frame into the water. A fish frame is a net of wire mesh about the size of a car door baited up with fish heads and innards. I'd used fish frames on other film shoots to great effect to draw smaller fish that in turn lured the big predators. I dived into the water weighed down with a huge amount of gear – scuba, powerful underwater lights, the fish frame and my brand-new Bolex in its casing.

The cavern walls created an incredibly strong current, sweeping me clear of the *doni*. I made my descent, struggling to hang on to all my gear. The sunlight played across the multi-coloured coral walls of the cavern, like the stained-glass windows of a cathedral. I had no time to admire it. The current seemed to gain strength the deeper I dived, causing the fish frame to brush up against me. Fish guts and mucus clung to the legs of my wetsuit. Near the sandy bottom, I wired the cage to an outcrop of dead coral that stuck out from the wall like an arm. Once I'd fixed it in place, I kicked away a good distance and lay down on the seabed. I turned my lights on and pointed the camera towards the fish frame as the current knocked it against the coral wall, spilling the fish bits into the cavern.

Within minutes, a huge swirling bait ball of golden trevally – big, hundred-pound GTs – swirled down the cavern like a tornado. The trevally were making an incredible din, thumping into each other and stirring up the water in a fanatical effort to devour the pieces of fish bait. I started filming. It took no time before the bigger fish picked up the huge vibrations the trevally sent rippling through the water.

The first shark to appear was a Galapagos whaler, a bulky nine-footer with the snubbed nose of a bull shark. He circled the bait ball and came within a few feet of my camera. He was close enough for me to see the gills of the little yellow pilot fish that rode the pressure wave off his nose.

The whaler sniffed around and then vanished. I'd seen this behaviour before, when I'd filmed a bunch of bronze whalers off Montague Island a few months previously. A single shark appeared, circled the bait ball several times, disappeared for a couple of minutes and then returned with a few mates. I figured the sheer number of trevally in the bait ball would lure a decent-sized gang of sharks. But I wasn't expecting over a hundred of them.

Whalers torpedoed into the heart of the bait ball, emerging with wriggling trevally in their jaws. The trevally bunched up tightly and started twirling about with greater velocity. Slowly, the bait ball migrated towards me. I lay flat on my back, pointing the camera directly up as it passed above only a few feet away.

Fish and sharks collided into each other with enough force for me to feel the vibration. It was the most thrilling underwater experience of my life, a front row seat to the beauty and savagery of nature. So long as I remained calm and still, the fish seemed oblivious to the light I cast on the scene.

At that moment of pure exhilaration, something latched onto my calf. I pointed the lights down. A giant moray eel was mouthing my wetsuit! The eel was at least eight feet in length, its body as thick as a man's thigh. I could feel pinpricks on the back of my leg as the eel's teeth penetrated the wetsuit. The eel had got a taste of the fish guts that had rubbed off on my leg and was trying to decide whether I was edible.

Panic started to rise from within. The instinct to kick the eel away or take hold of it with my hand was hard to resist. But acting on my fear in that way would end my life. The eel would take a chunk out of my leg with its long, razor-sharp fangs. My blood would draw the whalers like a magnet. They'd rip me to shreds in a second.

I could do nothing but watch as the moray eel moved its mouth up and down my leg. I slowed my breathing as the eel worked back down towards my ankle, wrapping its jaws completely around the lower part of my calf. The activity in front of me was getting more frenetic. The bait ball had now moved to within a foot of my camera. Occasionally a trevally would peel away from the group and cannon into me, nearly knocking the lights and camera out of my hands.

I looked down at the eel. I lived an eternity in those few seconds, almost convinced my end was near. But the eel didn't bite down and end my life. It detached itself from my calf and swam towards the baits and started to pick off fish bits attached to the frame. I watched on gratefully as a whaler took hold of the eel and tore it to pieces.

I remained at the bottom of the cavern for twenty minutes while the whalers continued to pick off the remaining trevally. They didn't stop until the bait ball was completely eradicated. When the last shark disappeared, the tranquil beauty of the cavern returned as if nothing had happened. I unhooked the fish frame and ascended to the surface. I passed all my equipment up to the Maldivians and hauled myself aboard.

I sat in the boat, euphoric. The footage I captured was groundbreaking. I knew with absolute certainty that I was on the brink of a new chapter in my life. I was going to bring wildlife to the world with my camera.

Part Three

CROCODILE MAN

14

A Genuine Croc Doc

By the mid-eighties, Sue and I were the proud parents of two beautiful boys, Luke and Adam. The dive school was doing incredibly well. I delegated more and more of the operations to my instructors. I now had the time and the money to devote myself to becoming a master underwater filmmaker.

As I threw myself into this new passion, my friend Mark Olding jumped on board as my assistant. Mark was a pilot for Ansett who had the poster-boy bronzed Aussie good looks that sent girls wild. Like most of my mates, Mark had come through the dive school. He was my sort of bloke – someone who acted on impulse and pursued his passions with great enthusiasm. When he expressed an interest in my film work, I invited him along for the ride.

We'd head off on weekend trips diving the reefs along the New South Wales coast. Sometimes we'd take a week off and explore the outer Barrier Reef off Far North Queensland. Having another person proficient in handling a camera underwater had huge advantages. I could interact more closely with the marine life or shoot scenes from different angles with two cameras running simultaneously.

It also allowed me to develop my skills as a presenter. I'd begin each dive with a piece to camera. My three-minute segments were suddenly becoming more sophisticated. I even started experimenting with voiceover narration and soundtrack. The overall quality of my work had improved out of sight, good enough to command five grand a film. That was good money for a couple of days' work, particularly back then.

And there was no shortage of buyers. At my peak, I was being broadcast three times a week, often on different channels. I started working with land-based creatures. I did segments on snakes, goannas and feral animals. The networks gobbled it all up. I was chock full of confidence, ready for my greatest challenge yet. It was time to produce something for cinema.

I dreamt of making a movie that set a new standard in wildlife filmmaking. To do that, I'd have to feature one of the world's most dangerous animals. I'd done good work with sharks. The only species that I hadn't shot were great whites and bull sharks and they were the domain of the husband–wife team of Ron and Valerie Taylor. Lions, tigers and the other big cats were old hat. The last great predator yet to be properly featured was the saltwater crocodile.

The time couldn't have been better for a genuine croc doc. Paul Hogan's brilliant portrayal of Mick 'Crocodile' Dundee had just burst onto the screens. International interest – particularly American interest – in Australia had never been so high. I did my research and couldn't believe how little was known of these ancient predators. Lifespan, migration, numbers and diet were largely a mystery. My time learning about grey nurse sharks taught me the best education comes from experience. I knew that jumping into a crocodile-infested river in the Northern Territory would be suicide. I needed an expert and I found him in Thailand. His name was Kamu Saru Suk and he was the craziest bastard I've ever met in my life.

Mark and I were in Thailand doing a piece on the Moken

People, a nomadic group who maintain a sea-based culture. I'd learnt from my research that some coastal regions of Thailand have large proliferations of crocodiles, so I made some enquiries about expert handlers. Kamu Saru Suk's name kept popping up. I found him working in a crocodile enclosure just outside Bangkok.

Kamu Saru Suk's crocodile compound was a large circular pit enclosed in a ten-foot wall with viewing platforms for spectators. At the bottom of the pit was a writhing mass of one hundred crocodiles taken from India, Thailand and Indonesia. Each day, Kamu would walk through the crocodile pen barefoot carrying a bamboo cane. It was insane. Crocodiles never lose their predatory instinct, even those bred into captivity. When I introduced myself to Kamu through a translator, he invited me to come inside the pen with him. Accepting that invitation ranks high on my list of foolish acts.

I'd already learnt that the higher the degree of risk, the higher my ratings. Footage of me walking amid scores of bloodthirsty crocs would be gold for the film. I justified the decision on the basis that every time I shot animals in the wild, I'd risked my life. But taking a calculated risk after careful preparation and observation is different to reckless stupidity. Early in my career, that line seemed pretty thin.

An announcement was made over a PA system that the show was about to start. Spectators crammed into the viewing decks as the gamekeepers threw hunks of raw beef into the pit. The crocs were crawling over each other to get to the meat. I could hear the sound of their jaws snapping from outside the pen. With the food devoured and the crocs all stirred up, Kamu entered the pit.

As casually as a man walking through a park, Kamu made his way along the four-foot wide concrete path that bisected the pen. Large ponds filled with murky green water lapped at either side of the path. As Kamu approached, the smaller crocodiles slid off the path and disappeared in the deep ends. Kamu turned around, smiling ear-to-ear, and beckoned me forward. With the crocodiles eyeing me off from the water, I elected to remain against the wall. I figured I'd at least have an avenue of escape in the event of attack.

Kamu shrugged and continued walking a few paces when a huge crocodile scurried out of the pond and blocked his path. With a lightning strike, Kamu struck the ground right in front of the crocodile with his bamboo rod. The crocodile was entranced. Kamu prodded the animal in the pit of its front legs until its jaws opened. With the crocodile's mouth agape, Kamu lowered himself until he was on his hands and knees right in front of the crocodile. Then, very slowly, he placed his head inside the crocodile's mouth. He remained in that position for a few seconds, before beaming at the adoring crowd.

The spectators erupted into applause. Kamu stood up, walked towards them and took a bow. With a swift strike across its head with the rod, the crocodile's trance was broken. It scurried back into the pond, ending the show.

I couldn't believe what I'd just seen. Through a translator, I said to Kamu I was worried for his safety. Kamu told me that he had been doing it for twenty years.

'I'm protected,' he said. He pulled up his shirt, revealing the tattoo of a tiger. I knew that the Thais revered the tiger, but this was ridiculous. What could I say? There's no point trying to reason with a man who believes a tiger tattoo will protect him from a saltwater crocodile.

I paid Kamu for taking me into the pen and wished him good luck. Two months later, Kamu Karu Suk was killed. One of the crocs he'd trained through cruel conditioning took Kamu's head off in front of a packed crowd.

Kamu's death was a reminder that, no matter a person's experience and confidence, handling crocodiles is incredibly dangerous. If I wanted to film crocs in their habitat at close range and for lengthy periods, I'd need protection. I came up with the concept of lowering a baited cage into a crocodile-infested river in Australia's far north.

I'd film the crocs from inside the cage.

Mark immediately signed up. My brother Michael also came along. We'd reconnected after a long period of estrangement following the birth of my first son. Michael had good knowledge of Australia's north after years working as a jackaroo. Information from a trusted source was always welcome.

Now all we needed to do was select a location. These days, finding crocs across northern Australia is easy. In some places, crocodile numbers have reached plague proportions. It was a different story in the mid-eighties. Unregulated hunting through the twentieth century had very nearly wiped the saltwater crocodile off the map. Bans on hunting had been in place since the early seventies and crocodile numbers were starting to rebound. But they were still scarce around regional centres. We needed to head off the map.

I selected the Drysdale River in the Western Australian Kimberley. This is remote country. The only ways in are by plane or boat. We flew into Darwin and chartered a floatplane. We took off mid-morning from Darwin, our plane loaded down with camping gear, food and a dismantled stainless steel cage. By noon, we were flying above the red cliffs of the Caroline Ranges. The plane followed the course of the Drysdale. From above it looked like an enormous black serpent snaking through the sparsely vegetated landscape.

The plane touched down on a wide section of the upper reaches of the river. After gaining permission from Aboriginal elders, I'd paid big dollars for a base camp to be set up with tents and generators for recharging cameras and lights. I'd also hired the services of an old Aboriginal cook who was waiting for us when we arrived. As I surveyed the camp, I was pleased to see a small twelve-foot tinny pulled up on the bank that would allow us to explore the remote parts of the river.

The next day, after assembling my croc cage, we loaded it onto the tinny and headed up the Drysdale into country that few white men had ever explored. We started to notice black shapes, like fallen tree branches with yellowy-green eyes, surfacing for a few seconds and then vanishing under the water. The further we went, the more crocodiles we sighted. At some points, huge numbers of them were sunning themselves on the riverbanks.

We eventually found a section of river that bent around a grassy promontory. The water rushing down from the ranges had burrowed out a deep channel. Step off the grassy edge and you'd find yourself in four feet of water. The bank rose steeply to a higher plateau, offering ideal vantage points to film the crocodiles attacking the cage from above. It was the perfect site.

The cage was lowered into the water and lashed to a couple of tree trunks on the bank.

Time to bait up. When people talk about the dangers of Australia's far north, the first things that come to mind are crocs and snakes. Very rarely do you hear people talk about scrub bulls. Let me tell you, they are *extremely* dangerous and this part of Australia is full of them. Scrub bulls are wild cattle descended from animals that escaped captivity decades ago. Their hard hooves dig up the delicate soil destroying vegetation, resulting in native animals starving to death. I had no problems ridding the Kimberley of scrub bulls and using them as bait. But they're not easy to hunt. The brown and white coats of these animals are perfect camouflage in the scrubby countryside. Stalking a scrub bull is a perilous task, particularly if you are caught out in the open. They charge with the fury of a Spanish bull. Setting up an ambush near a watering hole where they regularly come to drink is a safer option.

Sure enough, we found a scrub bull drinking from a billabong about a mile from our film site. I shot him dead and cut off his legs, dragging the butchered parts back to camp. Once the bait was secured, I fixed a wooden statue to the top of the cage. I'd bought the statue on a recent trip through PNG. It was said to be a crocodile totem, providing protection to those within its vicinity. I thought it added a nice bit of theatricality.

All was ready. I stepped into the cage wearing a long john wetsuit and holding a camera with underwater housing to shoot above and below the waterline. Mark, meanwhile, was shooting continuously from the shore above. I got inside, closed the hatch and waited. Had I known how long I'd be waiting, I would've called the whole thing off.

15

The Madness of the Kimberley

Two weeks passed and we didn't get a thing. I'd spend the entire day half submerged in murky brown water, a haunch of rotting bull meat inches from my face. We'd return to the cage the next day and find the bait devoured. The crocs battered the cage with such savagery they broke the wooden totem on the first night.

We tried shooting at night for a week, rigging up powerful water-resistant lights to illuminate the cage. It had no effect. So long as I was in the cage, the crocs wouldn't come near. It was as if these crocs were suspicious of our intentions. All I could do was wait day after day, melting in the heat while being harassed every second by those bloody flies.

After three weeks we packed up camp, utterly dejected. We all had families that needed us. But I didn't give up on the project. Expedition after expedition we'd set off with a different strategy in mind. We'd change locations, shoot non-stop for two days and even chum up the water around the cage with extra bull carcass. Once, I even tried changing the bait with near-disastrous consequences.

By then it was November, just before the start of the wet season. We were coming to the end of a particularly arduous expedition, having been camped on the edge of the Drysdale for weeks. The heat was unlike anything I'd experienced. We found that if you walked over rocks exposed to the sun all day the rubber would melt off your shoes.

Heading into the wild to find the scrub bulls was exhausting in the heat. The locals at Kalumburu, an Aboriginal settlement near the mouth of the Drysdale with a population of about 400, suggested using sharks for bait. Crocs, they said, wouldn't be able to resist shark meat. They told me hammerheads entered the mouth of the river when the tide started rising. I had nothing to lose.

I waded out to the sand flats carrying a stainless steel hand spear. The tide comes in thirty feet in this region, bringing an enormous variety of marine life. Swarming past in great numbers were all manner of fish, including small hammerheads. I dug my feet into the sand, lined up a shark and hurled the spear from point blank range. The spear entered the fleshy part of the shark behind its bony head. As I took hold of the spear, the shark flailed around in the water. The end of the spear went into my mouth, lacerating my tongue before lodging in my lower gum. Wincing in agony, I yanked the spear from my gum. Cuts, no matter how minor, suppurate quickly in the tropics. The deep laceration I suffered was oozing pus within a day. Soon I started vomiting, bringing an end to the expedition. Adding insult to injury, that fucking hammerhead failed to lure any crocodiles!

I returned home, sick and exhausted and found myself at a low point in my life. We'd been filming on and off for over a year and I'd chewed through tens of thousands of dollars of savings. I'd even had to take out a loan from the bank. I was in debt to the tune of $50,000 and, worryingly, the dive school was down on enrolments.

My marriage was beginning to suffer. Sue knew from the moment we got engaged that I'd never give up my life of adventuring. But being away from your wife and two infant children on a seemingly doomed project is hard to justify. My family needed me and the dive school needed me. But I didn't have it in me to quit. It wasn't just a matter of letting go of a dream. Giving up felt like caving in to the bullies and validating what the Knox headmaster had said about me in front of the school: 'David Ireland will amount to nothing.' Every time I thought about that day my teeth would grind and my resolve would turn to steel. I was going to finish this film, no matter the consequences.

Money was the major problem. The economy was beginning to flag and interest rates had skyrocketed. I was paying 27 per cent interest on the bank loan. External investment was out too. I couldn't find a production company that wanted to touch the project. I needed another source of revenue. The plan I put in place is an indication of just how desperate I'd become: I'd fund our expeditions by offering recreational fishermen access to our base camp for a fee. Fishing in the Kimberley holds a certain mystique for anglers. An exotic array of huge fish can be found in the river systems and estuaries, offering incredible sport. The problem has always been getting to these remote spots.

I took out a page in a nationally distributed angler's magazine, advertising a three-week holiday package for experienced fishermen. I'd organise transport, food and tent accommodation and offer suggestions about the best fishing spots in this remote wildernesses. There was space for ten people. I filled every spot within a few days of the ad's publication. My scheme was never going to turn a profit, but it would help recoup some of the costs of filming.

We took the first trip with guests in early February, smack bang in the middle of the wet season. The humidity was 100 per cent. You couldn't walk a few feet without becoming drenched in sweat. Against my advice, the fishermen we brought along hydrated themselves on beer. They were drunk by mid-morning, getting into fights with each other and completely trashing the pristine ecosystem.

I had no choice but to supervise them, losing all my filming time in the process. If one of these dickheads got himself killed, I could be found liable of neglecting my duty of care. Forget about the film being derailed. My entire future could be fucked.

My worst nightmare nearly came true towards the end of the two-week trip. One fisherman, a complete bogan who'd flown up from Tasmania, was nearly taken by a croc while having a piss. Luckily, he was blind drunk. The awful racket he made just getting out of his tent was enough to wake me. I pulled my shoes on, grabbed a torch and went to inspect. I heard him singing down by the bank. I shone my torch along the bank, eventually lighting up the clown pissing into the water off a small ledge.

'Fucking idiot,' I shouted. 'Get back from the river!'

He ignored me. As I ran towards him, something stirred in the river. I shone the torch out, the light reflecting the golden eyes of a crocodile the size of a tall man about ten feet from where the man stood. I'd learnt from countless failed attempts to film the crocs at night that they don't like torchlight. So I kept my torch pointed into the croc's eyes, sprinting the final few steps towards the fisherman. When I pulled him backwards by the collar, he pissed all over himself.

'What the fuck do you think you're doing?' he roared, shaping up to take a swing. I pointed towards the river and shone the torch on the crocodile. He flew out to Darwin the next day. By the time the last fishermen left the Drysdale, I hadn't shot a single frame of footage.

Mark, Michael and I put the whole bloody mess out of our minds and concentrated on luring the crocs to the cage. It was time to test one of my most harebrained inventions: the crocodile flapper. I came up with the idea after seeing a croc take a magpie goose after it landed on the surface of the river. The crocodile flapper was supposed to simulate a bird landing on the surface of the water. It consisted of a diving flipper attached to a battery-powered motor that drove a spindle-geared system. When the motor was switched on, the flipper flapped, hence the name.

After a positive test run in our swimming pool back in Sydney, I was confident of success. My confidence was misplaced. The flapper was a complete failure. The device flapped around for a few seconds on the surface before stopping abruptly. The motor had become detached from the flipper and sunk to the bottom.

The expedition was another disaster. I decided on taking Mark with me to film the birdlife that flocked to the billabong behind our camp. I needed something to show for the last three weeks. We set off around midday after loading up with a gallon of water and some food. I was taking extra precautions. Too much had gone wrong on this trip. But the heat must've got to my head. I'd forgotten one crucial thing.

It was now mid-March, nearly the end of the monsoon. The Kimberley was at its most hellish. The sky would turn black in a blink, bringing the heaviest rain before the clouds parted and the sun baked the ground dry. Lightning strikes started bushfires that the howling wind ripped across the landscape. Trees would burn and crackle until a cloudburst doused the flames.

Mark and I walked through the scrubby long grass. The fires had turned the sky blood orange and a ribbon of smoke streaked the horizon. It was like the end of the world. When we arrived at the billabong, a pair of brolgas was performing a mating dance. A beautiful crane with bluish-grey feathers and a splash of scarlet on the back of its head, a brolga doing its mating dance is one of the great spectacles of the Kimberley. The male struts about, puffing out his chest and extending his long legs while a female sits back and observes.

Mark and I both pulled out our Bolex cameras and started shooting. As quietly as possible, we entered the knee-deep mud around the billabong to get as close as possible without frightening the brolgas away. We were getting fantastic footage. Following the brolga was so engrossing that we didn't notice the threat looming behind us.

The first warning was the sound of snorting. I turned around, feeling sick with worry. Coming in from the stony desert that backed up to the billabong was an enormous scrub bull. It was about fifty yards from where Mark and I were filming. Nothing stands in the way of a wild bull and a drink of water. There was no safety for us in the billabong. We'd seen a crocodile burst out of this billabong on a previous expedition, taking hold of a wallaby that was quenching its thirst on the bank. We weren't going anywhere near that water.

'Mark,' I said, keeping the panic out of my voice. Mark looked up and I motioned with my head towards the bull. The bull started pawing at the ground with such force that I could hear his hooves from fifty yards away. Mark went pale. I handed my camera to him and reached around for my thirty-thirty rifle.

'Lay flat on the ground,' I said. 'And don't move.'

I opened up the chamber of the rifle and my heart sank. I only had one bullet. How could I be so careless? I had one shot to kill him, instantly. If I wounded the bull I'd only succeed in stirring him up. We'd be gored or trampled to death like those thrillseekers that run with the bulls in Pamplona. I had one shot. I couldn't afford to miss.

I took a few deep breaths, closed the chamber and put the bull in my crosshairs. I was a good shot over this range. Problem was, the branches of a couple of paperbark trees obscured my view. The thirty-thirty is a small-bore hunting rifle that uses jacketed soft point bullets that flatten out like a fifty-cent piece when they strike a target. The wound that such a bullet inflicts generally proves fatal. But unlike full metal jackets, these bullets will deviate off course if they strike an object. If my bullet hit a tree leaf it could nudge it a few critical millimetres from the intended target.

I'd have to wait for the bull to move. Mark was sprawled across the mud in front of me, his eyes trained dead ahead. With a sudden snort, the bull dropped his head and charged. He burst through the paperbark trees, kicking up a cloud of red dust as he rapidly closed the gap between us.

'Shoot the bastard!' Mark screamed. 'Shoot him now!'

I ignored him. I had to wait to the absolute last second to make certain I didn't miss. I also had a plan. On other bull hunts, I'd noticed these big animals had a habit of raising their heads when they entered mud. If this bull wanted to take us down, he'd have to charge through fifteen yards of mud. Not only would the mud slow him down, the change of terrain might result in the bull exposing his chest.

The bull was now only twenty yards away, close enough for us to see the beads of sweat trickling down his muscly flanks. I could hear the huffing and snorting from his nose above the clap of his hooves striking the desert ground. He was about one second away when his front hooves disappeared into the mud bank. The bull stumbled, bringing his nose to within a few inches of the ground. He let out a furious snort, kicking up his hind legs to keep himself from falling. The action caused his head to rear up, exposing his chest.

A split second before I shot him dead, the bull looked directly at me. The madness I saw in his eyes is something I'll always associate with the Kimberley. The bull crumpled to the ground, his lifeless body tumbling through the mud and stopping a few feet from Mark's head.

I was now in debt to the tune of $100,000. Another unsuccessful expedition would likely result in me defaulting on my loan. Losing the house was a real possibility. So was losing my wife. But I pressed on. I was too far down the rabbit hole to turn back.

I returned to researching in the library and found an interesting reference to 'crocodile calling'. Long-forgotten Aboriginal tribes passed on the knowledge to early European hunters who sought ways of luring crocodiles out of rivers and estuaries. Here was the solution to my problem. The question was whether anyone still possessed this knowledge. I asked a mate who had done a lot of filming with Indigenous communities if he'd ever heard of Aboriginal people luring crocs out of the water. He said he'd heard of a bloke who'd acted in a few films in the seventies and early eighties who knew how to croc call.

My hopes soared. I managed to track the bloke in question to a community on the Fitzroy River in Queensland. Not only was he prepared to share his knowledge, he also played a starring role in my film. We shot some great scenes on the banks of a creek near his home as he taught me the ancient ways of crocodile calling.

The technique involves making a muted trumpet-like sound with the throat and mouth, which simulates the call of a baby croc. It took a couple of days for me to perfect the technique. Afterwards, I shot a couple of scenes of the two of us walking through mangroves as if searching for crocs. I'd edit those images into the film and add a stirring soundtrack.

I returned to the Drysdale River, certain I'd cracked the code. The monsoon season was over. Conditions were bearable. Mark and I went out with my fully loaded thirty-thirty and killed a scrub bull. We attached two haunches of meat to the cage. I got into my wetsuit and lowered myself into the cage. There was so much at stake. My career hinged on whether this ancient technique worked or not. I cleared my throat, moistened my lips, cupped my hands over my mouth and started crocodile calling.

A loud splash came from the other side of the bank. Before I knew it, pairs of golden eyes were popping up from the brown surface. I started my camera rolling, continuing to call the crocodiles. They were gliding a few feet from the cage before a croc attacked. Suddenly, the attacks were coming from everywhere. The smaller crocs started fighting over the scraps of bull carcass that came loose from the cage, while the big fellas rapped their jaws on the cage. In a few seconds, I recorded more useable footage than I'd got in the previous year.

The bait was devoured and the crocodiles disappeared into the murky Drysdale. I emerged from the cage triumphant. Mark, Michael and I all got into a three-way hug. We shot for another week, using the crocodile call to great effect. Once we'd exhausted all our supplies, we flew to Wyndham – a town about 200 miles away – to stock up.

Rather than end production, the breakthrough with the crocodile calling made me hungrier. The crocs of the Drysdale River weren't huge, only ten- or eleven-footers. I wanted to film a real monster. By now, I'd gained a certain celebrity status through the region. After a couple of feature articles, I was known throughout the Kimberley as the 'Crocodile Man'. People approached me with stories of close encounters and near misses wherever I went. But nothing captured my imagination quite like the story of Fergus.

16

The Blood Drain

The first time I heard about Fergus was from the mouth of a retired croc hunter by the name of Max Bowman. Max was a local legend. For nearly forty years, the police contracted Max to shoot crocs once they exceeded a certain size. Nobody knew crocodile behaviour and habitats better than this man. I got his address and, with Mark and Michael tagging along, drove to a shabby old home at the edge of Wyndham.

Max was a rough-diamond adventurer with leathery brown skin and a mouth like a truck driver's. After we stated our business, Max took us into his garage to show us his collection of crocodile skulls. From the size of their jaws alone, I could tell that these animals were far larger than those I'd encountered on the Drysdale. Max had a story for every skull in his house. He even claimed that a couple had taken humans.

'This fucking bastard here,' he growled, pointing at a skull with a perfectly preserved row of teeth, 'took a Malayan fisherman who jumped off a trawler in the Cambridge Gulf.'

According to Max, the fisherman was trying to illegally migrate to Australia. He must've figured his best chance was to swim to shore when his trawler came near the coast. He couldn't have picked a worse spot. The Cambridge Gulf is an enormous ocean inlet into which five major rivers flow. At high tide, the ocean laps against huge hundred-foot sandstone cliffs that form a barrier around much of the gulf. When the tide goes out, dense mangroves and mudflats are left exposed. The massive tidal surges flush nutrient-rich water into the gulf, attracting fish and bigger predators.

'The captain of the trawler told the police he wore a distinctive ring on his finger,' Max said, holding up the skull. 'I found a distinctive ring inside the stomach of this croc a few weeks later.'

According to Max, many people had been taken by crocs in the Cambridge Gulf, particularly near Wyndham. As the Kimberley's oldest and largest town, this was hardly surprising. But Max believed that the main reason was the old Wyndham meat works. Closed only a couple of years before we arrived, the meat works had operated since 1919. For six decades, every station owner across the Kimberley plateau would employ drovers to herd their cattle to the meat works. The cattle would be slaughtered and the meat shipped to Perth or into Asia. According to Max, the meat works provided regular meals for the marine life of the Cambridge Gulf.

Situated on a creek to the north of the town, the Wyndham meat works consisted of two concrete buildings. One building was for slaughtering, the other for processing. Once the cattle were slaughtered, the carcasses would be hung on hooks that were connected to a steel cable. The cable ran down the length of the building where butchers would slice away skin, excess fat and gristle. The two buildings were connected by a shallow concrete groove in which blood, bits of meat and offal collected. At the end of each day, a powerful hose flushed the groove clean. Cattle remains washed down the gutter and into a drain that fed directly into a creek bed at the back of the meat works. Twice a week, the huge thirty-foot tidal surge flooded the creek.

'The blood and guts sent the fish wild,' said Max. 'They'd stir up the water bringing eagles, sharks, barramundi, bloody everything – including crocodiles.'

On a few occasions, an enormous crocodile entered the creek late at night to feed. The crocodile was so fierce that the others took off when it approached. Nobody had an exact fix on his length, but those who saw him said he was by far the biggest crocodile they'd ever seen. The locals called him Fergus.

Max claimed that Fergus was responsible for at least three human fatalities in the Wyndham area. The most recent fatality was Paul Flanagan, a truck driver who breezed into town one night in 1980 and nearly emptied the pub of beer. Pissed as a fart, Flanagan thought it a good idea to have a night swim. He piled a couple of ladies into his truck and drove to the meat works. The tide was coming in fast and the creek was nearly full. Flanagan stripped naked and walked down to the red water where the discharge pipe pumped blood and guts into the creek. The two women he'd brought along warned him not to enter the creek. Flanagan, who was flailing about in waist-deep water, turned around and roared, 'The Wyndham crocodiles are all bullshit!'

A second later, a huge crocodile clamped his jaws around Flanagan's waist. The crocodile thrashed about for a few seconds and then disappeared. The next day, the cops found the truck driver's leg lodged in a mangrove tree. The crocodile literally shook Flanagan's limbs off. Fergus had struck again.

Since the closure of the meat works, sightings of Fergus had been less frequent. Some blow-in took the pub owner's pet dog for a walk down near the wharf. He returned to the pub an hour later covered in the dog's blood. An enormous crocodile had exploded out of the shallow water and ripped the dog apart. The locals were convinced it was Fergus.

A year earlier, a cow being herded onto a boat of live cattle headed for Java got out of the pen and fell in the water. As the whar-fies tried to guide her back to shore, a big croc latched onto the cow's neck and took her down. Goodbye cow! The wharfies had never seen a crocodile as big. But I'd heard this sort of thing before. Rumours snowball into legend pretty quick in the deep north.

'Fergus is still out there,' Max said.

'How do you know?' I asked.

'I've seen him.'

Although Max's croc-hunting days were behind him, he contin-ued to fish the Cambridge Gulf for barramundi. A few years back, he'd seen an enormous crocodile stalking the mud flats at low tide for stray wallabies and scrub bulls.

'Fergus is alive,' he said.

'How do I find him?'

'The blood drain.'

The meat works might've been closed for four years, but the creek still stank. A couple of crocs always came in at high tide. Max was confident that once we started baiting up a cage, the crocs would come in greater numbers. Fergus would show up sooner or later. But how long would I have to wait? I wasn't even convinced Fergus existed. Remaining in Wyndham indefinitely on the off-chance that we got a big croc on camera wasn't an option. Another week up here and I'd be declaring bankruptcy and Sue would be fil-ing for divorce!

Max had a solution. We'd select a site near the blood drain and anchor the cage in the creek. Mark, Michael and I would then head back to Sydney while Max baited up the cage before high tide. He'd keep an eye on the crocodiles that came into the creek and ring me the moment he saw Fergus. All he asked in return was a modest fee for his services. We agreed on the amount and shook on it.

With Max's help, we spent the next day selecting a site behind the meat works about twenty feet from the blood drain. The sea had receded beyond the horizon. Beyond the mouth of the creek towards the Cambridge Gulf, all I could see were a few pools of water, shimmering in the sunlight. It seemed unbelievable that within a day the water level would be above our heads.

We settled on a site with a slight muddy slope that backed up to a fringe of mangrove trees not far from the discharge pipe. We drove four six-foot star pickets into the mud to anchor the cage into the creek bed. I attached water-resistant lights to the cage and fed the cables back to a generator high up on the bank. The following morning we all flew home.

I arrived back in Cronulla in the midst of an unfolding global catastrophe. The stock market crash of 1987 hit everyone hard. Times were already getting tough in Australia. Inflation was out of control, interest rates were sky high and unemployment was in double-digit figures. The decade that began so positively was ending in doom and gloom. It wasn't just that people had lost their confidence to spend. They'd lost their sense of adventure.

The dive school was burning through money. I had no choice but to scale back the business. That meant letting people go. It was agony. Some of these people had been working at Cronulla Dive for fifteen years. It was like firing family members. With fewer diving instructors on hand, I was working harder than ever. Slowly but surely, I started to balance the books.

At the very moment Cronulla Dive started to show signs of turning a profit, I got a call from Max. Fergus was back.

17

Fergus

I rang Michael and Mark and told them to get ready: we were head-ing back to the blood drain. Both said they wouldn't be going. Michael's family needed him at home. Mark had lost his nerve.

'But I'm the one in the cage,' I said.

'We've taken too many risks,' he said. 'Our luck won't last much longer.'

Mark was right. It was dangerous, even for those people film-ing from the bank. But I sensed something else at play. Mark had recently got engaged to a real beauty. The voice at the other end of the line was Mark's, but the words he was speaking belonged to his fiancée. It was bitterly disappointing after all the work we'd done to get the film shot. But I had overcome greater setbacks.

I found replacements in Sydney and we all flew up to Wyndham. Sue was really worried that something tragic was about to happen. I told her that if I got Fergus on camera, then I could make the film great. Nothing else was said. It was a lousy way to leave things, but I was determined to get it finished, even if that meant risking everything.

We landed in Wyndham and I went straight to Max's house. He

told me that huge numbers of crocodiles had been feeding off the cage. They were turning up now at high tide and had become accustomed to the powerful lights.

'A couple of nights ago,' he said, 'the crocs all scattered and everything went silent. A few minutes later, Fergus ripped the baits off.'

'You're sure it was Fergus?'

'Absolutely,' said Max. 'He looked twice as big as his mates.'

Max advised me to take extra precautions before I entered the cage. My thirty-thirty rifle was next to useless. Firing a bullet under water probably wouldn't penetrate the croc's hide. So I invested in a 12-gauge powerhead. Spearfishermen use powerheads when hunting sharks. Powerheads are long tubes with a spring inside that fire a shotgun shell on contact. I'd seen a spearfisherman blow a hole the size of a basketball into a bull shark. I didn't like the idea of using it. But that sort of firepower could save my life.

I'd also take a sharpened hunting knife. From what Max was saying, Fergus was bigger and more powerful than any croc I'd ever encountered. If Fergus, or any other croc for that matter, started to pull the cage over, I'd simply cut the rope that held the bait.

I was ready to go. It was time to head to the cage. It was creepy down at the blood drain and even creepier inside the meat works. Aside from a couple of broken windows everything was in decent condition. The hooks that carried the carcasses down the line for processing were still attached to a heavy steel cable. Despite a layer of dust coating the equipment, the place was clean. I knew a bit about factories, but the thought of working in this place made me shudder. Screaming cattle, the smell of blood and guts, and the oven-like conditions must've been horrific.

Outside, the tide was surging up the creek. I set up the film crew on the shore about forty feet from the cage. I waded out through the mudflats with a couple of Bolex cameras that I'd fitted with high-speed motors that shot a greater number of frames per second. It meant that I'd be able to capture, in great detail, a crocodile's jaws clamping shut.

Once the cameras were in place, I returned to shore and got dressed. The temperature was nudging fifty degrees, but I decided to wear a wetsuit long john to protect the lower part of my body against the cooler water that the tide swept in from the ocean. I filled up on sandwiches and fruit and drank about a gallon of water. I did a final check with the onshore camera crew, shook everyone's hand and then set off for the cage.

Out of nowhere, the police came to spoil the party. By now, everyone across the Kimberley knew what I was attempting to do. A few Wyndham locals had even come down to the blood drain, hoping to catch sight of the legendary Fergus attacking the Crocodile Man's cage. The police didn't like it. But there was nothing they could do. Or so I thought . . .

'Those things are illegal in Western Australia,' said the senior sergeant, pointing at the powerhead attached to my belt. 'I'm going to have to confiscate it.'

'C'mon, mate,' I protested, 'can't you see what I'm about to do?'

'The law is the law,' he said, with a smirk. I handed over the powerhead. The cop made a big show of checking everything on shore, as if I might be concealing a cache of illegal firearms. He looked out towards the cage as though he was preparing to make an inspection, but decided against it. He sauntered back to his car with his mate and took off.

Losing the powerhead was a blow. If a croc managed to rip apart the meshing that encased the cage, all I had to defend myself was a bowie knife. The knife would barely penetrate a crocodile's skin. So I decided to take my thirty-thirty rifle along. It was more to boost my confidence. A rifle was completely useless underwater.

By now, the creek had filled to about two feet of water and was rising fast. The sun was low on the horizon. I waded out to the cage. I made a final check, pushing hard against the star pickets that anchored the cage to the creek bed to make sure it was stable. Once I was satisfied, I leapt on top of the cage and slipped inside, making sure the hatch was locked above.

The tide swept up the creek with great speed. Within half an hour, the water was above my knees. At sunset, I turned on the lights. The slight buzzing sound the lights emitted was a worry. Standing waist-deep in water in a steel cage attached to high-voltage lights was a sure-fire way of being electrocuted. But I had more immediate concerns. As the water continued to rise, spiders started falling onto me.

I first noticed them floating on the surface of the water inside the cage. They were brown with flecks of black. The larger spiders had bodies about the size of a twenty-cent piece and a leg span about the size of a palm. At first, I thought they'd fallen from overhanging trees and swept into my cage. Then I noticed a whole family of them scurrying out of the hollowed-out steel supports of the cage. I'd drilled holes into the supports of the cage to prevent it floating away. Inadvertently I'd created the perfect home for a spider colony.

As the water level rose, more spiders spilled out of the supports. They scampered up the cage to escape the rising water, some falling into my hair and scurrying across my face and shoulders. I doubted very much that they were venomous. Not that this made it any easier. I fucking *hate* spiders!

Three hours in the cage and the water level stopped rising. Standing up, the water came up to my chest. The gap between the surface of the water and the roof of the cage was less than two feet. It was incredibly claustrophobic. Standing upright in a cage for so many hours was bad enough. The insects that were drawn to the lights and attacked my exposed skin made life miserable. There was absolutely nothing I could do. Stepping out of the cage and swimming to the bank would be a potentially fatal mistake. I just had to tough it out.

Around midnight, an olive sea snake paid me a visit. I heard him striking the side of the cage. The snake would launch out of the water, fangs bared, striking the lights. Obviously the snake had mistaken the lights for prey and was attempting to inject venom. If that venom found its way into my body I'd be in serious trouble. With my eyes firmly fixed on the snake, I carefully hooked the end of my Bolex to the cage, and reached for my bowie knife. The olive-brown of the snake's skin melted into the muddy water, making it very difficult to see.

'Everything okay?' Max asked from the bank.

'Sea snake!' I shouted. There was nothing anyone on the bank could do. Launching the tin boat to come get me in the event I was bitten was out of the question. If crocs were lurking, they could quite easily capsize the boat.

The snake launched at the lights again, striking with staggering speed. It circled round and started biting at the lights on the other side of the cage. I didn't dare take my eyes off it. Each side of the cage was fitted with a wire-grilled security door with the fly-wire meshing removed. I'd designed it to keep out crocodiles. A snake would have no problem slithering through the gaps in the grille.

The snake eventually suspended its attacks. It circled the cage and then vanished underwater. I lowered my eyes to water level in the hope of seeing movement on the surface. Nothing. I stood to my full height, breathing a sigh of relief. I sheathed my bowie knife at the very moment the snake entered the cage.

Number one rule when in close proximity to venomous snakes is to not make sudden movements. I followed the snake with my eyes as it explored the confines of the cage. As it brushed past my body, seemingly unaware of my presence, I slowly raised my left hand above the surface of the water and quickly grabbed hold of the snake behind its head. The force of my thumb pressing into the snake's throat caused the animal to open up its mouth. The lower half of the snake was wriggling around furiously, desperately trying to wrap itself around my arm. I raised my knife and sliced it in half. The lower part of the snake fell into the water, inert. The top half went mad, causing blood to splash over my chest.

A snake cut in two is capable of living for minutes and those fangs could still deliver a lethal bite. I pinned what remained of the snake's body against the cage and sliced its head off. Its mouth twitched a few times then went still. I fed the remains of the snake through the grille and then sounded the all clear to those keeping watch from the bank.

Not long afterwards, the crocs showed up. They approached cautiously, their eyes a luminous gold in the lights fixed atop the cage. Although my crew on the bank knew to keep quiet so as not to scare the crocs away, I could hear the flurry of activity as they scrambled into position.

The crocodiles responded instantly to my calling. They converged on the cage in twos and threes, tearing away the baits I'd attached. The crocs were a similar size to those I'd encountered on the Drysdale River, but the experience in the blood drain was much more frightening. I was learning that a cage fixed to a riverbank is far sturdier than one held in place by star pickets. The crocs, hammering their heads against the cage, causing it to rattle and shudder, tore at the bull haunches ferociously.

The tide changed around two o'clock. The crocs had devoured all the bait. Now I just had to wait for the water to flow out to sea and the sun to come up. The last few hours before dawn were exhausting. I'd been on my feet since dusk. Remaining upright against the slow-moving current for hours on end was like standing against a riptide. I made a note to myself to install a bench before the next night's shoot so that I could periodically rest my legs.

By daybreak, a foot of water was all that remained in the blood drain. The temptation to get out of that cage was hard to resist. But there was still a chance that a crocodile had burrowed into the creek bed. I waited for two torturous hours until the remaining water evaporated into a few puddles and then pulled myself out of the cage. It was mid-morning when I made it to the bank, nearly collapsing from physical and mental exhaustion. I'd been in the cage for over twelve hours.

I handed the cameras to the crew and fell into the passenger seat of my car. Max drove me to the pub where I'd booked a room. I took a shower, scouring myself clean of mud and snake blood, and then collapsed into bed. I awoke late in the afternoon with a blistering headache and terrible aches in my joints.

Wincing in pain, I stumbled into the bathroom and wrapped my mouth around the tap. After filling up on water, I popped a couple of aspirin. Feeling marginally better, I went downstairs and had a feed before returning to the blood drain for another long night of shooting.

The second night of shooting proceeded much like the first. The crocs showed up in great numbers just before midnight. My crew had attached more bait to the cage and they buffeted the grilles with incredible force. Some of the bigger crocs pulled at the ropes that held the bait, causing the cage to lean over. On several occasions, I reached around for my bowie knife, preparing to cut the rope if I sensed the cage was about to topple. But the star pickets held.

The footage was incredible. At times I was completely surrounded, four crocodiles attacking the cage from different sides, tearing away at the haunches of meat. But Fergus stayed away that night, as he would for the rest of the week.

—

It was hard to establish a routine. We were completely at the mercy of the tides. I generally had a fifteen-hour window before I'd be back in the cage. This meant we sometimes shot during the day. For different reasons, daytime shoots were just as hard as nighttime shoots. The heat was obviously more oppressive, and without any shade my skin got badly burnt. The crocs were a bit shy during the day too. Sometimes I'd spend an entire day in the cage without seeing a single croc.

After a couple of weeks, I was completely knackered. Keeping my lower body submerged in coolish water while my top half sweltered in forty-degree heat was extremely taxing. Even with the aid of the wooden bench, I was barely able to stand at the end of each night's filming. It was no surprise I got so sick.

The alternative name for dengue fever is breakbone fever, and for good reason. It felt like someone was taking a power drill to my body and boring holes into every bone and joint. My headaches started morphing into full-blown migraines. I did my best to ignore the symptoms, passing off the aches and pains as cramps and dehydration. When I started vomiting up my guts, Max suggested I see a doctor. I stupidly ignored him. I was worried a bad diagnosis would cause further delay.

To get through it all, I called up my happiest memories. One minute I'd be diving the Barrier Reef with Sue, the next I'd be in the backyard with our two boys. It kept me mentally balanced and the tedium of waiting for the crocs to show was kept at bay.

After ten nights of shooting, having filmed ten separate twelve-hour sessions from the cage, my condition took a turn for the worse. On the last shoot, I staggered out of the blood drain and had to be helped to the car. I'd developed a cough that wracked my body for minutes on end. It was like an asthma attack, only I was hocking up green mucus.

My camera crew begged me to take a week off. I told them I'd be okay. I knew that if I let up for any extended period, my body would shut down. Only two things would bring the film shoot to an end: capturing Fergus on camera or dying. That's how deep my obsession went.

I woke up ten hours later feeling worse than I'd ever felt in my life. I literally crawled to the bathroom and took a shower sitting down. I forced down a sandwich for breakfast even though I had no appetite. Somehow, I managed to drive to the blood drain – pulling over at one stage to vomit up the sandwich I'd just eaten. When I arrived, the film crew looked very worried.

I understood their concern. Making it in this business requires more than resilience and courage. You also need to be adaptable and quick-thinking. I might be required to cut one of the baits if a croc threatened to pull the cage over. Or another olive sea snake might slither into my cage. There were all manner of things that might go wrong. I knew what my film crew was thinking because I'd be thinking the same thing if I were in their position: should someone step in and end this madness?

I pulled on my long john wetsuit, sheathed my bowie knife, took hold of my camera and rifle, and made my way towards the blood drain. As I approached the bank, I noticed that Max's tin boat had been taken off the trailer, as if ready to launch into the creek in an emergency. It was probably there to boost my confidence even though I would never let that happen. I took one last look at the crew and then walked out to the cage.

I won't pretend that the reasons that motivated me to be so reckless weren't ego driven. But it's also true to say that I believed then, as I do now, when you give up on your dreams your spirit dies. To me, that's a fate worse than death.

It started the same way as always. The mosquitoes swarmed as the tide came in and the spiders started spilling out of the hollow steel supports of the cage. By sunset the water was up to my chest. At high tide, the crocs showed up. The smaller ones attacked the baits first, eager to get their fill before the ten-footers muscled them out. I started calling to them, stirring up their aggression. With the cameras rolling, I got about twenty minutes of good footage. There were six big crocs savaging the baits. Then they vanished.

A strange calm descended over the creek. Everything fell deathly silent. Something big was happening. I could sense the members of the camera crew holding their breath. I peered into the darkness, searching for movement on the surface. That's when I saw him – a pair of golden eyes two hand-widths apart, just beyond the pool of light. The stories were true. Fergus was a monster!

He slowly moved into the light and went still, eyeing me off for seconds like a gunslinger waiting to draw. With a sudden whip of his massive scaly tail, Fergus charged the cage. His head struck the grille with such force that for a horrible moment I thought the cage was going to keel over. Fergus went in again and again. Somehow, the star pickets withstood the onslaught. After a minute, he gave up and started circling the cage.

The size of the animal was hard for my mind to comprehend. His entire body could have enveloped the cage. His teeth hung threateningly out of his mouth and below his jawline. I was in the presence of a very old creature. Reports of an abnormally large croc terrorising the Cambridge Gulf started way back at the beginning of the twentieth century. Nobody knows how old these animals can live in the wild. I had every reason to believe that this was the same crocodile.

Fergus struck the cage with the side of his head. The jarring caused my ears to ring. It was like someone was hitting the cage with a sledgehammer. A single blow would easily kill a man. Eventually, he gave up on the cage and focused on the baits. When his jaws opened, a nauseating stench of rotten flesh washed over me. It was the smell of the dead wallabies, scrub bulls, sharks and human beings that had rotted in Fergus's mouth for decades.

Once all the baits were gone, Fergus floated alongside the cage eyeing me off. The scrub bull was entrée. I was the main course. Fergus was going to wait me out. He didn't move for the rest of the morning. Every so often, he'd thump the cage with his head to remind me he was waiting.

But time was on my side. The tide began rushing out. Before dawn he disappeared under a few feet of water. I couldn't see anything, but I knew he was still there. I stayed in the cage well into the day. I wasn't going to leave that cage until every last drop of water had left the creek. Finally, just before noon, after a marathon fifteen hours in the cage, I hauled myself out. The coast was clear. I gave a triumphant fist pump to the guys on the shore, who responded with a cheer.

Max walked out to the cage with a measuring tape. Alongside the cage, Fergus had left his imprint where he'd burrowed into the mud. We measured the imprint at 17 feet 10 inches. We could see his massive paw prints in the mud. They looked like dragon prints leading out to sea.

I was seriously unwell. Exhausted from the ravages of the day, I decided to leave the cameras in the cage. I'd get them the next day.

I slept a full twenty-four hours, waking up bathed in sweat and feeling like death. I knew at that moment that the film was finished. There wasn't much else I needed. The footage I'd gathered over the previous night was brilliant. All that was missing was a demonstration of Fergus's raw power. I'd hoped to catch Fergus lifting himself out of the water or attacking the cage with jaws agape. But there was no guarantee Fergus would return. Besides, another night in the cage would probably kill me.

I returned to the blood drain early that afternoon and broke the news to the camera crew. They were overjoyed with relief. We were going home. I'd already told Max that he could have the cage. All I needed were the three cameras that I'd left inside.

The tide was ebbing, having swept in and gone back out while I was asleep. The creek was not yet drained of water. I calculated that the cage was standing in about two feet of water. There hadn't been any bait on the cage for over twenty-four hours and those members of the camera crew who had arrived on the bank earlier hadn't seen any croc activity.

I scrambled down the muddy bank and waded into the water. It came up to my knees. I'd never been in the creek when it had any water in it and was surprised by the amount of effort it took to pull my feet out of the muddy bottom. I felt uneasy. Something felt wrong. I managed to convince myself that my concern was just the product of tiredness. On I went.

The sun was high in the sky and I could feel the sweat trickling down my neck. The closer I got to the cage, the greater my sense of unease. I stopped halfway and took my bearings. Nothing at all stirred. On the surface, the little water that remained in the creek appeared millpond calm. I could feel the gentle tug of the current pulling at my calves. I looked back to the bank. The only person watching me was one of my camera crew, a young woman who'd come down from Darwin. She waved encouragingly. I waved back and pressed on. I should've listened to my instincts.

I increased my pace. About ten yards from the cage I heard an ear-piercing scream from the bank. I lifted my legs high out of the mud and ran for the cage, not daring to look back. I could hear the water splashing behind me and smelt a foul breath. I leapt on top of the cage like a jackrabbit as Fergus brought his jaws down in a bloodcurdling clap. He'd come within inches of ripping off my arse. I toppled inside the cage, tearing skin off my arm against the sharp wire meshing of the cage roof, and landed hard on the bottom. I looked through the grille, directly into Fergus's eyes, close enough to see the flecks of green and gold around his black pupils.

Fergus stalked the cage for several minutes, whacking it with his head and loosening one of the panels from its hinge. Staring into the jaws of one of the largest saltwater crocodiles on the planet through a flimsy cage is most people's idea of hell. I saw it as a privilege. My yearlong effort to capture these incredible animals on camera led me to this conclusion: saltwater crocodiles are the greatest predators that walk the earth. Millions of years of evolution have honed them into the perfect killing machine.

Within an hour, the water emptied from the creek, leaving it a muddy bog. With one final bang against the cage, Fergus made his way out of the blood drain and followed the water as it retreated into the Cambridge Gulf. When he was thirty yards from the cage he turned back and stared straight at me as if to say, *You got away this time, mate!*

18

The
Southern Right

I returned to Sydney sick as a dog. The doctor diagnosed dengue fever and double pneumonia and prescribed a course of antibiotics and plenty of rest. My body took time to recover. After a couple of days, I found the energy to play with my kids, giving them the attention they deserved after I'd spent months away from home. I also started the job of whittling down hundreds of hours of footage into a 76-minute film.

But I was a long way from fully recovered. I found the most basic tasks confusing. I'd forget people's names and have trouble adding up money. The pneumonia also brought on asthma attacks for the first time in years. I wasn't in any condition to start filming in the wild again. But when a mate who worked for the National Parks and Wildlife Service rang to tell me a whale had been seen off Wanda Beach, I went straight back to work.

I'd never lost my fascination with these giants since watching Queequeg harpoon the whale in *Moby Dick*. I'd applied for a permit to dive with whales years earlier, but never had a chance to use it. I told my wife that I might not get a better opportunity to film a whale. That was an exaggeration. But Sue didn't stand in my way.

She knew that the wild was calling me back.

My mate arranged a boat with a crew on the wharf at Gunnamatta Park. As we cleared the calm waters of Gunnamatta Bay and headed into the open sea, I felt fatigue wash over me. I found the normally simple effort of keeping balanced in a large swell exhausting. If I couldn't stand, how was I supposed to film a whale underwater?

I was all set to call it off when I saw the whale break the surface. The whale's enormous tail flukes loomed before us. The tail remained suspended above the sea for a few moments before slapping hard against the surface. Curious at our arrival, the whale drew up alongside the boat, a fully-grown female measuring about fifty feet in length. The callosity – the white, calcified patches around the head – indicated that this was a southern right whale. Nearly hunted to extinction in the nineteenth century, it was rare to sight southern rights along the coast and even rarer to film them up close. There was no way I was going to miss this chance.

I did a final check of my scuba gear and equipment. Atop the underwater housing that held my video camera, I'd fixed a 35mm Nikonos still camera. Satisfied that everything was ready, I stepped off the boat. The whale dipped beneath the surface when I entered the water. She swam to the bottom and I followed her down. This was my first dive since returning from Wyndham. The experience of being in the clean ocean was exhilarating. I felt like I was washing off the muck from the blood drain.

Then the water went cloudy. At first, I thought I was suffering blurred vision. My concern gave way to great excitement – the whale was about to give birth! Exerting as little energy as possible so as not to disturb the pregnant whale, I swam to the bottom and positioned myself about ten yards away. I buttoned on with the video, filming the whale as she rubbed her belly against the sandy bottom.

RIGHT: Me, Mum and my older brother Michael.

BOTTOM: Dad and Chester. Dad was the classic strong, silent type. He was not one for overt displays of affection, but he was a good man and he doted on me in his own way.

TOP: An advertisement for Don Athaldo's mail order strength program. This was the program that set me on my path from sickly asthmatic kid to dive instructor and wildlife film producer.

LEFT: Me and the greatest of companions, Shek.

TOP: Taking a dive course in 1972 during the heydays of Cronulla Dive.

RIGHT: At the dive shop. The employees of Cronulla Dive became some of my best mates.

TOP: Filming shipwrecks on the Great Barrier Reef in 1974. The first film I shot with 16mm cameras.

BOTTOM: Filming at the Darwin croc farm. Obviously I paid no attention to the warning sign in the background.

TOP: In my cage at the Darwin croc farm, completely surrounded by crocs.

LEFT: My view from inside the cage. This is a huge seventeen-foot croc taking the bait.

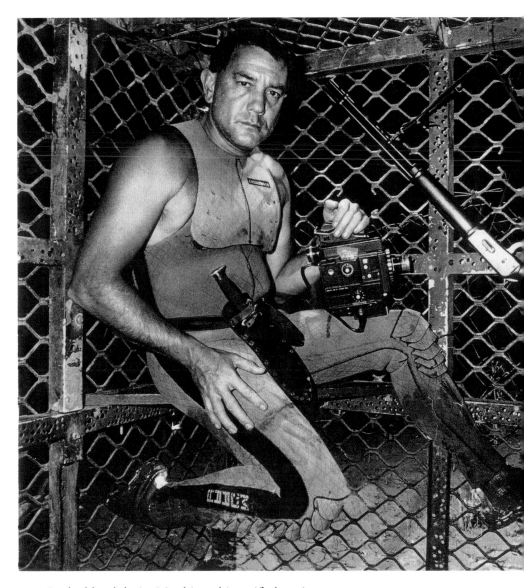

TOP: In the blood drain. My thirty-thirty rifle hanging behind me was next to useless – I was really hoping the cage would hold.

OPPOSITE TOP: Transporting the croc cage up the Drysdale River. I'm on top of the cage, my brother Michael is at the motor and my cameraman, Mike Olding, is at the rear. If the boat had flipped, we would have been in real danger.

OPPOSITE BOTTOM: Fergus.

CROCODILE MAN

THE MOTION PICTURE ...a true wildlife adventure

"For the Man and his Dragon to survive... One must Surrender"

LEFT: The original poster for my film *Crocodile Man*, which screened on both Channel Seven and Discovery Channel in 1990. It was one of the highest-rating documentaries that year.

BOTTOM: Kamu Sari Suk from Thailand, one of the craziest bastards I've ever met. Kamu's death was a reminder that no matter a person's experience and confidence, handling crocodiles is incredibly dangerous.

TOP: Elephants are beautiful and intelligent creatures, but they can be dangerous. I got a little too close for comfort to this one – it charged me while I was filming in South Africa. Thankfully I survived to tell the tale.

BOTTOM: Joe the Irishman (left) with one of his hunting mates. Joe taught me how to hunt, and his death had a huge impact on me. Joe is never far from my thoughts whenever I have a bow in my hands.

TOP: I fell head over heels in love the moment I met my wife, Sue. Here she's on a dive in the waters off PNG.

BOTTOM: Lions killing a wildebeest in South Africa, filmed from the bonnet of a Land Rover. When I told the driver to get as close as possible, I didn't think he'd rest the bull bar directly on the kill!

ABOVE (BOTH): Filming bull sharks for my film *Sea God*. Over thirty sharks came in for a feed while we were shooting this footage, including the biggest bull shark I've ever seen.

ABOVE (BOTH): Hitching a ride on a lemon shark for the filming of *Shark Rider*.

OPPOSITE TOP: Getting up close and personal with a wallaby. I fell in love with the Australian bush as a child, and am committed to protecting it from the unbelievable damage wrought by introduced species.

OPPOSITE MIDDLE: Catching an olive python in the Kimberley, Western Australia.

OPPOSITE BOTTOM: Me and my cameraman Abraham Joffe in the jungle of a headhunter island in the Solomons, the same island where my grandfather was taken captive and his mate killed.

PREVIOUS PAGE: Me, Sue and our four boys (left to right): Jason, Adam, Luke and Nathan.

TOP: I owe so much to this wonderful woman. Me and Sue, November 2014, aboard a pearling lugger sailing ship off the coast of Broome.

LEFT: A lace monitor caught in outback NSW during the filming of *Wild Boar Attack*.

The swirling current enveloped the whale in her own fluid, concealing her from view. Concerned that I might miss the birth, I swam closer. I was now within a few yards of the whale as she rubbed herself with greater vigour against the seabed. I was concentrating intently on filming and didn't notice the whale reposition her tail above me. Having been underwater for a couple of minutes, the whale was preparing to surface for air. She brought her tail down on top of me to push off from the bottom.

In all my years of shooting wildlife, nothing has come close to the pain of being crushed between the seabed and the tail of a fifty-ton right whale. The blow forced my diaphragm up into my chest, completely knocking the remaining air out of my lungs. I felt my body go limp. Every part of my being craved oxygen. Stars started to appear in my field of vision. I'd survived months filming the most ruthless and cunning man-eaters in one of the world's most inhospitable environments. I was going to die at the hands of one of nature's gentlest mammals in waters I'd been diving for years.

I wasn't ready to die. I wanted to hold my wife again and see my boys grow up. But how would I survive this day? I was paralysed fifty feet below the surface and having trouble inflating my lungs from my regulator. There was no way of letting those above know that I was in trouble. I felt myself giving in to fear. My heart felt like it was beating out of my chest. From out of nowhere, a voice entered my head. It was the voice of Don Athaldo telling me to be calm. I managed to slow the crazy tempo of my heartbeat. Even when my arms and legs refused to follow the commands of my brain, I didn't give in to panic.

I felt pins and needles in my arms and feet. Feeling was returning to my body. I managed to kick weakly off the bottom and began the long journey to the surface. My field of vision started to narrow. Energy sapping away, I started to sink. This was it. The end was near.

About three feet from the seabed I felt a gentle pressure at the small of my back. I turned my neck and stared directly into the eye of the whale. Out of instinct, I raised the camera and took a photograph with my Nikonos. The whale retreated behind me and placed her nose on my backside. With ever-increasing momentum, I started to approach the surface. Right whales are incredibly playful creatures, known to push human vessels around. The whale riders of New Zealand are said to dive the depths of the seas on the backs of this very species. Some would say she was just being curious. But in my heart I believe that this whale knew I'd been injured. She was rescuing me.

I broke the surface and took in a lungful of air. The whale disappeared below to finish her labour. The boat crew immediately knew something was wrong. I was practically motionless and starting to sink. Two guys dived into the water and pulled me towards the boat. I was dragged aboard, tightly clutching my camera gear, unable to speak.

X-rays would reveal that I'd suffered bruised ribs and hairline fractures to two vertebrae. My body, already weakened from tropical maladies, was now coping with serious internal injuries. I was lucky it wasn't much worse. The doctor said I came within millimetres of severing my spinal column, an injury that would've put me in a wheelchair for life.

The picture I took of the right whale's eye ran on the front page of several daily newspapers. The money earned was a welcome boost to the coffers. But the picture meant more than its financial value. It was a treasured keepsake of one of the most spiritual experiences of my life – the day a southern right whale carried me from the clutches of death.

19

Croc Farm

While recovering from my broken back, I worked on the crocodile film. I edited countless hours of footage shot on the Drysdale River and in the blood drain. With growing dismay, I sensed something was missing.

We'd done well to capture the raw beauty of the northern wilderness and the foreboding atmosphere inside the cage. There were also some excellent shots of Fergus chomping down on the baits and the crocs responding to my calling. But the raw power and ferocity of the crocodiles I'd witnessed at close range didn't come across in any of the footage. The film was lacking a frenetic climax, something that shortened the breath and got the heart beating faster. I had to go back up north.

The idea to shoot at the Darwin Crocodile Farm had been floated early in the production, back when we were struggling to get anything decent on the Drysdale. I'd dismissed the idea on the basis that the premise of the film was to shoot crocodiles in the wild. The experience of filming Fergus in the blood drain, however, provided an opportunity to slightly change the narrative. The manner in which the other crocs disappeared when Fergus turned up suggested that I was dealing with a territorial animal. In all the research I'd conducted, there was no mention of this behaviour. Taking a baited cage into an enclosure that held over a hundred crocodiles seemed the perfect place to prove that theory. Of course, this was just a pretence. The main objective of the shoot was to capture crocodiles going mental!

The major hurdle was getting Sue on board. Our financial situation remained precarious. The bank loan hadn't been repaid and interest rates were still high. Plunging further into debt to fund yet another shoot was beyond risky. It was bloody crazy. Sue was also worried about the battering my body had copped over the previous year. I assured her that I was in tiptop condition and that the shoot shouldn't go for longer than a month. All we needed to do was set up a new cage and start filming. She reluctantly consented. God, I love that woman!

I headed to Darwin. Before leaving I managed to get Mark Olding back on board. I was delighted when he agreed to return to the production and finish what we'd started together. We met up at Darwin Airport, hired a car and drove directly to the site.

The Darwin Crocodile Farm consists of a massive barbed wire fence surrounding a man-made lake. The animals in this place had either killed livestock or shown aggression towards humans. Since hunting crocodiles had been made illegal, the number of residents in the farm had increased. There were, at that point in time, over a hundred mature saltwater crocodiles with a record of misbehaviour.

The lake was the obvious place from which to film. The problem was safely getting the gear out there. As ambush predators, crocodiles will not willingly reveal themselves to prey unless they are certain they have the advantage of surprise. Learning the art of crocodile calling and being prepared to film at night had been the only way I could lure these crocs to the cage.

At the Darwin Crocodile Farm, I would have the opposite

problem. After years spent in captivity, these animals no longer feared humans. Worse still, the crocs had formed a direct association between humans and eating. I observed this during a feeding session that the croc handlers periodically put on for the benefit of the tourists. The moment the handlers arrived at the edge of the fence, the crocs started jostling for position. That was before the raw meat and chickens had even been brought out and hurled into the enclosure.

Witnessing the seething mass of crocodiles crawling over each other to get to the food, I knew I was in exactly the right place to get the climax of my film. These crocs were real monsters: vicious and ferocious. Given the complete disregard they had for each other, it was hard to imagine that there was a dominant order. But there was only one way to find out.

By now, my exploits in the blood drain and the Drysdale River had spread to Darwin. Some people were calling me the Crocodile Man to my face. I used my newfound fame to convince the management of the farm to allow me to use their lake. I told them that shooting the final act of my film on their site would likely draw greater numbers to the place. They agreed. They even supplied gear and personnel to help set up. I had one ten-foot aluminium boat at my disposal. With lookouts posted on the edge of the fence, we lifted the boat over the fence and rowed onto the lake. Although unafraid of humans, the crocs were wary of boats. That wouldn't last for long.

I selected a spot about twenty yards from the shore to set up the cage. Just as I'd done in the blood drain, star pickets were used to anchor the cage to the lakebed. Once the cage was secure, we returned to the shore to collect the bait and the camera equipment.

The manager of the farm and I paddled out to the cage on our own. I tied the slaughtered chickens to the cage with heavy ropes so that the crocs had to fight for their food. I figured the struggle would add to the spectacle. Once the bait was in place, I lowered myself inside, the water coming up to my armpits. The manager then handed over the camera gear, wished me luck and made the arduous return journey.

I worked methodically setting up the cameras. I had three Bolex cameras inside the cage – one filming me and two filming out, as well as a handheld 16mm camera adjusted for slow motion filming inside a waterproof casing, plus a single Canon still camera. I'd added a feature to this cage. I'd cut three large holes at eye level, big enough to fit my head. The design was intended to allow the camera an unimpeded view of the crocodiles without the obstruction of the grille.

Once everything was in place, I buttoned on with the handheld and started calling out to the crocs. In a blink, crocodiles were everywhere. I'd had scarier experiences in the cage – the showdown with Fergus in the blood drain being the obvious example. But readjusting to the claustrophobia of the cage was a challenge. The crocs didn't touch the baits that first day. Instead, they just stared at me. It was like they were sizing me up.

The same thing happened the next two days. Five or six crocs would gather within a five-yard radius of my position. Ten yards back, there was another group of twenty. Beyond them was an outer layer of maybe fifty of the monsters. Only one or two crocs came up to snatch the baits. The rest remained utterly still, staring directly at my face, only slinking away when the tin boat was put back in the water to come fetch me. I didn't exactly get the most compelling footage.

The fourth day was a different story. By then, the crocs no longer seemed alarmed at the presence of the boat on the lake. They started thumping their heads against the hull of our boat. At first, I thought we'd hit rocks. It was terrifying – sitting completely vulnerable at the bow of a ten-foot tinny with fourteen-foot dinosaurs each weighing up to a ton threatening to capsize the boat. Paddling out to my cage was now ridiculously dangerous.

Once the hatch of the cage was secure and the cameras started rolling, I started calling the crocs. I was instantly surrounded. My hopes that the escort of crocodiles we'd received from the bank to the cage hinted at a change in behaviour were quickly dashed. I panned the surface with my handheld, the crocs doing little beyond staring at me from a safe distance. The thought entered my mind that maybe the Darwin Crocodile Farm wasn't the best place to shoot the climax after all.

Everything changed when the storm came. The first sign that we were in for some weather was a lightning flash on the horizon. I lowered my handheld and looked out beyond the cage. Huge black thunderheads were rolling directly towards us. Every few seconds, forks of lightning split the sky, touching down behind the bank of eucalyptus trees that surrounded the farm. The rumble of thunder followed seconds later.

'Do you want us to come get you?' shouted Mark.

'No,' I shouted back. 'Just a passing shower.'

I was more worried than I was letting on. The last place I wanted to be during a severe electrical storm was standing in an aluminium cage up to my armpits in water. But sending out the tinny would put others in danger. I'd wait it out, putting the thought of death by electrocution out of my head. It was one of the best decisions I've made.

When the storm broke, the behaviour of the crocs changed instantly. The teeming rain brought all the animals on the banks into the water. Crocs started bumping into each other. They crowded into the lake, pushing closer and closer towards the cage.

The moment the first croc's head touched the cage, the spell was broken. The feeding was on. Crocodiles were coming from every-where. The footage was insane! The water around the cage became a churning mass of chicken innards and blood. In the background, lightning streaked across the black sky and thunder clapped with enough power to rattle the cage. It was exactly the sort of thing I needed to end the film. But it wasn't enough. I hadn't captured any evidence of territorial behaviour or the presence of a dominant male in the film. All I'd done was confirm what everyone already knew – crocodiles were incredibly violent predators.

I ended up spending seventeen days in that cage. The crocodiles were now completely at ease with my presence. Life for me became more frightening. There was heavier bumping on the boat trip and more thumping on the cage. Mark was getting very worried about my safety.

On day seventeen, the largest crocodile – a sixteen-foot monster with scars etched across his head – started exerting his influence over the cage. He thrashed wildly at the others with his head. This fella was the maddest and baddest bastard in the lake. Once he'd cleared an area around the cage, he mopped up the remains of chicken carcasses left floating on the surface.

Then he turned and faced me. He came in with blistering speed, attacking the largest bait. He took it in his jaws and swam a few yards from the cage until the rope went taut. I couldn't keep the smile off my face as the croc thrashed about. He seemed intent on pulling the chicken off the rope and devouring it in private. The force the crocodile exerted pulled his whole body out of the water like a marlin breaching the surface in an effort to sever a fishing line. Infuriated, the croc performed a death roll – a manoeuvre where the croc spins itself violently while clutching tightly to its prey. I'd attached the baits to ropes with a breaking strain of one ton. Not even a massive croc in a death roll could snap that rope.

With his energy nearly spent, the croc started tugging at the rope with a jarring motion that made the cage shudder. I was so fixated on capturing the action on my camera I didn't notice the cage start to tilt.

'It's going over!' someone shouted from the shore.

If the cage went over I was dead, pure and simple. Even if I managed to pull myself out through the hatch, there was no way I'd make it to the shore. There were at least ten crocs between the cage and the shore. That twenty-yard swim might as well have been twenty miles.

I dropped the camera and reached for my bowie knife that I'd strapped to my chest. I thrust the knife through a hole in the cage and severed the rope. The cage snapped back into a vertical position and the crocodile catapulted away. He looked at me with the chicken guts spilling from his jaws, his eyes full of menace. He gobbled what remained of the bait and swam to the bank.

The boat came out to get me. With the baits all devoured and the extra people in the enclosure, the crocodiles kept their distance, enabling us to retrieve the cage. Safely back on the bank, a full inspection of the cage revealed just how close I'd come to death. The force the dominant male had exerted as he pulled on the rope had bent the star pickets to an angle greater than 45°. Luckily for me, the lakebed was made of clay. Had the lakebed had the soft consistency of the mud in the blood drain, the cage would've been pulled over.

I suddenly felt overwhelmed with emotion. I'd risked life and limb for this project. I'd sunk every penny I owned, jeopardised the business and my marriage, all in an effort to film the world's most dangerous predator. I roared with excitement and hugged Mark. I'd done it!

There was just one last thing to do. For a while, I'd been kicking around the idea of finishing the film with me on a Harley Davidson riding one of the deserted roads of the Northern Territory, disappearing into the heat haze. I had in mind the heroes of Western movies – the hero riding off into the sunset after saving the day.

The problem was finding a bike. On the advice of a couple of locals, we found a pub on the outskirts of Darwin. The pub had a reputation for danger, and for good reason. It was a filthy old dive full of bikers. We must've arrived after happy hour, because the place was packed with extremely heavy men, all covered in tattoos and piercings. Everyone was shitfaced. The floor was layered with broken glass and blood, and writhing on stage to heavy metal turned up full were four women wearing nothing but high heels.

Every head turned when we walked inside. I felt like I was back in the croc cage; hundreds of eyes were boring into me. Luckily, I was recognised.

'Fuck me!' someone shouted. 'It's the Crocodile Man!'

These blokes were fringe dwellers and risk takers. Most had probably had a run-in with the law. They had a soft spot for people who did crazy things, and jumping into a crocodile cage seemed to qualify. We were shouted beers the whole night.

I asked one bloke if I could borrow a bike for the film. He told me I had to speak to the president, a frightening-looking guy with ink-covered muscles, long hair and a goatee. He was seated at a table, surrounded by scantily clad women. After someone introduced me as the Crocodile Man, the president got to his feet, extended his massive paw and pumped my hand.

'I was wondering if I could borrow your bike for the film?' I asked

'You can have my girlfriend,' he said, 'but you can't have my bike.'

'I'll make you a deal,' I said. 'If I beat you in an arm wrestle, you lend me the bike. If you beat me, I'll shout you a round of drinks and leave you in peace.'

The boss was a few inches taller than me, twice as heavy and had arms far more muscly than mine. Still, I felt I could take him. Since breaking my back, I'd been working out every day for six months. I'd never felt as strong. When I left Sydney I was bench-pressing twice my body weight.

There was nothing in it for the president. Why risk losing face for a couple of free drinks? It wasn't as if he was paying for any. But I'd been studying the behaviour of dominant males for a year. This was more than just a sportsman's bet, it was a challenge to the president's authority on his own turf. It's not in the nature of the dominant male to decline a challenge.

'You've got yourself a deal,' he said, with a smile.

A loud cheer broke out. A table was cleared and Mark went to get the cameras from the car. There was no way I was going to use the footage. I'd have to change the rating of the film. But it was an awesome scene: two wild men, faces strained with effort, locked in an arm wrestle in front of the roughest-looking blokes in Australia's north. In the background, naked women writhed about to outrageous music.

The boss was as powerful as he was unfit. Like a prize-fighter trying to end a bout with a right hook, he put everything into the first few minutes. It felt like I was holding back a freight train. He slackened off eventually and we were locked in a stalemate for another few minutes. I could sense the fight seeping out of him and transferred every bit of power left in my body to my arm. It took about a minute, but eventually I put the back of his hand on the table with a thud. There was a second of disbelief before the boss broke the silence.

'Bike's yours, Crocodile Man,' he said.

After a massive night of drinking, we met at a pre-arranged spot the following evening. I rode the Harley helmetless into the sunset along an abandoned road. My mood matched the euphoria of earlier triumphs – harpooning the bull ray, spearfishing in Glenelg, smacking down the bullies, opening the dive shop, marrying Sue and becoming a father. I couldn't wait to get back to my family and share in the success of the film.

I was absolutely soaring. If you'd told me then the setbacks I was about to face, I'd have said you were crazy. I was about to be reminded that life is savage sometimes.

Part Four

A NEW
BEGINNING

20

The Black Dog
and the Wild Boar

We titled the film *Crocodile Man*. It ran for seventy-eight minutes and was exactly the sort of production I'd dreamt it would be, capturing the raw beauty of the far north and the power of the saltwater crocodile. Proving that crocs are territorial animals was a premise that tied in nicely with the massive struggles we had in simply luring them to the cage. But the live action, the constant threat of death and the ancient Aboriginal method of crocodile calling were the things that made it memorable.

The press loved it. They started calling me 'The Real Crocodile Dundee'. I was on television and radio, and was featured in all the major dailies and magazines. Discovery Channel bought the rights and took it around the world. Locally, it was a massive hit. Channel Seven broadcast it on a Sunday night at prime time. It was one of the highest-rating documentaries ever shown on Australian television. *Crocodile Man* screened in a Townsville movie house to sold-out sessions for over a year! That sort of screen time is rare for a Hollywood blockbuster, much less a wildlife documentary.

With the film's commercial success, you'd have thought I'd be rich. But I didn't make a cent. The distributors stitched me up.

I had a somewhat naïve way of conducting business. My philosophy was simple. When you make an agreement and shake on it you stick to it, no matter what. I was about to learn a valuable lesson about business: read the bloody contract! The fine print effectively cut me out of any profits of the film. I blame myself for not thoroughly reading the contract.

Let me be clear. This wasn't about getting rich. I'm a believer in setting goals and working hard to achieve them. I encourage other people to do the same. But if your sole aim in life is to become a multi-millionaire, I think you need to get your head checked. Greedy people crush everyone and everything around them to slake a thirst that can never be quenched. I'm not saying money doesn't matter. Money pays the bills, puts food on the table and puts clothes on your kid's back. It's important. So when I say that I was devastated to be cut out of the profits, it's not because of greed. It's because I desperately needed the money.

My financial woes coincided with one of the worst economic downturns in Australian history. Nobody was hit harder than people in small business. The dive school went from $50,000 turnover a month to $5,000 a month. It wasn't nearly enough to pay staff wages and operating costs or service an overdraft that was approaching $200,000 at 25 per cent interest. I also had one extra mouth to feed with the arrival of another beautiful son, Nathan.

I had no choice but to shut the doors of my beloved dive school. Having creditors swoop in and liquidate the business that had sustained me for nearly twenty years was heartbreaking. Worse was still to come. Eventually we had to sell our beautiful home in Caringbah. It was a decision I'd live to regret. I had $60,000 left to pay on the mortgage for a house that would these days be valued at nearly $1.2 million. But the bank was baying for my blood and it seemed the fastest way of clearing my debts.

I'm not sure if the economic policies of the government of

the day ultimately led to greater prosperity for this country. But Treasurer Paul Keating's infamous statement that it was the 'recession Australia had to have' nearly made me spew.

Despite the large-scale selling off of my assets, I managed to hang on to the dive shop. The shop had always worked in tandem with the dive school, but as a business operated as a separate entity. Sue and I ran the shop on our own. I continued to teach diving and Sue kept the company books. Although returns were fairly meagre as the recession bit, I could still put food on the table and pay the rent on a reasonable house in Cronulla. In the fire sale of all the dive school's equipment, I managed to hang on to the boat and enough scuba equipment to take divers out to sea.

Financially, it was touch and go. But we managed. Emotionally, I was a mess. Shek, my greatest friend in the whole world, had been struggling for a few weeks. Shortly after he turned seventeen – a mighty age for any dog – he became lethargic. Within days he could barely stand. I put him in the car and drove him to the vet. I spoke to him the whole way, reflecting on our unbelievable journey together. He looked at me with an expression of deep sadness and pain. I think he knew his life was coming to an end.

The vet examined Shek and said he had cancer. The only humane thing to do was to put him down. I was so choked up with emotion. The best I could do was nod my head. I held the old dog as he was given the needle and he quietly died in my arms. I cried the whole way home. Shek's life as my pet bookended a wonderful period for me: the success of Cronulla Dive, meeting Sue, the birth of three sons and the excitement of filmmaking. It felt like Shek was checking out at the moment my life was getting really tough.

Around this time, Joe the Irishman walked into my shop. Some men are blessed with a magnetic personality. They enter a crowd anonymously and leave as everybody's best friend. Joe was that kind of guy. A strapping six-foot dark-haired bloke in his late twenties, Joe had a twinkle in his eye and a winning smile. And, God, he was funny. It didn't matter if you were a businessman from the top end of town or a tradie propped up at the bar, he'd leave you clutching at your sides, gasping for air.

Joe and I hit it off the moment we met. He was an outdoorsman and adventurer with a passion for hunting feral animals in the Australian outback. He was keen to learn how to dive and heard that I was the best spearfisherman going around. He wanted to strike a deal: I'd teach him how to spearfish and scuba dive and he would teach me how to hunt.

'I've been hunting since before I was a teenager,' I said.

'Yes, but have you ever hunted with bow and arrow?' he shot back.

Ordinarily I would've politely declined the offer. But Joe had brought a smile to my face for the first time since Shek had died. I was in need of positive company. So I agreed.

Joe helped me select a compound bow to buy and taught me archery. After I'd mastered a fixed target, he said it was time to go hunting. He suggested Wilga Downs, a huge cattle station about 400 miles north-west of Sydney on the way out to Bourke. He said that feral goats and pigs were destroying the habitat and that the property owners welcomed hunters to help sort out the problem. It sounded like great sport, roaming the countryside with bow and arrow, taking out pests. Joe was in high spirits. He'd just got engaged to a beautiful girl and wanted to celebrate with one of his mates.

First, I had to run it by my wife. I hadn't left Sydney since returning from Darwin after shooting the final scene of *Crocodile Man*. The primary reason was to make up for lost time with the family. I sensed Sue was reluctant to let me go off on another crazy adventure and not because she thought I needed to be around for the weekend. We'd had such a challenging year she felt something bad might happen. I told her that I'd be fine. 'Compared to standing in a cage in crocodile-infested rivers,' I said, 'this will be a cakewalk.' Sue, to her credit, never stopped me from going on my wilderness expeditions.

Wilga Downs is in the New South Wales red country, a sparse and flat landscape with outcrops of eucalypt, weird rock formations and lots of mulga bushes – stunted-looking trees that seem to flourish in dry conditions. Dotted around the station every five or six miles, large man-made water holes measuring over fifty yards across have been dug into the ground. The locals call them 'tanks' and their purpose is to hydrate sheep and cattle. Otherwise it's unremarkable with very few distinguishable geographical formations, making it easy to get lost.

Joe was ready for a new challenge. He wanted to hunt wild pig. These creatures wreak havoc in the Australian bush. There are huge swathes of the wilderness where there isn't a square foot that hasn't been dug up by wild pigs. It looks like a backhoe has gone through the whole place. Wild pigs also carry brucellosis and leptospirosis, diseases known to be fatal to horses, cattle or sheep. Even those animals that survive are often rendered sterile. Boars regularly kill lambs or attack a ewe when she's lambing. They feed on all ground-nesting animals, which has led to the localised extinction of a variety of native fauna.

Worst of all, feral pigs carry *coxellia burnetii*, a bacterium that leads to Q fever in humans. Q fever is a nasty disease that can remain in the human body for years. Sufferers experience nausea, confusion, respiratory problems and many other ailments. Those that hunt and eat these feral animals also run a heightened risk of contracting tapeworm, flat segmented worms that live inside the intestines.

All told, wild pigs are among the most destructive species ever introduced into Australia. The problem is getting worse. If you thought the federal and state governments were committing resources to combating this catastrophe, think again. The areas worst affected are remote and, as with any serious issue unfolding in our midst, if there aren't any votes in it for the government of the day, bugger all happens. Little wonder farmers welcome hunters onto their properties to cull the bastards.

All that can be said of wild pigs is that they are great to hunt. Quick tempered and agitated, to experienced bow hunters like Joe, these feral animals are far more challenging to kill than goats. But Joe didn't want to hunt any old pig. He wanted to take down a great big boar.

And he had a plan. The best way to hunt pigs is to wait for them to come to you. Wild pigs are extremely wary of humans. So Joe planned to set up a 'blind' – a wooden platform that you build into a tree. The blind should be located above a 'pad' – a patch of land where the hunter's quarry is known to congregate. Joe had already constructed the blind and found a river red gum situated on the banks of the man-made tank. It was the perfect pad. Prints around the softer edges of the tank indicated plenty of pig activity.

Joe scaled the gum tree and installed his blind about fifteen feet above ground. Once he'd finished setting up, he came back down and collected his bow and arrows. I never doubted Joe's experience as a bow hunter, nor did I doubt the sturdiness of the blind. But I had a bad feeling about what he was doing.

'Relax,' he said. 'I've done this hundreds of times before.'

My instincts were telling me that Joe shouldn't go up to that blind.

'Why don't we just go free-ranging?' I said.

Joe wouldn't have a bar of it. Had it been my expedition, I would've insisted. But Joe was the leader. It was his call. I watched him scale the tree. Once he was happily seated on the platform, he gave me the thumbs up. I gave him a wave and did my best to ignore the insistent voice in my head telling me that something was wrong.

I decided the best thing to do was go hunting on the far side of the tank. If I came across any wild pigs on that walk, I have no memory of it. My mind was firmly fixed on Joe. I wasn't in the mood to hunt. The temperature was getting hotter. I learnt later that the mercury tipped above fifty degrees Celsius.

I stopped to take a swig from my water bottle when a feeling of dread surged up from the pit of my stomach. Never had my internal alarm sounded so strongly. It was simply impossible to ignore. I sprinted back towards Joe. It wasn't a long way back, only a couple of hundred yards. Everything was utterly still and silent: no sound of birdsong and no breeze to rustle the leaves.

I arrived on the pad and looked up. Joe's legs were dangling over the side of the blind.

'Joe?' I said. 'Are you alright, mate?'

I hadn't finished asking the question when Joe toppled forward. The area around the base of the tree was red clay, baked granite-hard in the sun. He was unconscious before he fell, having succumbed to heatstroke and dehydration. The vision of his arms flailing about uncontrollably just before his head struck the ground will stay with me forever. I ran to my mate. His face started changing colour and blood trickled from an ear and an eye. Crouching low above him, powerless to help my mate, I heard him softly moan. I couldn't find a pulse, so I spent the next thirty minutes trying to resuscitate him. But Joe was gone.

I closed his eyes, covered his face with his hat and went to raise the alarm. My head was a swirling storm of emotion. I did my utmost to keep the grief at bay by concentrating on the job at hand. I eventually made it back to the homestead and tracked someone down. An ambulance was dispatched from Bourke to come and get the body.

I drove the twelve hours back to Sydney utterly devastated. At intervals, I'd have to pull over at the side of the road, the tears distorting my vision. A week later I went to his funeral. The size of the congregation was a mark of Joe's popularity. There was standing room only. I went looking for Joe's fiancée after the coffin was carried out to the hearse. I lost it when I saw her. No words were exchanged between us. We embraced, tears streaking down our cheeks.

I'd experienced the tragedy of watching my dad die in agony from throat cancer. But holding someone while they die from fatal injuries was a different kind of trauma. I doubt anyone can prepare for that sort of shock.

The family doctor told Sue that she should keep an eye on me. He even suggested I see a psychologist. I told her not to worry.

'I'm too strong,' I said. 'It won't hit me.'

But I was more vulnerable than I was letting on. I'd been copping it from all angles. The business I'd started was gone, my dog had died and the film project for which I'd sacrificed so much earned me nothing. Joe's death tipped me over the edge.

I had a pretty uncomplicated attitude towards depression. I just thought it meant feeling down. This doesn't come close to describing how totally transformative the black dog can truly be. Not only was I feeling bloody miserable, I couldn't sleep, I couldn't concentrate, my motivation was sapped, I lost my appetite, and I became moody. Where I was once a person who sought out tough challenges, now the most menial of tasks seemed insurmountable.

Sue's support through that period was huge. After staggering through the fog of depression for several months, I booked in for a check-up. The doctor wrote out a prescription for antidepressants. I thanked him and left. Once I was outside, I scrunched the script into a ball and threw it in the rubbish. I don't judge people for going down the path of antidepressants. Depression is a disease that affects people differently and therefore managing the condition will vary from person to person. In my case, I firmly believed that the drugs, at best, would treat the symptoms. At worst they would make me dependent on prescription medication, making a bad situation worse.

That's not to say that the consultation with the doctor was a waste of time. In fact, it spurred me on to address the problem. My solution was not the sort of thing you'll find in a psychologist's textbook and I doubt any medical practitioner would recommend it. But I figured the only way to overcome my depression was to return to the place where it all started.

That night, I packed food, water, camping gear and my bow in preparation for a few days at Wilga Downs. For three days, I hunted that property, free-ranging the same places Joe and I had been only a few months earlier. I didn't get much initially, only a few goats and a small pig. What I really wanted was a big fat boar. The hunt was like a metaphor for overcoming depression: staying alive, not getting lost and remaining focused.

At the end of the second day I was exhausted. The initial plan was to return to Sydney the next day. But I still hadn't got a big fella. There was no way of knowing that there was a big boar to be found on the property. I was going on instinct that the beast I was after was lurking in the undergrowth, cutting up the ground with his hard hooves and poisoning the water tanks. There was only one place I hadn't yet hunted and that was the place where Joe had died.

I went out there first thing the next morning. It was another stifling hot day, just like the day of Joe's death. There wasn't a breath of wind or a cloud in the sky. It was still and silent. I found the tree where Joe had set up the blind. My pulse quickened as I approached the spot where his head had cracked on the hard clay. I looked around at the ochre colour of the ground, the burnt orange of the sky at dawn and the earthy green of the eucalypt leaves. For the first time since I'd set foot on Wilga Downs, I realised that it was beautiful country.

That's when I saw him: a huge spotted boar, trotting out of the tree line and heading down for a drink of water on the far side of the tank. I crept around the tank, concealing myself in the trees, all the while keeping a close eye on the boar. Once I was behind him, I stepped out of the trees and walked directly towards the water. The tree line was about thirty yards from the tank. I paced fifteen steps and looked back. If my arrow missed, I'd have to run back and climb a tree. I was confident that fifteen yards was enough of a head start, even from a fired-up boar at full tilt. If I didn't make it, a boar this size would tear me open with his tusks and wouldn't stop until I stopped moving.

I raised the bow. The boar was busily drinking, his snout deep in the water. As I nocked my arrow, the red dust caught in the wheels of the compound bow, producing a high-pitched squeak. The boar swung around, locked his eyes on me and charged.

Had I run, I would've made it to the trees. But I'd been turning my back on this problem for too long. It was high time I killed the boar. I waited until he was five yards away before I released the arrow. It disappeared deep into his neck, the very spot where Joe had always instructed. The boar squealed in fury and pain, but kept coming.

I turned around and ran. I could hear the boar squealing and snorting a few inches behind me. I lined up a tree that had a branch solid enough for me to grab onto and clamber up. Just as I was preparing to launch myself at the branch, I heard the boar stumble and collapse. I turned around and saw him take his final breath.

I nudged the boar with my foot, making certain he was dead. Then I sat down alongside him, exhausted, my hands trembling with the adrenalin that had flooded my body. I reached into my backpack for my water bottle. As I twisted off the lid, I realised I was drinking from Joe's bottle. I must've packed it with my gear without noticing. I raised the bottle to the sky.

'Here is your boar, mate,' I said.

I took a long swig of water. As the tears ran down my dusty cheeks, I felt the grip of the black dog releasing. The feelings of depression lifted. I was free! I can't describe how amazing it felt to be myself again.

I ended up teaching my sons and all my mates how to bow hunt. It has been a massive part of my life and would become a staple of many wildlife documentaries. Whenever I have a bow in my hands, Joe is not far from my thoughts. I have also dedicated a huge amount of time to raising awareness about the destruction that feral animals are wreaking in the Australian bush. The wild pig is often in my crosshairs.

21

The Breath of
the Lion

Bill Tucker approached me towards the end of 1993. Bill was a big player in Australian publishing. His biggest success was the annually updated Tucker's Encyclopedia. Publishers like Bill hadn't wised up to the opportunities the newly created internet presented. They were instead focused on another form of electronic media: the Compact Disc Read Only Memory, more commonly known as CD-ROM.

The CD-ROM is designed to store computer data in text, graphics and images. Bill believed CD-ROM had huge potential. For one thing, consumers would flock to an encyclopedia that didn't require a bookshelf to be cleared to make space for an updated volume. But this was hardly revolutionary. Other encyclopedia brands had already duplicated their content on CD-ROM. Bill's vision was to tailor each CD to a specific market. This way he could target demographics and interest groups – a CD-ROM for sports lovers, a CD-ROM for music lovers, a CD-ROM for arts enthusiasts and so on. The possibilities were endless.

One of his biggest hopes was for a nature and wildlife CD-ROM. Bill wanted to make full use of the multimedia potential without having to buy video and images. He wanted to own it. So he went looking for a cameraman and still photographer. Bill was an admirer of *Crocodile Man*, so I was his first port of call.

Bill rang and wasted no time getting to the point. I immediately liked what I was hearing. Bill offered to put me on a generous retainer to shoot and produce wildlife material. Additionally, he'd give me a 17 per cent cut for all the material he sold that featured my work. The retainer was a good, reliable income. But the real money would come from the royalty cheques from sales.

Given the amount of travel and work involved, accepting the offer would mean closing down the dive shop. I asked Bill to give me the night to talk it over with my wife. There was no doubt in my mind that Sue would want me to accept the offer. The retainer would clear any outstanding debt and allow us to rent a house big enough to accommodate a family of five. The way I saw it, accepting the offer would get me doing what I loved above all else – filming in the wild.

If I had any hesitation, it was the specifics of the deal. I'd been so badly burnt by the distributors of *Crocodile Man* that I wanted to make sure I wasn't being misled. I wanted to meet the man in person. So I showed up at his offices. After we talked over the contract, I stood up, looked him in the eyes, and shook his hand. My instinct told me that this was a man of great integrity. It was one of the few times that my instinct let me down.

But that was much later. Initially, it was a period of great excitement. Sue and I closed up the dive shop without any regret. We rented a big house in Cronulla and I started putting together an itinerary for a series of film shoots for Tucker's Publishing.

Excluding crocodiles, I'd only ever dabbled in filming land animals. My strength was filming marine life. The Tucker deal allowed me to master the craft of wildlife photography on land. The deal also presented an opportunity to choose locations I'd only ever dreamt of visiting.

Top of the list was Africa. The Mala Mala Game Reserve in South Africa was *the* place to go for any wildlife lover. Covering about a hundred square miles, Mala Mala is located within the Greater Kruger National Park. It's South Africa's largest big five game reserve. 'Big five' refers to the African elephant, the Cape buffalo, the African leopard, the rhinoceros and, of course, the African lion.

Mala Mala's gamekeepers were famous for driving their Land Rovers to within feet of big game. From a filming perspective it was perfect. I pitched the idea to Bill and he loved it. Not only would he use my footage for promotional material for the release of his world encyclopedia, he'd fund the trip and pay all expenses.

I left for South Africa within a week of signing the contract. I took along my own cameras, lights and recording equipment. This would be an altogether different experience from previous film shoots. I wasn't going to be a presenter. This was all about getting the best footage. When I arrived at Mala Mala, I was given my own Land Rover, Kalahari trackers and a guide. I told them that my priority was to film lions hunting.

'We know exactly where to find them,' my guide said.

We set off before nightfall the following day, tracking down the pride within an hour. The pride comprised three adult females, a bunch of cubs around twelve months old and a huge male. We followed them night after night – the period they like to hunt – hoping to film a kill. My driver lived up to the reputation of the Mala Mala gamekeepers, driving his Land Rover to within several feet of the lions. Sometimes we were close enough to reach out and pat them on the head. It was uncomfortably close. Our truck was roofless, windowless and doorless. Oddly, the lions behaved as if we didn't exist. I figured that they were oblivious to our presence because they were so fixated on hunting. On the fourth night, I'd revise that theory.

That night it was utterly clear. There was no need for the car lights. The full moon illuminated the females as they stalked the tall grasses looking for prey. Led out by the matriarch, the three lionesses prowled alongside the Land Rover, keeping low to the ground. The male was up the back, keeping watch over the young.

The driver had the truck in the lowest gear, barely touching the accelerator as we inched forward with the three females. Without warning, the matriarch stopped. I noticed her ears flatten to her head. All three females crouched low into the grass.

'Kill the engine,' I hissed to the driver.

Everything fell silent. I took out the spotlight and pointed forward, lighting up a lone male wildebeest on his haunches about fifty yards away. I turned off the light and took out my handheld camera. Without the light, I was pretty certain that the footage would be terrible. But I couldn't care less. I was about to witness an epic battle between very powerful animals.

The three lionesses seemed to be acting on a single consciousness. The matriarch pressed on ahead very slowly. One of the other lionesses went left. The other went right. The wildebeest was cornered in a pincer movement. No matter which way he ran, one of the females would be waiting. While the wildebeest was stalked, the cubs crouched low together in the grass a few yards behind our car. There was no sign of the male. I guessed that he was patrolling beyond the sight of the bull, creating another impediment to escape.

I had the camera following the matriarch as she inched closer. The wildebeest seemed to register that danger was present. His head was arched high above the grass, desperate to see the direction from which the threat was coming. The wildebeest started stomping the ground. The matriarch's approach was relentless, pawing closer and closer. The wildebeest looked like a coiled spring, preparing to make a mad dash for freedom. The drama was incredible. I was so transfixed that I didn't see the big male stalking me from behind.

The first warning I had of approaching danger was in the change of temperature. The night was bitterly cold and I'd draped my legs in a groundsheet. From nowhere, I felt a gentle wave of warmth across my face. I turned around and locked eyes with the male lion. His face was about two feet from mine.

Two thoughts occurred to me at that moment. The first was that the pride hadn't been oblivious to our presence, as I'd initially thought. They'd been patiently waiting for us to be distracted before mounting an ambush. The second thought I had was that I was about to die.

Strangely, I felt no fear. I was resigned to my fate. The sky above was filled with a billion stars. It was so peaceful. I returned my gaze to the lion, losing myself in his glorious mane and his powerful aura. I estimated his weight at over 500 pounds, putting him in the highest weight percentile of his species. In the surreal glow of the moonlight, I could see scars across his face, the battle wounds he'd sustained in fierce scraps with rival males. This lion was a survivor, a great warrior – the king of the jungle. He'd make mincemeat out of me in seconds.

But I saw no malice in his eyes. I sensed curiosity. The lion was so close I could feel his hot breath on my neck. Maybe he meant me no harm. A gust of wind stirred the groundsheet that covered my legs. It started flapping hard against my leg. The lion extended his paw and hit the blanket firmly, striking my leg. It felt like a heavy-weight boxer was punching my thigh. Concerned that any sudden movement might prompt an attack, I tried not to wince.

The flapping groundsheet obviously bothered him. I'm certain it wasn't an aggressive act, because his claws weren't extended. He kept his paw on my leg for a second, removing it with a sudden jerk. His head swivelled in the direction of the wildebeest and his ears flattened. Above the breeze I could hear the whispering patter of lions' paws racing over the grass. The attack was on.

The wildebeest's distressed grunts echoed into the night. That

was the signal for the lion king to spring to life, sprinting ahead
to aid his lionesses as they struggled to bring the powerful bull to
ground. The driver turned the ignition and started the engine.

'Stop!' I said. 'Don't move. Don't move!'

The driver turned around, bewildered. Earlier I'd instructed him
to drive the Land Rover as close as possible just before the wildebeest was felled so that I could get good close-up footage of the kill.
I tossed off the groundsheet, stepped out of the Land Rover and
climbed onto the bonnet.

'Okay,' I said. 'Get moving!'

The Land Rover surged forward, jolting me backwards. I managed to steady myself with one hand on the top of the bull bar,
while clinging tight to my camera with the other hand. Once we
were within twenty yards I told the driver to slow down so as not to
frighten the pride away.

By now, the four adult lions had cornered their quarry. The
wildebeest was prancing about in the middle of a shrinking circle.
The noose was being tightened. But he still had some fight in him.
Whenever a lion leapt forward, the wildebeest would turn his back
and kick out his legs to close down the attack. It was a futile last bid
for life. Two lions launched at him with lightning speed. The wildebeest managed to kick back the lion coming from his rear, leaving
himself vulnerable to a frontal attack. One of the females leapt up
and took hold of the wildebeest's muzzle inside her mouth. She was
going to suffocate him. The other two lionesses jumped onto his
back, bringing him to the ground. All the while, the big male waited.
He was letting the ladies prepare his dinner.

'Get me closer,' I said over my shoulder.

As we moved forward, I swivelled around on the bonnet so that
my elbows were hanging over the bull bar. One of my guides had the
spotlight zeroed in on the fallen wildebeest, which was madly struggling to get free.

'Closer!' I shouted over the engine. 'Get me in tight.'

We were now within ten yards, the perfect distance to capture the wildebeest's final seconds. I wanted to capture the lions tearing up his innards with my 15mm wide-angle lens. I needed to be closer. The driver obliged. He took me in close. Way too close . . .

'What are you doing?' I said, in a voice just above a whisper.

The last thing I wanted to do was alarm the lions by shouting. They might turn on me. So I can only assume the driver didn't hear me, because he ended up resting the bull bar on the wildebeest's still-breathing body. My head was less than a foot away from the action. One of the lionesses pulled away from the wildebeest, looked me in the eyes and started growling.

'Bugger off!' she seemed to be saying. 'This is our kill.'

There was nothing I could do. Given the position of my body, the only movement I could make was towards the wildebeest. I didn't want to move an inch closer. They'd be eating the wildebeest for main and me for dessert. All I could do was stay still and keep filming.

It was some of the best footage I'd ever captured. I was so close the camera picked up the full moon reflecting in the wildebeest's moist eye. You could see, with incredible detail, the wildebeest's cheeks puffing up as he tried to suck in air. It took about two minutes for the wildebeest to die.

The driver finally cottoned on to how close I was. He backed up ten feet as I filmed the lions ripping into the carcass. We left for the hotel once the wildebeest was little more than bones. Back in my room, I went straight to the bar fridge and, on one of the very few occasions in my life, poured half a glass of scotch and downed it in one go. I'd have preferred a beer, but the scotch thawed my frozen body. It also allowed me to get some sleep after the closest of encounters with the king of beasts!

22

The Elephant and the Baboon Army

The next destination on my itinerary was Mashatu Game Reserve in Botswana. I'd been told that Mashatu had the big five in greater numbers than Mala Mala. Some even believed it had a wider biodiversity. I flew in on a light aircraft directly from Mala Mala, landing roughly on a makeshift dirt runway towards the end of the day.

As I stepped out of the plane I was presented with an endless vista of wide open grassland dotted occasionally with umbrella thorn acacia. I could see a herd of zebra scampering away in the distance as the setting sun turned the horizon pink and orange. This was the Africa of my dreams – the sort of place you could imagine pith-helmeted explorers on safari.

Accommodation on Mashatu was very basic. It comprised a group of small, medium and large tents. I was immediately struck by how flimsy they appeared. It came as no surprise when the camp manager, a white South African who lived full time on the reserve with his wife, told me that the camp had recently suffered a tragedy.

'Our barman was recently taken by a lion,' he said in a matter-of-fact manner. 'We were going to close the camp down until we heard you were coming.'

I noticed several grim-faced people loading their belongings onto the plane I'd just disembarked. They looked like refugees. While giving me a tour of the campsite, the manager said that he'd be leaving the camp once I was finished filming. We arrived at my accommodation. It was the sort of cheap tent you'd take on a weekend camping holiday in a fair climate.

'Dinner will be ready once you've unpacked,' he said, with a smile.

It was dark by the time I left the tent. It was easy enough to find the campfire. It was roaring away about 150 yards from where I stood. Over an excellent dinner of steak and vegetables, the camp manager described what had happened to the barman. A lion had come into the camp late at night as he was cleaning up. He leapt on him from behind and ate him.

'Where exactly did this happen?' I asked.

'About ten feet from where you're sitting,' he said.

By now it was after midnight and everyone else had gone to bed. For the first time, I heard the low rumble of a lion growling. I picked up my torch and shone it beyond the field of light cast by the fire. The torch was just strong enough to light up a pride of at least seven adult lions prowling about seventy yards from where we sat. I got to my feet, feeling the effects of the beers we'd been drinking to stay warm.

'Do you realise we're surrounded by lions?' I asked.

'Yeah,' he said. 'They're waiting for us to go to our tents so they can warm themselves by the fire.'

I suddenly remembered that cats – domestic, feral or big – are attracted to warmth. All this time I was thinking that the fire would keep lions at bay. It was doing the opposite.

'That's why I always keep this close at hand,' said the manager, picking up his rifle before getting to his feet. 'I'm off to bed.'

I wanted to ask, *Where's my rifle?*

The walk from the campfire to my tent may have only been 150 yards, but that's a long way in the dead of night when you're surrounded by lions. I went looking around the campfire for something to use as a weapon. All I could find was a small fire extinguisher. I doubt it would've scared a fully-grown lion, but it was something. With the extinguisher tucked under my arm and my pathetic little torch lighting the way, I set off for the tent.

There was no attack. I leapt inside my tent and zipped it up. God knows what a zipper was going to do. I slipped into my sleeping bag and eventually fell into a restless sleep. I awoke the next morning to find lion prints around my tent. That day I decided to relocate my accommodation alongside the camp manager's tent.

I'm glad I resisted the temptation to fly out of Mashatu the next day. The next two weeks of filming would be some of the most exceptional of my career. I got footage of African animals that very few others, if anyone at all to that point, had captured. But there were some hairy moments.

I went to extraordinary lengths to get the best shots. With a local guide, I set off in a truck in search of a leopard. This guy knew exactly when and where to find them.

'At night,' he said, 'near the long grass.'

We went out just before midnight with cameras, lights and rifles. About half an hour from our camp he pulled the truck to the side of the road. The guide shone his torch along the sandy surface until he found what he was looking for.

'Here!' he shouted. 'Leopard prints!'

We followed the prints off the road, across a plain and into a field of native grass that came up to shoulder height. My guide told me to stay low. We crawled for several minutes, my camera rolling.

'We're close,' whispered the guide, pointing at a section of flattened grass that indicated a struggle. With a sudden jerking motion, he held up his hand. I heard it too: a low growl and the sound of jaws tearing apart flesh. We both got to our knees, peering over the grass in the hope of catching sight of a leopard feasting on his quarry. We saw nothing. It was the strangest thing. Although not loud, the sounds were distinctive and close. It was as if they were emanating from right on top of us . . .

After a further few seconds of confusion, I felt a drop of rain land on the back of my hand. Funny, I thought. There wasn't a cloud in the night sky. I looked up. Directly above, only about fifteen feet up, a leopard was pulling apart an impala with his teeth. The impala carcass was draped over the branch of a tree. There was no danger. The leopard was completely preoccupied with his catch. I turned the spotlight on and started filming as the leopard happily tucked in.

Once I'd got what I needed, we quietly retreated back to the truck. Walking out of the tall grass and stepping onto the open plain, we were greeted with the horrific cackling and offensive stink of hyenas. There must've been ten of them, skulking about in the dark on their oversized front legs, baring their hideous teeth. The smell of impala blood must have drawn them out.

'Keep walking,' said my guide. 'Don't look them in the eye.'

We marched through the pack and made it to the truck without incident. I sighed with relief once we sped away, leaving the hyenas in our dust. Although cunning, hyenas very rarely attack humans unless they come across a person who is asleep, injured or immobile. Still, the sight of them made me shudder. They looked positively evil. Of course, in the animal kingdom, outwardly appealing animals can be the most dangerous.

Take elephants for example. Beautiful and intelligent creatures, these big fellas are mistakenly regarded by many people as gentle giants. In fact, they are extremely dangerous. I'd repeatedly been told to be wary of elephants, to only ever film at a distance while remaining close to the truck just in case I needed to make a swift getaway. I was told that few people survive close encounters with elephants in the wild. Given what happened to me, I guess I was one of those lucky few.

We'd been driving along a plain, searching for anything of interest when I spotted baboons frolicking in a pond at the base of a sheer cliff wall. Baboons were a species of animal that had until that day eluded me. I pulled out my camera and tripod and turned to my driver.

'Wait here,' I said. 'You watch out and make sure nothing comes from behind.'

The driver turned off the engine while I went and set up. To get to the pond, I had to walk along a creek that bisected two fairly high cliff walls. The distance between the cliff walls was very close, only about five yards. It was a tight squeeze. As a safety precaution I set the camera about fifty yards from the pond. Baboons have been known to be aggressive towards humans when approached. I was getting some great shots until I heard something coming from behind.

I turned around and clapped eyes on an enormous bull elephant trudging towards me. I calculated that he was about fifty yards from the truck. I was about twice that distance. I waved my arms frantically above my head, desperately trying to get the driver's attention. There was no movement from inside the truck. His feet were up on the dash. The idiot was fast asleep.

Hemmed in between two walls, with a family of baboons behind me, I was trapped. My only option was to try and run back to the truck. I dismissed the idea as quickly as it came into my head. A charging elephant can hit twenty-five miles per hour. The elephant wasn't charging yet, but if I made a sudden dash, he'd probably see that as a threat. I'd be trampled to death quicker than you could say Babar.

You see, elephants *hate* humans. Despite the best efforts of authorities, the illegal trade of ivory tusks is as robust as ever. If poachers aren't killing elephants, then gamekeepers are tranquillising and relocating them for the protection of their species. The fear of humans is deeply ingrained in the elephant.

By now, the elephant had gone past the truck. I could see his curling white tusks were several yards long. He seemed to skip a step for a second, his trunk extended directly towards me. I'm sure it was a signal that he'd seen me blocking his passage to the water because the next thing I knew, he accelerated. Facing the very likely possibility of death, there's really only one thing I could do: keep the camera rolling. In my view, if you're about to shoot your last ever shot, make sure it's good.

The elephant came at me, moving at a decent clip. I distracted myself by keeping the camera focused on his every move. Once he was a few yards away, the elephant slowed and then stopped. He was huge, six or seven tons at least. Head to toe, he stood about twelve feet high. His tusks curled around his trunk and ended in sharp points.

With his ears spread, the bull extended his trunk high enough for me to see into his mouth. He then curled his top lips back. It seemed to me he was asserting his dominance. I just kept on filming, expecting at any moment for his trunk to sweep me aside. After a terrifying fifteen-second stand-off, the elephant lost interest. He walked past me towards the water.

The driver was goggle-eyed when I returned to the truck. The sound of the elephant trotting past had obviously woken him up. Clearly, his mind was struggling to grasp what his eyes had just seen.

'Thanks for the warning,' I said, hurling my gear into the back.

Close to the Limpopo River, very near the border of South Africa and Botswana, a mountain of heavy boulders and jagged peaks soar into the sky. It's a very strange place, a lonely mountain standing in the middle of a savannah that stretches as far as the eye can see.

Local legend has it that a long extinct race known as the Leopard People once inhabited the mountain. They lived in stone structures on the slope of the mountain. The ruins have survived the centuries. Archaeologists have been visiting the site for many years. Despite their excavations, little is known about the early inhabitants of the mountain.

I insisted on being taken to the mountain. Although shooting footage of ruins from a lost civilisation was beyond my brief, I couldn't resist this sort of stuff. It was *Raiders of the Lost Ark* and *King Solomon's Mines* rolled into one. Even if the footage didn't interest Bill Tucker, I was bound to get something worth using for another project.

It took us several hours to drive to the mountain from our camp. I saw the mountain from a distance, its summit disappearing into the mist.

'We cannot go up there,' said my driver once we'd arrived at the mountain's base. 'I brought you here to see it, but I can't let you go any further.'

'Why not?' I asked. 'Are there leopards up there?'

'Sometimes,' he said. 'But the real danger is baboons. They own the mountain. You cannot go up.'

'What if I take the thirty-thirty with me?' I asked, pointing towards the boot of the Land Rover where the rifle was kept. The guide shrugged, as if to say, *You're welcome to take the rifle but I'm still not coming with you.*

With the guide looking on fearfully, I took a bottle of water, my Bolex camera and the rifle. Before I left, the guide told me that there were stone stairs that led up to the summit.

'I'll be back in a couple of hours,' I said.

I climbed for a few minutes, losing sight of the Land Rover behind a huge cluster of boulders that formed a ring around the base of the mountain. The terrain became increasingly inhospitable the higher I climbed. On one side of me the path fell steeply into a dark ravine. On the other side a fast-flowing river roared over rapids.

Eventually, I came onto a set of stone stairs carved into the side of the mountain. They were in good condition given they were said to be many centuries old. Moss-covered thanks to the spray of water from the river, the stairs were dangerously slippery. It was now high noon and the temperature had increased. It took all my focus to keep upright.

After about thirty minutes, the stairs levelled out and I decided on taking a short rest. I'd made good progress. Looking back, I had an unimpeded view across the savannah. I could see elephant herds marching slowly across the plains many miles in the distance. After briefly admiring the view, I continued my climb.

A further ten minutes of climbing the steps, the mountain levelled out to a large shelf that led to a cave. The opening of the cave had been built up with rocks, some of which looked like they'd been mortared with clay. I found a passage through the rocks and ventured inside. The smell inside the cave was rancid. Clearly, something lived inside here. The cooler temperature raised goose bumps on my exposed arms and legs. I pulled my torch from my pack and played it around the inside of the cave, bringing the beam of light to rest on a pile of human skulls. I walked over towards the skulls to inspect, nearly tripping over a spear and a discarded drum. I set my pack down on the ground and filmed inside the cave for a few minutes, then a shiver rippled through my body.

I turned quickly. I could've sworn someone or something was watching me. I did a thorough examination of the inside of the cave and saw nothing. But the feeling persisted. I turned off the Bolex and quickly gathered up my pack before a sound stopped me dead in my tracks.

The bark of a male baboon is sonorous and disturbing. Some call it the 'wa-hu' shout: the word a close approximation of the sound. It is very loud. Even though the barking was coming from outside the cave, it seemed to echo inside the hidden chambers of the mountain. There was no way of hiding inside the cave. This was clearly the place where they dwelt. Besides, if I needed to shoot at the baboon, better to do it outside.

When my eyes adjusted to the sunlight, I saw the baboon standing up on his haunches, staring straight at me. I'd seen numerous baboons across the savannahs and in the trees since arriving in Mashatu. But this one struck me as being different. It wasn't simply his size – easily the equivalent of a well-built man of medium height – it was his presence. He exuded dominance. If ever I were to break into the headquarters of a bikie gang and steal something, this was the look I'd get from the leader if he caught me in the act.

The baboon barked again. The sound echoed down the mountain. From far away, I could hear screeching and more barking. The general was calling his army. In a blink, fifteen warrior baboons emerged. They leaped over the rocks and swung down from the trees that rimmed the plain. I was surrounded.

The leader started making quick, jerking motions with his arms. He rolled back his gums, baring his razor-sharp canines. I knew it wouldn't be long before he launched an attack. It was time for me to flash my own teeth.

I put the camera down very slowly and took the rifle off my shoulder. I levered the chamber open and took a quick peak inside to check the number of bullets. What I saw nearly caused me to topple over. I had one bullet.

I only had myself to blame. You'd have thought I'd learnt my lesson after exactly the same mistake nearly resulted in Mark Olding and me being trampled by a scrub bull in the Kimberley. In my defence, I felt it was safe to assume that a rifle kept permanently in the game reserve's Land Rover was always fully loaded. Then again, whoever said that assumptions are the mother of all fuck-ups might have been talking about preparing to film in the wild. I should've checked my ammo before leaving.

In the few seconds I'd spent checking my bullet situation, the baboon leader had moved to within twenty yards of where I was standing. I could see now that when he stood up to his full height, he was as tall as me. I could imagine his teeth ripping my neck apart and severing my jugular.

I raised the rifle and aimed at the baboon's head. None of the baboons responded. This was bad news. Clearly, the baboons of this mountain had never been shot at before. Of course, at a range of twenty yards, I'd have no problem blowing his head off. The question was how the others might react with their leader down: would they scurry away in frightened confusion or would they rise up to vanquish their fallen hero? I didn't want to find out.

One of the things that I'd learnt after spending years in the wild is that animals – like people – are responsive to the emotions of humans. Aggressive animals such as these baboons respond to fear and panic. It's almost as if they can smell it. If I were to run, I'd be ripped apart before I'd even got into stride. If I were to whimper or cower, back away or hold up my hands in meek defence, they'd descend on me in a hail of clenched fists, ripping off my flesh with their teeth. They are like bullies. And you should never cower or run away from a bully.

Obviously, I wouldn't be muscling my way out with brute force. But I stood a chance of winning a battle of minds. I needed to assert my dominance. The way to do that was projecting an aggressive aura. Although I'd had next to no experience dealing with primates, I figured that if any creature in the animal kingdom were to respond to my aura it would be an animal with whom humans share a common ancestor.

I picked up the camera with one hand, slipping my head through the neck strap. With the camera secured, I raised the rifle and aimed between the leader's eyes. It was the leader I had to intimidate. My fate rested with his actions. The others wouldn't attack until he moved.

'Back off!' I shouted. 'Or I'll kill you!'

The leader barked at me in response. I kept shouting at him, throwing in a few swear words for good measure. I didn't move towards him. I just channelled all my anger and hate and full-on aggression into my aura. At first, he didn't flinch. But I persisted. I wasn't going to fire that rifle until I was absolutely certain he was going to attack.

Finally, I detected a change in the tone of his bark. It sounded like he was barking at a higher pitch. He became less inclined to stare me in the face. He was becoming confused, less certain of himself. I knew I'd made progress when he stopped baring his teeth. Buoyed up by the change in atmosphere, I shouted and swore at him with even greater gusto.

His bark changed again. This time it was the sound of an animal that was frightened. The other baboons started to scamper away. After a minute, they'd all melted back into the mountain. Eventually, the baboon turned his back and disappeared behind a rock.

I gathered up the camera and made my way back down the steps. It was a dangerous descent, but the rush of adrenalin had sharpened my senses. I felt eyes watching me all the way down that mountain. Every so often, I'd see a movement at the corner of my eye. I'd stop and look around, catching sight of the baboon. Sometimes he was behind me, next second he was beside me and then he was above me. But he never got too close.

I made it down those steps in record time, eventually passing through the rim of rocks at the base of the mountain. When I was about fifty yards from the Land Rover, I noticed the driver pointing over my shoulder in warning. I looked back and raised my rifle. The baboon was standing up on one of the rocks, staring down at me with murder in his eyes. He looked like a warrior standing high on a rampart, defending his castle.

I could've shot him easily. But the way I saw it, that mountain belonged to him. I was a trespasser who he'd let live. I lowered the rifle and the baboon disappeared.

23

The Volcano

The Africa trip was a major success. Bill Tucker was elated with my work. He planned to include snippets of my work on a whole variety of CDs – *Tucker's Guide to African Animals*, *Tucker's Guide to Mammals* and many more. It's fair to say that I was expecting a windfall. Not right away, of course, but eventually.

While I waited for the CDs to go on sale, Bill sent me off on more adventures. I was basically given free rein to film whatever I wished. Best of all, I got to spend some meaningful time with my ever-growing family. By now Sue had given birth to our fourth son, Jason. When the money was getting tight, I'd saddle up and head into the great unknown. I fulfilled a lifelong ambition to shoot bird-life of the Cape York Peninsula. I filmed a variety of shark species along the length of the east coast of Australia. And I filmed the unbelievable damage wrought by introduced species in the Australian outback.

One trip that particularly stands out during that period was to Pentecost Island in Vanuatu. I'd long wanted to witness the island's famous land divers. The land divers are the precursor to modern-day bungee jumpers, with several key differences. The land divers jump from platforms that jut out of a man-made wooden structure rising up a hundred feet. They attach vines to one leg and tie the other end to a pole on the top of the tower. Unlike the elastic cords used in bungee jumping, the vines have no recoil or give. Most startling of all, the vines are cut to a length that result in the divers striking the ground headfirst.

It's a ritual fraught with danger. Some men have been killed or permanently injured. Although the land divers were well known to the outside world, I was among the first to capture them on film. It was difficult to watch. While the women chanted, several men would scale the flimsy wooden structure. At the top, someone would help each man fasten the vine to his leg, and then after a bit more chanting, he'd leap out keeping his arms to his sides. If they did it properly, their bodies would strike the slope of a mudslide at the bottom, the force of the landing diffusing through their shoulders. The vine would go taut and their bodies would jerk backwards, coming to rest at the base of the tower. If they got it wrong by a matter of inches, they'd break their neck. More often than not, the men would spring to their feet, grinning ear-to-ear and acknowledging the cheers of the crowd.

After filming the land divers, I ventured to Tanna Island to film dugong, the sea cows of the deep. For many generations, these creatures had interacted peacefully with the local inhabitants, swimming into the shallows and allowing children to ride on their backs. All that changed after a cyclone ripped through Vanuatu, levelling the farmers' crops and forcing the people to feed from whatever they could plunder from the sea. In desperation, one man trying to feed his starving family harpooned a female dugong. The male went crazy and, with that, the peace was broken.

I found the village on Tanna Island where the locals once swam with the dugong. I tracked down the chief of the village who spoke a few words of English.

'I want to dive with the dugong,' I said.

'Too dangerous,' he said, shaking his head. 'The big male will bite you and drown you.'

'I've come a long way,' I said.

'Only I can dive with the dugong,' he said.

I tried appealing to his ego, asking if I could be allowed to film the chief swimming with the male. The chief agreed and later that afternoon – wearing mask, snorkel and fins – I followed him into the sea.

The male dugong was circling us in an instant. The chief was intent on swimming between the dugong and me. Although he was acting in the interests of my safety, he blocked my view, completely ruining the footage. Even more frustrating was the chief's habit of fending the dugong away with his hands and feet if the big animal ever threatened to get too close.

Eventually, the dugong swam away. Once we were out of the water, the chief looked up at me with a smile.

'Thank you,' I said.

It was useless footage. All I got were glimpses of the dugong between the arms and legs of a half-naked islander. I'd have to try again. Without telling the chief, I returned to the shallows with my gear and went in search of the dugong. The big male must've heard me enter the water because, within minutes, the dugong appeared.

I'd been in the presence of predators of the deep countless times and I couldn't believe the creature swimming lethargically around me was dangerous. He seemed more curious than anything else. So when he started nudging me, I didn't react with any concern. I just kept the camera rolling, smiling at the awesome shots I was getting. I wouldn't be smiling for long.

The attack wasn't vicious. One second the dugong was rubbing his nose along my calf, like a dog detecting a scent, the next he had my lower leg between his jaws. Luckily for me, a dugong's diet is mainly sea grass. Evolution has not given them sharp teeth because they don't tear food apart. But they are equipped with powerful jaws to wrench plants and weeds out of the seabed. He'd bitten down hard enough to perforate my skin. That was not nearly as troubling as the fact that the dugong was taking me down.

I was low on breath and we were at least thirty feet down and getting deeper. I'd still managed to hang on to my camera gear throughout the attack. The camera was encased in brand-new aluminum underwater housing. The last thing I wanted to do was injure the dugong. But I had no other option. I brought the camera down on his head. The dugong immediately released me and I headed up to the surface.

The moment I'd filled my lungs with air, I swam quickly towards the beach. I was more concerned about the blood I was leaching out into the water attracting the attention of nearby sharks than a repeat attack of the dugong. I made it safely to shore. Even though the footage was excellent, I was worried I'd done little to mend the rift between the villagers and the dugong!

Tanna's volcano dominates the island. As one of few active volcanoes around the world that can be viewed safely from the mouth, it's a big driver for the economy. I was desperate to view one of nature's great phenomena at close range.

The problem was finding someone to take me up. The volcano's unusually high level of activity had everyone spooked. Some locals were worried the rumblings constantly felt across the island were a precursor to a massive eruption. When a Japanese tourist was killed by a white-hot rock the size of a ping-pong ball that went through his head, tours were suspended.

I thought the concern was overcautious. I figured the solution to my problem would be paying extra money. But the fear across the island was palpable. I couldn't find a single tour operator willing to risk a journey to the mouth of the volcano. In the end, I had to settle with an old man who'd heard I'd been making enquiries. He was clearly not a tour operator. In fact, it was possible he'd never climbed to the top. But he had a four-wheel drive Jeep and was obviously in need of a quick buck. He'd have to do.

We set off that night. There were absolutely no cars on the ascent and for good reason. The volcano was in a constant state of eruption. The orange glow of molten lava that reflected in the clouds and occasional bursts of light reminded me of Sydney Harbour on New Year's Eve. I could feel the earth tremors shaking the car. The further up the mountain we drove, the worse our visibility became. Ash was haemorrhaging out of the volcano and covered the road. The Jeep was quickly coated in white dust. The old man stopped the car.

'We walk from here,' he said.

We were still 300 feet from the summit, but the road was layered with ash deep enough to bog the car. We took as little gear as possible on the ascent – torch, water and camera gear. It was terrifying stuff. The rumbling volcano shook the mountain, causing us to stumble and trip. It sounded like crashing waves, only louder. But the worst was the ash. It clogged up the air, making breathing difficult.

We pressed on. The heat was incredible. The surface around us was literally baking, tendrils of smoke snaking up from the ground. Nothing lived up here. It was like walking through hell. Huge smouldering rocks lined the path we were walking. Some were the size of footballs. Others were about the size of a car. They radiated a fierce heat. Clearly, these rocks had been jettisoned from inside the volcano itself.

My instincts were screaming at me to turn back. I'm not sure why we kept going. But I was desperate to get that footage. As we neared the mouth, the eruptions got louder and the surface became less stable. I could see great jets of orange lava shooting into the air. I took the camera out and started filming the final steps to the ascent. I got to the lip of the mouth and looked down.

It's one thing to know that we live on a thin crust of rock that covers the molten heart of our planet. But actually seeing it makes you realise the fragility of our world. It makes you feel that at any moment, the ground beneath our feet could explode. I spent several minutes filming the cauldron of orange lava bubbling away below. I wanted to do the job properly because I wasn't planning on coming back here.

Just before leaving, the wind changed. The old man had taken us along a route that had placed us upwind of the breeze. In a blink, we were suddenly downwind and engulfed in a swirling mass of sulfurous cloud. With each breath I took in more of the noxious gas. My throat constricted. The bronchial tubes in my lungs swelled up and the little openings to the alveoli sacs in my lungs filled with mucus. It was the start of the worst asthma attack I'd suffered in years.

In the agony and chaos, I was struck with the thought that I'd lived this moment many times before. I'd envisaged these swirling black clouds as an infant, slowly suffocating to death. It was like waking up into a nightmare.

We ran down the mountain, the ground shaking with greater force. Above the sound of my own desperate wheezing, I could hear the old man struggling to breathe. With visibility down to a couple of feet, we were incredibly lucky not to tread on one of those molten rocks that had been spewed from the volcano. Had one of us done so, that person would've lost whatever part of his body struck the rock.

We made it to the Jeep, leaping inside and slamming the doors. Even though we were out of the ash cloud, I still couldn't get any air.

'Drive,' I gasped to the old man.

I needed to get off the mountain and into my hotel room where

I'd left my ventolin puffer. My guide drove like the wind. To me, he couldn't drive fast enough. I was desperate for oxygen. I was beginning to black out.

The old man pulled up outside my hotel. I staggered through the lobby, fumbled for my key and burst through the door. I found my ventolin and emptied the entire puffer in two goes. It had no effect. I could feel panic rising in my chest, my body tensing into a ball.

From the deepest recesses of my memory, I heard that familiar voice from my past. 'Don't panic, David,' said Don Athaldo. 'You'll be okay. Just breathe.' I sat on the bed, closed my eyes and focused on taking slow, deep breaths. I started to visualise, just as I had in my younger days, imagining myself in a happier place. I was putting back into practice the teachings of the old circus strongman. Eventually, my vision returned and my breathing normalised.

Don Athaldo was firmly in my thoughts when I returned to Sydney. Not for the first time, I owed my life to him. I believed then, as I do now, that Athaldo's wisdom could be life-changing for a lot of people. So when the coach of my son Nathan's under-11's soccer team resigned and I was the only person who could take on the job, I decided to base my coaching on the lessons learnt from the circus strongman.

The fact that I'd never played the game didn't faze me. I did a short course in coaching soccer, learning the basics of the game. Afterwards, I put together a training schedule, worked out some soccer drills and got a run-down from Nathan about the team. He gave me the impression that the team was okay, but would probably lose more games than they would win. I was determined that the boys would do much better. I wanted them to exceed their own expectations. Just like when teaching students how to dive, the first and most important thing was to get the boys to believe in themselves.

At the beginning of every training session, I channelled Don Athaldo and told the boys to repeat after me – 'I can be whatever I want to be! I can do whatever I want to do!' The kids got right into it. I'd tell them not to be afraid of making mistakes and that through hard work they'd be able to achieve remarkable things.

Before every game, I'd sit the boys down and conduct a visualisation session. I'd address each player according to his position. If he was a defender, I'd tell him to imagine laying a goal-saving tackle; if he was a midfielder, I'd tell him to imagine dribbling the ball down the wing on a fast break; if he was a striker, I'd tell him to imagine the ball smashing into the back of the net. We'd talk about what each player was going to do in great detail. Then they'd go out and do it.

If anyone – parent or player – thought that these techniques were rubbish, nobody was thinking it when we won the grand final. We went through the season undefeated.

I have to admit, the boys exceeded my expectations. It proved that Don Athaldo's teachings were more effective on children than adults. That says to me that the limitations people place on themselves worsen later in life.

24

Ireland for the Prosecution

The enquiries I made to Bill about the 17 per cent cut I was promised for the sale of each CD-ROM were always met with the same assurances. 'I'll write you a cheque when the sales figures are all tabulated,' he'd say. I never really pressed him on it. That blind trust would cost me dearly.

Bill called me into his office for a chat. I had no reason to be concerned. He'd done this sort of thing before to toss around ideas.

'I want to hire you as a full-time employee,' he said, straight off the bat.

I hadn't been in anyone's employ since Surf Dive 'N' Ski, and for good reason. I just couldn't imagine a scenario where I didn't have final say over how I spent my time. I told him I was happy with the present arrangement.

'In that case,' he said, 'I'm going to terminate our business relationship.'

It was a real shock. Losing the retainer was a massive blow. But there was nothing I could do.

'That's fine,' I said, doing my best to hide my disappointment. 'But what are you going to do about my 17 per cent?'

'You're not getting anything,' he said.

It felt like the oxygen had just been sucked out of the room.

'What?'

'I'm not paying you and I don't believe I have to.'

There was nothing in the contract that I signed that referred to 17 per cent. An agreement had nonetheless been made which was binding. The problem was proof. All I had were a couple of emails that obliquely made reference to our deal.

'Bill, I've been a good friend,' I said. 'But if you don't pay me what I'm owed, I'll be your worst enemy. I'll take you to court.'

'I don't think you can,' he said. 'You don't even own a house.'

He was saying that I didn't have the means to go after him. I resisted the temptation to punch him in the face and left his office without saying another word.

The sensible course of action would've been to let the matter rest and get on with my life. Tucker was no doubt banking on my common sense prevailing. Before I'd left his office, I noticed his smug look of entitlement that I used to see on the faces of schoolyard bullies who'd made my childhood a living hell. The ratbag had duped me, plain and simple. But he hadn't counted on one thing – I hate bullies.

I trawled through all my correspondence with Tucker – letters, emails, notes – and printed off and copied any reference made to the deal. I collated the material and then found a law firm prepared to represent me on a no win–no cost agreement.

First, we had to establish exactly how much I was owed. It was an enormous job. Obviously, Tucker Publishing wasn't prepared to release any information. That meant we had to ring up all the major retailers in Australia and request sales figures. Some complied, others didn't. Of those companies that were prepared to supply information, we multiplied the total number of Tucker CD-ROMs sold by the wholesale price. Seventeen per cent of the total amount came into the hundreds of thousands of dollars. It was a conservative estimate. Not only had we been unable to get all the sales figures across Australia, we had none from around the world. Only Tucker knew the countries where his CDs were sold.

My lawyers sent copies of spreadsheets with all our calculations along with a strongly worded letter demanding the immediate payment of all monies owed. Tucker's lawyers refuted my claim and things got dirty. After several months of claim and counterclaim, I indicated to my lawyers that I wanted to take the matter to court. My lawyers bailed out.

'Nobody ever beats publishers,' they said.

I think their real concern was my capacity to cover all the costs in the event of a loss. I didn't blame them for being worried. But there was no way I was backing down from this fight.

I fronted up to court in a borrowed suit without a clue of what I was doing. At the other end of the table, Tucker's serried ranks of lawyers – some of them noted QCs – stared across at me. I saw in their eyes the same ruthlessness I'd seen in the eyes of the crocodiles of the Cambridge Gulf. The only difference was that, in here, there was no cage to protect me. These bastards were going to eat me alive.

When the court came to order, the judge – a severe-looking woman who I'd come to admire as a person of great integrity – looked down at me with a frown.

'Mr Ireland,' she said. 'It is highly inadvisable for you to be representing yourself.'

'I'll be fine, judge,' I said.

I'll admit that I didn't impress too many people in those first few court hearings. I had to endure the snickering and audible groaning from Tucker's lawyers as I fumbled around for papers, interjected at inappropriate times, asked for clarification on points that a first-year law student would understand. I came to loathe those bewigged fuckers. It was clear they saw this as a game, and the name of the game was manipulation, concealment and lies. These so-called 'officers of the court' weren't in it for justice or principle. They were in it to assert their intellectual dominance and for the fat cheque at day's end.

At the conclusion of the first session, I went for a walk in nearby Hyde Park to clear my head. I felt completely drained. I eventually came to the statue of a sword-wielding naked warrior grasping the severed head of a Minotaur, a mythological creature with the body of a man and the head of bull. The statue came to symbolise my own struggle in the courts – naked against a monstrous and powerful beast, my only weapon the sword of truth. I'd visit the statue often. It gave me the strength to handle the hardship of that three-year battle.

Being in and out of court meant that there was no time to do any freelance filming or photography. Although I wasn't paying lawyers, I still had significant financial demands. Sue was caring for the kids full-time and managing to work part-time. Our savings vanished in a matter of months. I needed cash and I needed it fast. I managed to get work jackhammering tiles off swimming pools while I read up on publishing, contracts and court procedure at night. People have asked me how I got through that period.

'I had incredible support from my wife,' I say.

I also had to dig deep into my reserves of courage. It was a different kind of courage to that which I'd used in the wild. I was burning the candle at both ends, living off the smell of an oily rag and bearing the constant worry of not being able to provide food and shelter for my family.

I was also facing constant humiliation. The hardest thing about that time was listening as my name was dragged through the mud. I couldn't believe the lengths to which these people went to trash my reputation. But I had the courage to withstand it and truth was on my side. No lawyer, no matter how many letters he has after his name, can stand up against truth and courage. It's an unstoppable force.

Sure enough, I started to come to grips with court procedure and legal jargon. I felt that I'd proven to the court that an arrangement existed between Tucker and myself that guaranteed me a 17 per cent royalty from every CD sold. But I couldn't prove the actual figure I was owed because Tucker's lawyers refused to provide information on sales. I argued that, given this arrangement existed, I should be granted full discovery – a legal term that requires, in this case from Tucker Publishing, the full disclosure of requested documents. I chipped away and, slowly but surely, there seemed to be a subtle momentum shift.

Around this time, the press started following the story. David and Goliath court battles always generate publicity, particularly when David is representing himself. When a journalist asked my thoughts on Bill Tucker, I couldn't resist.

'Bill's an absolute shark,' I said, and left it at that.

A day after the story was published, a writ turned up at my house informing me that I was being sued for defamation. I'd opened up a second front. On one especially memorable day, I had the strange experience of turning up at the Supreme Court to fight Tucker's lawyers for the money I was owed, before heading to the Federal Court to defend myself against the same lawyers.

I won't forget that defamation case in a hurry. Bill's lawyer got up, prattling on about how my comment was deeply offensive to his client, claiming my statement would do his publishing business untold damage. Sitting quietly alongside his lawyers, Bill had the look of an animal preparing to go in for the kill. Bill Tucker might be a deceitful prick, but he isn't weak. I'm certain that he'd been called far worse things in his life than a shark. He had probably seen it as a compliment.

This wasn't about Bill's feelings or the negative impact on his business. This was about Bill delivering a knockout blow. If I lost, I'd be forced to pay him damages. Not only would it bankrupt me, it'd force me to drop my own suit. So when the judge asked me to explain, you can imagine I was feeling a little concerned. The stakes couldn't have been higher.

'Your honour,' I said, 'it's true that I referred to Mr Tucker as a shark. But I don't consider the comment insulting or defamatory.'

'And how do you arrive at that conclusion, Mr Ireland?'

'I'm a wildlife expert,' I said. 'I've been filming marine animals for many years. It is my firm belief that the shark is one of the noblest creatures in the animal kingdom.'

I then went on to detail the work I'd done to highlight the dangers that overfishing posed to shark species, including wobbegong and grey nurse. I was tempted to say that in comparing sharks to Bill Tucker, I'd actually defamed every shark that swam the seas. But I kept that thought to myself. The judge threw the case out. Bill was furious. His eyes flashed with anger and his face went purple.

The other case dragged on. On the day I was due to be cross-examined, I walked into the courtroom and realised with a shock that the whole affair had consumed three years of my life. That was time that could've been spent with my family or in the wild. My feelings of resentment towards Bill Tucker were now white hot. I was determined to bring the matter to an end.

Sitting in the dock with Bill's number one barrister hitting me with everything he had was one of the hardest experiences of my life. It went on for hours. His strategy seemed to be based around knocking me off balance. One minute he'd be aggressive and threatening, the next he'd be cordial, even friendly. He bandied about terms that three years earlier would've left me scratching my head. He also reeled off every half-truth and lie about the case in an effort to trip me up. But I'd now developed a decent understanding of the law and I knew the case better than any of them.

Then, just before he was finished, the barrister pulled out his trump card. He revealed a photocopy of a spreadsheet my former lawyers had put together as part of the package we'd sent to Tucker Publishing demanding the money I was owed. Tucker's lawyers had found a mistake in the spreadsheet. When we were adding up all the sales of Tucker's CDs, we'd inadvertently included several that didn't feature any of my footage. I looked over the spreadsheet closely. The barrister was accusing me of falsely claiming damages on the basis of this one mistake. It was a far-fetched claim. But the document could potentially damage my credibility.

'Mr Ireland?' said the judge. 'What do you have to say?'

'Your honour,' I said, 'I would like to apologise to the court and Mr Tucker. This item should not have been included in the spreadsheet. It is a mistake.'

Rather than being the silver bullet, my response seemed to disarm them. If anything, the sincerity of my apology had the opposite effect of what Tucker's lawyers were wanting. It proved that, no matter how the evidence reflected on me, I'd tell the truth. The barrister sat down and I stepped down. We took a short break while I made my final preparations. It was my turn to play my trump card.

Weeks previously, I'd contacted a friend who lived in New York City. I asked her to buy a single copy of Tucker's World Encyclopedia on CD-ROM, which I knew contained my footage. I'd send her the money if she could send me the receipt. With the CD-ROM and the receipt in hand, I went back into court for the last time.

'Your honour,' I said, 'despite what Mr Tucker's barristers have said, I believe I've proven that an arrangement was reached that I was entitled to a 17 per cent commission on every sale of a Tucker CD-ROM that featured my work. Implicit in any such agreement is the requirement that Mr Tucker must be accountable for all those sales.'

I reached into my pocket and extracted the CD-ROM purchased at Walmart and the receipt.

'Here is a CD-ROM bought in Walmart in New York City. It was sold for $12.99 and here is the receipt to prove it.'

'Your point, Mr Ireland?'

'Your honour, I don't have any accountability from Bill Tucker for that one disc. He has not been accountable to me.'

The judge looked over at Tucker.

'Were you accountable for that one disc?'

I could see Bill's teeth grinding. He was trapped. If he was caught in a lie then the consequences could be disastrous.

'No, your honour,' he said.

'Do you see any reason why the court shouldn't order full discovery of all Tucker's CDs?'

Bill shot a look at his lawyers, but there was nothing they could say. They dropped their eyes. Bill was speechless. They say that you should only ever negotiate from a position of strength. My position had never been as strong.

'Your honour,' I said, 'I'd like to request a recess to speak to Mr Tucker in person.'

The judge seemed only too happy to comply. Bill and I met in an anteroom outside the court. Tucker's barristers had wanted to come inside.

'Fuck off!' I shouted. 'This is my meeting.'

With his face turning red, the leading barrister was about to refuse when Bill told them to leave.

'What do you want?' Bill said.

'One hundred thousand.'

'Fine.'

I could've gone higher, I suppose. God knows I was owed much more. I also hadn't factored in the loss of income over the last three years. But the truth was, I wanted it over. I couldn't stomach another day in the presence of those lawyers. My feeling was that Bill felt the same. My $100,000 would've paled in comparison to the legal fees he'd have to stump up.

I returned to the courtroom triumphant.

'We've settled, your honour,' I said.

The stenographer's jaw visibly dropped. The judge, for all her experience, took a moment to regain her composure.

'Very well,' she said. She brought down the gavel and the case was closed.

Before I rang my family, I walked through Hyde Park one last time. The weight was off my shoulders. I practically floated across the ground. When I arrived at the statue of the swordsman and the Minotaur, my mind drifted back to that little boy with the broken voice box, scared of the sound of his own voice. That same boy had just stood up to the smoothest-talking silks in the land and won.

Bill's leading barrister rang me up a few days later.

'I just wanted to congratulate you on the settlement,' he said. 'Next time you're in town, I'll buy you a beer.'

I couldn't believe what I was hearing. This guy mightn't have instigated what had been a rotten period of my life; but he was certainly the architect of a campaign to smear my name and deny me what I was entitled. Worse still, he'd tried to do it with lies. I'd never been more disgusted in my life.

'I only have a beer with people I respect,' I said. 'Fuck off!'

I slammed the phone down and with that, it was over. I took a deep breath. It was time to head back into the wild.

Part Five

I AM THE
WILDLIFE MAN

25

Wild Boar Attacks!

Having been tied up in the courts for three years I'd barely had time to work. While remaining fully invested in raising our boys, Sue was working two jobs, which helped supplement the pittance I made from jackhammering. But we weren't making enough to put food on the table and pay the rent. I'd been forced to go back to the bank with hand extended. My victory against Tucker was a relief, but the settlement wasn't enough to service my debt and keep the family going. I needed money fast and I had a good idea where I might find it.

Having pored over Tucker's sales figures, I'd seen the public appetite for CD-ROMs. There was money to be made from this form of media. I went in search of companies producing CD-ROMs and found Jerry Baxter. Baxter owned a multimedia company that specialised in content for children. Kids are fascinated with animals. Yet, when I researched Baxter's material, I found no wildlife content.

I teed up a meeting with Baxter and gave him my pitch. The deal was twenty hours of Great Barrier Reef marine animal footage for $20,000. It was a one-off payment with no commission. He agreed.

God, it was good to be back in the wild. Diving the reef's pristine waters cleansed my body of the filth I'd gathered in the courts.

I came back with some of the best marine footage I'd ever shot. Baxter was elated and suggested expanding the business relationship. While I'd been away, he'd been doing background work on me. He'd bought a copy of *Crocodile Man* and liked what he'd seen. He asked me if I'd considered doing a film for television. Had I what!

Baxter offered to help fund six one-hour films. He'd pay $60,000 for each production and I'd get a cut of the profits. What he was asking was impossible. The cost of post-production – editing, music, voice-over narration – came to about $30,000. Now, let's consider the costs of shooting in the outback. I'd have thirty grand to finance the hiring of a film crew; travel costs; the hire of camera equipment, sound gear and at least one four-wheel drive; and the cost of room and board for the crew. I'd learnt one thing about long shoots in the wild from bitter experience: what can go wrong, *will* go wrong. We'd most likely be out there for weeks trying to get what we needed.

If we miraculously wrapped everything up in a couple of days, I'd take whatever was left over as a fee. In a best-case scenario, I'd be paid a few thousand dollars. More likely I'd get nothing. So the sensible course of action would've been to politely decline Baxter's offer. Instead I accepted without hesitation.

If you want to achieve something significant, adversity is unavoidable. There are usually millions of reasons why you can't pursue your ambitions. So rather than immediately dismiss a dream as impossible, accept that you're going to encounter some obstacles along the way. The trick is finding a way around them.

Finding corporate sponsorship was the key. I'd learnt from *Crocodile Man* that if a company knows that your film will give it television exposure, they'll clamber over each other to give you stuff. I needed a guarantee from one of the networks that someone would broadcast my films. I rang every contact in television and started pitching the show. By lunchtime, I'd stitched up a deal with Channel Nine. They agreed to buy all six one-hour films in advance. All the money made in the deal went to Jerry, partly paying off his original investment. But the value of the Channel Nine deal had less to do with money than it did with exposure. Within days, Sony came on board and upgraded my camera gear, Akubra gave us some hats and Driza-Bone provided branded clothing and boots.

The next problem was finding a film crew. Again, this was a money issue. The sort of film that Jerry and I had in mind would require a director, producer and at least three cameramen. The going rate for each of those jobs is about $1,500 a day. That's $7,500 a day for all five. I'd have them for four days before my $30,000 was spent and that was before paying for a researcher and a writer.

Now, let's compare my production to, say, a David Attenborough film. Attenborough's productions typically employ over twenty staff per film. Each will have multiple directors, producers, cinematographers, consultants and an army of writers and researchers. Often he'll send the crew out to shoot the footage and he'll maybe do a few pieces to camera and the narration. These productions cost a fortune, so it helps that Attenborough has a budget of several million dollars.

Don't think that I'm dirty on David Attenborough. I absolutely love the man's work. Luck doesn't keep you at the top for six decades. He got there through sheer hard work. The way I see it, he's fully deserving of the privileged position he has enjoyed in recent years. But the fact that I had no staff and only a fraction of the budget meant nothing to Channel Nine. They'd be expecting Attenborough-quality stuff. In signing up for this gig, I knew I'd be working as a director-producer-writer-narrator-presenter. I'd also have to do all the dangerous camera work.

Although I was confident I'd be able to shoulder the workload,

I'd still need at least one cameraman. Unlike the work I did for Bill Tucker, these films would place me in the centre of the action. I've been working in this industry for decades and if there's one cardinal rule about filming in the wild, it's that you never scrimp on the cameraman.

There are many things that distinguish a brilliant cameraman. Let's start with concentration. A crew might be shooting for weeks before something happens. Out in the wild it's a case of blink and you'll miss it. Physical endurance is important too, particularly seeing as my films are usually shot in extremes of climate and geography. And don't forget the importance of a trusting relationship between presenter and cameraman. Knowing when to follow or when to hang back can make or break a shot.

But nothing is more vital than having an intuitive sense of animals and the wild. This work is dangerous. Knowing your animals back-to-front might just save your life. One mistake, a lapse in concentration or lack of awareness, can result in tragedy. This, of course, applies to everybody on your crew.

Steve Irwin was killed when a bull ray's barb pierced his heart. I never met Steve. All I knew of him was what I saw on television. Here's what I thought: Steve was a great wildlife presenter. The energy he exuded on screen was infectious. Obviously, Steve made his name with crocs. He was also an animal handler without peer when it came to land-based creatures, particularly reptiles. His death was felt deeply among all of us who love the wild and was a profound tragedy for his family.

Wild animals are by their very nature unpredictable. You can take all the precautions in the world, but Steve's death is a sobering reminder that in this game things can go badly wrong. This is therefore the final thing you need from a cameraman: a person prepared to put himself in harm's way. All told, great wildlife cameramen are bloody hard to find.

Nor do they come cheap, but Jerry wasn't willing to increase the budget. I needed to find a gutsy, highly skilled person happy to work for a pittance. Into my lap fell Abraham Joffe. Someone at Channel Nine must've told him that I was looking for a cameraman. Abe was a young cameraman who'd worked freelance for several news bulletins. He was tired of working with people in urban settings. His dream was to film animals in the wild and he was looking for someone to give him a start.

'I'd like to take you on,' I said. 'But I can't afford to pay you much.'

Abe told me he wasn't interested in the money. At this stage, he wanted to get experience. Before signing him up, I pitched my idea for the first film.

A few years earlier, I'd done some volunteer work with at-risk Aboriginal kids from broken homes. They were from remote communities near Goodooga, a town in New South Wales near the Queensland border. My brief was to give them the sort of experience they'd never get at home. I taught them how to snorkel, took them bushwalking through eucalyptus forests, showed them local fish markets and entertained them with adventure stories. They particularly loved the story of Fergus and the blood drain, so much so they nicknamed me Croc.

'Hey Croc,' they used to say. 'You should come to our place. We've got snakes, goannas, spiders and lots of feral pigs.'

What they told me about the behaviour of the feral animals really piqued my interest. Australia was in the grip of one of the worst droughts in recorded history. The drought had made the feral pigs a real menace. They tore up the ground in search of water and slaughtered ewes and lambs. Most disturbing were the reports of an increase in attacks on humans.

The kids told me about a boar attack on an Aboriginal elder. This bloke was an expert in 'dogging', a hunting method where pig dogs are used to take the boar down by the ears before the 'dogger' rushes in and sticks the pig with a long-pointed hunting knife. The elder had turned a tidy profit selling the slaughtered wild pigs to market. That was before he came across a monster.

'He was a real big spotty pig without any ears,' said one of the Aboriginal boys. Other pig dogs had probably ripped off the pig's ears. Evidently the pig had fought the dogs off or killed them. Oddly, the injuries the big boar suffered in each skirmish helped him survive subsequent attacks.

A pig with no ears is a nightmare scenario. With nothing to latch onto, the dog has no choice but to go for the pig's neck. Bigger pigs with thicker necks are usually strong enough to shrug off most dogs. The elder's pig dog was ripped apart. The boar then launched himself at the elder, bringing him to the ground. The boar went to work with his tusks, tearing up the old man's feet, calves, groin and hands. Panicking, the old man tried to protect himself, rolling onto his back. The boar went mental. He ripped apart the man's back and even stuck a tusk through his throat.

Luckily, the old man had brought along his Jack Russell. The little dog was barking like mad in the back seat as the attack unfolded. He somehow managed to prise open the window and rushed over to defend his master. The boar swiped at the Jack Russell with his tusks, but missed by miles. The little fella was too quick. He spun that boar around and around, nipping away at his balls. Exhausted, the boar lost interest and took off.

The elder was alive, but only just. He dragged himself to the car and drove to the nearest town with his little saviour in the back seat. Helicopter ambulance flew him to Brisbane and somehow he survived. He'd spent months in intensive care, recovering from toxaemia – blood-poisoning from the injuries sustained by the boar's filthy tusks.

It was excellent background material for a film. The idea of working with pig dogs also appealed. Not only would there be plenty of action, it was the perfect way to cast light on two catastrophes unfolding in the Australian outback: the drought and the damage wrought by feral pigs.

Abe loved the idea. The next day we loaded up the Jeep with the new camera equipment and set off on the ten-hour drive to Goodooga. We managed to track down the elder and interviewed him on camera. He was a fantastic storyteller. On camera, he showed the scars of the horrendous injuries he'd suffered.

Then Abe and I went hunting with dogs. A local pig dog named Blue was loaned to us for the film. Blue was fearless. He'd run in snarling and barking at the fiercest-looking animals. We took out about ten pigs on that first day. It was awesome fun. It was also way too violent for television. There was a huge amount of blood and the pigs' squeals made my blood curdle. Any wildlife presenter will tell you that kids are the backbone of your audience. If parents forbade their children from watching my shows, I'd be jackhammering pool tiles again. So I came up with a way of filtering out the distressing material without losing the action.

Once the dogs had latched onto the pig, I'd race in and grab it by the front legs and jam my knee behind its neck. Once the pig was secure, a couple of local teenage doggers – who we'd recruited as helpers – would call Blue away and then Abe would rush in with the camera and start filming inches from the pig's snout. With the pig very much alive, I'd talk directly to the camera about the menace feral pigs posed in the outback. When I was done, Abe would button off and I would kill the pig.

The new method increased the danger to me tenfold. If my knee slipped or the pig wriggled free, I'd be savaged by one seriously pissed-off feral animal. It meant we had to be careful about the pigs we chose to capture. For the first few days of shooting, it worked beautifully. Abe was a natural behind the camera. He also had a good eye for detail, suggesting that we highlight the damage feral pigs did in the outback. He filmed lamb carcasses that had been ripped to shreds and acres of land that had been dug up.

To add another dimension to the film, we did some work with local fauna. I captured a few goannas and lizards, and tailed some of the world's most venomous snakes – black snakes, tiger snakes, king browns and, the most deadly of all, the inland taipan. It was destined to be an awesome show – a gritty, action-filled adventure that actually highlighted a major problem while exploring the mysteries of the outback.

Then it went bad. We came across a large mob of pigs grazing at the side of a road. I brought the Jeep to a screaming halt. Abe opened up the back door to let Blue out and then the rest of us followed at breakneck speed. Blue had a boar secured by the time we were on the scene. I came in knees first and held him down. Blue let go and chased another pig. With the pig firmly under my knees, I waited for Abe to turn up with the camera before launching into my spiel. But Abe was nowhere to be seen. He was off following Blue with our two doggers.

No drama, I thought. I'd stick the pig and catch up with the others. But when I reached for my knife it wasn't there. The squeal of a distressed pig is ear-splittingly loud. I discovered on that day that a pig's squeal is loud enough to drown out the sound of a man shouting for help. It didn't matter how loudly I bellowed, Abe and the boys couldn't hear me.

The boar beneath my knees was forty pounds heavier than me. If he got free, those tusks would rip me to pieces. The boar started bucking around, wriggling himself out from under my knees. With a sudden jerking motion, his head smashed into my sternum plate. I managed to get him under control, pressing down on the back of his neck with my right forearm. I yelled out to the others until it felt like my head was about to explode. Just as I was losing feeling in my arms, one of the boys came back brandishing my knife. He ran in and stuck the boar. With one last scream, the monster died.

I was completely spent. My right arm had gone to jelly and I was having trouble breathing. Worse was to come. I woke up in the middle of the night with a searing pain in chest. It felt like an elephant was sitting on my sternum. The pain blossomed out to my shoulders and neck and all the way down my back. I was having a heart attack and I was absolutely in the middle of nowhere with no satellite phone to raise the alarm. I didn't think to alert any of the crew. I just got in the car and drove myself to hospital. I wasn't thinking straight – the nearest hospital was a couple of hours away in Walgett!

It was a nightmare. Kangaroos were everywhere, feeding at the road's edge. The dew that collected on the road each night ran off and nourished grass fronds. The grass was one of the only things growing across the drought-stricken land. Had I driven faster than twenty miles per hour, I'd have had roos bouncing off my screen. My slow progress meant that a drive that normally takes two hours took me five.

God, I was in pain. I genuinely thought each passing minute would be my last. But I made it to Walgett, staggered into the hospital and nearly collapsed on the bench at reception. My pulse was spiking. A nurse rushed out, took one look at me and agreed with my self-diagnosis – I was about to have a cardiac arrest. They hooked me up to an electrocardiograph (ECG) to confirm the obvious. I waited an excruciating twenty minutes, begging the nurses to let me call my wife, fearful that I'd not get a chance to tell her one last time how much I loved her.

Finally, a registrar turned up holding the results with a strange look on his face.

'There's nothing wrong with your heart,' he said. 'What in the hell have you been doing?'

An X-ray revealed the boar had shattered two of my ribs – one at the point where it joined the sternum and the other where it joined the spine. We suspended filming for two months. We could've left it at that point. There was more than enough footage to put together an excellent outback story. But I decided to return to Goodooga. I wanted revenge, and the focus of my revenge was that bloody boar that had killed the elder's dog. The only question was whether I'd be able to find him.

Abe came back out with me. We came onto a mob within an hour. But when I set Blue loose onto a big black pig, the unthinkable happened. I froze. The sound of the pig squealing raised the hairs on my back. I could feel sweat on my brow and my hands started to shake. Even though I'd been pain-free for weeks, my sternum started to ache. I was terrified.

Uncontrollable fear manifests in all sorts of ways. I was in the grip of indecision. In this game, indecision is catastrophic. The pig was desperately trying to shake Blue off. That brave pig dog was hanging on with everything he had. Every so often I'd catch his eye. He seemed to be asking me a question – *What the hell are you doing?* Either I overcame my fear or I got another job. It was that simple.

I gritted my teeth and ran in to help my mate. I lifted up the boar's back legs, bringing him crashing to the ground. With my right knee dug in deep behind the boar's neck, I unsheathed my knife and drove it into his heart. The boar's squeal faded to a raspy wheeze. I could feel his life draining away and taking my fear with him.

I must've stuck about forty pigs that week. We got way more footage than we needed. But we still hadn't got the dog killer. My determination to find him had become an obsession. It also felt like the right thing to do. This feral animal was more than just a menace to a delicate ecosystem. He was a genuine threat to the Aboriginal community. The problem was, I couldn't find the bugger. We searched high and low and found no evidence of his whereabouts. I was beginning to think the whole thing was a myth. Just when I was about to throw in the towel, my luck changed.

I couldn't believe it when I first clapped my eyes on the boar. The monster was just like the Aboriginal elder had described: a big fat spotty pig with thick tusks that tapered into razor-sharp ends, a deeply scarred head and shoulders, and no ears. And it was huge! It was also fearless. Unlike the other boars we'd culled, this tough warrior stood his ground. He turned towards us when we approached, and scraped his tusks along the dirt like a bull pawing at the ground. He was ready for battle.

Blue ran straight at the boar. With a perfectly timed swipe of his tusks, the boar brushed Blue aside like a man swatting away a fly. Blue went at him again, this time leaping onto the pig's back and biting hard into his neck. The boar let loose a deep, throaty growl and threw Blue to the ground. Then he went at him with his tusks. Blue's mouth was cut up and he was slashed just under his eye. The dog scampered away, barking like crazy from a safe distance.

With Blue out of the picture, the boar lined up the two men spectating. Abe and I clambered up the nearest tree. The boar circled the tree and then started ramming the trunk. When that failed to bring us down, he took off over sandy loam country. I was furious at myself for not having a rifle close at hand. Not only was the pig dangerous, it had undoubtedly sired hundreds of piglets. He needed to be destroyed. There'd be no way to track the bastard. The loam was a crosshatch of prints left by other feral pigs.

But a dusting of rain changed our fortunes. Who would've thought? It was the first rain for months and it was perfect: a light shower to sweep away the older, shallower tracks without washing away the deeper, fresher ones. I got my 8mm rifle from the car and went hunting. In no time we were hot on the boar's trail. We followed the tracks for about two miles and found the bastard in an open field. With Abe filming over my shoulder, I lined up the dog killer and shot him dead. It was the perfect way to end the film.

I called the film *Wild Boar Attack!*. It was exactly what I'd hoped: a gutsy, tough, action-packed film that had a strong message. Channel Nine saw it differently. The program director rang me after watching the final cut.

'David, we can't show this film,' she said. 'It's way too violent.'

'You should show it,' I said. 'It'll educate city people about what's going on out there.'

We went back-and-forth like this before she rang off without making a firm commitment. Weeks passed and I heard nothing. Eventually, I came to accept that the film would never see the light of day. I was gutted. But there was no time to feel sorry for myself. I had another five films to make.

Before turning my mind to the next project, I wanted to spend some quality time with the family. Christmas was upon us. It was the first time in three years I was celebrating the festive season without serious financial worry or an impending court date. I remember sitting with Sue as our kids tore the wrapping off their presents, the joy they experienced lifting our hearts.

We'd left the television on in the background because Channel Nine was showing a Christmas pageant. After the pageant the boys wanted to watch a live broadcast of an Iron Man event in Queensland. As it happened, the weather in Queensland that Christmas was horrendous, forcing the event to be cancelled at the last minute. In the mad dash to find something to fill the one-hour gap in programming, a young intern was sent off into the archives to find a show that would appeal to a male audience. He returned with *Wild Boar Attack!*.

'Fucking hell,' I whispered. Proud though I was of the film, it wasn't exactly Christmas Day material.

'Well, that's the end of your career,' said Sue.

The kids were transfixed. That was a good sign. But it wasn't until the phone started ringing off the hook that I knew I had a hit. Channel Nine ended up re-broadcasting *Wild Boar Attack!* four times over the next twelve months. It was one of the most popular documentaries in the network's history. It was the best Christmas ever.

26

Whales and Militiamen

Wild Boar Attack! was the first of six very successful films, all shot on a shoestring budget. They'd become known as the Wildlife Man series. Beyond International – a production company with global reach – bought the series and sold it to several big networks, including Discovery in the United States and Canada. The films were a huge hit internationally, scoring a viewership well into the millions. I now had the backing to pursue the subjects I'd wanted to film for years. Whales were high on my list.

I'd always felt a special connection to whales after being saved by the southern right off Cronulla. That bond grew stronger after I went whale-watching with my sons in a grey inflatable. Low and behold, we came upon a southern right whale with her calf. Just one look at her distinctive markings and tail and I knew it was her.

'That whale saved my life,' I said to the boys, tears in my eyes.

Ever since, I'd been determined to film whales at close range. Problem was, the government had banned swimming to within twenty metres of a whale. That wasn't close enough for me. I wanted to get in tight for filming.

Tonga was a different story. In the winter months, this tiny

Pacific nation annually hosts the humpback whale mating season. The Tongan tourist office was delighted to hear I was coming to shoot a film in their country. In addition to arranging room and board, they paid for the hire of boats and guides.

Abe's busy schedule meant he had to sit out the shoot. So I hired a freelancer and we flew out to Tonga. It was magic to be back in the South Pacific. I'd almost forgotten the vivid blue of the water and the pristine white of the sandy beaches. The locals gave us the royal treatment, driving us directly from the airport to our hotel and putting on a big feast. They clearly saw our film as a potential tourist boon and were anxious that everything ran to plan.

Our hosts took us out to the Tonga Trench the following day. The Tonga Trench is an underwater valley where the seabed drops down a staggering 37,000 feet. The humpback whale has come here to breed for millennia. The warmer waters are not only ideal for calving, but the depth provides greater safety for the young. Humpbacks can dive to 700 feet, well beyond the range of a human, particularly on snorkel. I was banking on most of the action remaining on the surface. And I wasn't disappointed.

The behaviour of male humpbacks during breeding is something to behold. They charge into each other, presumably as a way of proving themselves worthy of the females. Weighing up to forty-four tons, the force the males exert when they collide reverberates like a concussion wave. Through this incredible demonstration of strength, other humpbacks sing to each other. The humpback song seemed to make the ocean vibrate. I felt like I was physically immersed in it. I swam closer, camera raised, drawn magnetically to the symphony.

The first sense of danger was a sudden change in pitch to the whale song. Another humpback had joined the chorus. It was getting louder and louder. I turned around and saw a big bull barrelling towards me out of the deep blue. Behind me, another male rolled so that he was now facing his challenger. I was right in the middle of the charge.

With a swish of his tail, the whale nearest to me accelerated towards the oncoming whale. A humpback at full speed can reach speeds in excess of fifteen miles per hour, very quick indeed underwater. There was no time for me get out of the way. At the very last moment, the humpback deviated a few inches, lifting one of his pectoral fins so it didn't smash into my head.

I wasn't out of danger yet. In his eagerness to match the speed of his opponent, the whale was violently swishing his tail, leaving me in extremely turbulent water. I was spun around in the vortex, desperately clutching my camera. I was only vaguely aware of the terrible impact of the two males colliding nearby. My main focus was orienting myself. It felt like being dumped in huge surf, only I was much deeper – maybe sixty feet – and very much in need of air.

After being spun around for a few seconds in his turbulent wake, I was now beginning to experience the first stages of hypoxia. Hypoxia is the dread of all divers. Brought on by oxygen deprivation, the condition induces a feeling of contentment and lethargy, like being pleasantly drunk. Some divers talk of hallucinating or losing all sense of urgency. I knew the early signs. I was entering the stage where splotches of bright colour start dancing before the eyes. In a little while I'd either black out or the body's urgent need for air would trigger a gag reflex and I'd inhale a lungful of water. Either way I'd be dead.

When the churning sea calmed, I turned myself towards the surface and kicked with everything I had. There was no strength in my body. It felt like I was swimming in molasses. My field of vision became narrower. The sunlight that broke through the surface looked like a distant light at the end of the tunnel. I was right on the brink of passing out. I felt like I was losing my grip on the real world.

I floated to the surface as if in a dark dream. When I inhaled, an explosion of light and colour filled my senses. During a lifetime spent beneath the waves, I'd been in some perilous situations. In those situations, remaining calm was the key to survival. This was no different. But I have to say, diving in the Tonga Trench with humpbacks was one of my closest calls.

The film looked great, a delicate mix of powerful action with something more spiritual. The money shot was a whale breaching. I'd been filming the whale from about twenty feet below as he headed to the surface at full speed. My surface cameraman – who was filming from the boat – had the camera trained on the exact spot where the whale breached. I spliced the shots together just before the final, most memorable scene.

I'd seen the female humpback suckling her newborn from the surface. This was exactly the sort of thing I'd been chasing – the perfect counterpoint to the shots of heavy males violently bumping into each other. I'd snorkelled over very slowly, remaining absolutely calm. Had I gone too quickly, the mother might have lashed out at me with her tail to protect her young.

I'd made it to within a few feet when the curious calf detached from his mother and swam within inches of my camera, milk leaking from his mouth. After a brief inspection of my lens, the little fella returned to his mum. It was a stunningly beautiful sequence to end the film.

We called the film *Swimming with Whales* and it was another huge hit. Channel Nine was delighted, which meant Jerry would green-light any idea I had. I looked at a map of the world and was immediately drawn to the newly created nation of East Timor.

Where better to break new ground than in the newest country in the world?

Civil unrest in East Timor persisted for several years after she won independence from Indonesia. By 2002, the Australian-led peacekeeping force quelled the worst of the violence and foreigners were being let in for the first time since 1975. Apart from the film's commercial appeal, I hoped the project might drum up some tourism for the fledgling economy.

On arriving in Dili it was clear that I couldn't simply do a wildlife film. Massive refugee camps surrounded the capital. The camps were filthy, full of discarded rubbish and human shit. Soldiers and army trucks roamed the streets, keeping an eye on the gangs who skulked around looking for trouble. This needed to be shown to the world. But filming the continuing humanitarian crisis in East Timor was beyond my brief. I was here to film wildlife.

So I came up with the concept of staging a massive Wildlife Man show for the children. Every company we approached – whether it was media, oil or electronic – jumped on board. We even had the backing of the United Nations. Acres of canvas tarpaulins were laid out to provide a sitting area for up to two thousand kids and huge screens with oversized projectors were sourced from the Australian army. The idea was to project film clips from my earlier productions onto the screens. I'd then get up with a microphone and tell stories about each clip. While this was happening, Abe would film me talking to the kids, and that footage would be incorporated into our film.

Abe and I left our hotel before dusk in an open-top Jeep on the scheduled day. Word had spread about the show. Local interest was massive. Families were bringing their kids in from surrounding camps. The UN told us the night before they were expecting a crowd of 10,000 people! This was going to be a day I'd never forget.

It was memorable, alright . . .

We could hear screaming children and gunfire before we even entered the camp. Then people of all ages started sprinting past us looking terrified. Fires were burning out of control and the air was filled with smoke. Driving into the field where the screens had been set up, three hundred thugs were waving large machetes around.

There was no way I was going to put the Jeep in reverse and get to safety. These kids had come to hear me talk and watch my films. I felt responsible for them. I drove into the centre of the field. The Jeep was surrounded in seconds. The thugs started chanting and banging on the hood of the car with their machetes. In the dying light of the day I could see the red stain of betel nut on their teeth and the mad glint in their eyes. These boys were keyed up and spoiling for a fight. Whether they were Indonesian-backed militiamen or a gang of bored young men was unclear. Whoever they were, they didn't want us around.

Abe and I hopped out of the car. The Jeep was now totally surrounded and the thugs were getting louder and more aggressive. One or two of them brandished their machetes inches from my face. It was frightening. I caught sight of the UN-appointed refugee camp manager about twenty feet away. His arms were raised in a pleading gesture as he spoke to one of the young leaders of the gang. The chanting was getting louder and louder and seemed to draw all of the thugs towards us. A couple of them shoulder-charged us.

'What are they doing here?' I shouted to the camp manager.

'You must leave,' he warned. 'They are chanting, "Kill the foreigners".'

I stole a glance at Abe, who had gone white. I didn't blame him for being scared. All it would take was one madman to strike us and we'd be cut to pieces.

'Tell them we're here for the children,' I shouted.

The camp manager did as I'd instructed. It didn't so much diffuse the tension as redirect it. The chanting stopped and the men started arguing among themselves. Clearly, there was some indecision as to what they were going to do with us. The manager bought us some time. Nothing more. Whatever happened, we weren't going to be allowed to leave quietly.

Above the screams of the children and the shouting of the men, a new sound boomed across the field. A Seahawk helicopter swooped overhead. The rotor wash kicked up the red dust and caused everyone to instinctively drop low to the ground. Another Seahawk followed close behind. Screaming people ran everywhere, smoke and fire swept across the camp, choppers streaked across the sky and heavily armed soldiers poured into the camp. The Aussie diggers had arrived. I felt like I was in Vietnam during the Fall of Saigon.

The mood of the men changed from one of violence to fear. Here was our chance. Abe and I jumped back into the Jeep. I turned the ignition and floored it. People scattered before us as we drove across the field and made it to the relative safety of a road that cut through the camp. On the way back to our hotel, we passed a huge convoy of armoured cars.

Abe and I returned to the camp a couple of days later. The situation had cooled down, but the fear of raids from violent gangs persisted. The army advised us against rescheduling the show. Large-scale public events ran the risk of attracting unwanted attention.

Abe and I were heartbroken for the kids. We were determined to do something for them. We spent the next three days hopping from tent to tent with a laptop. The computer was a poor substitute for the massive cinema-sized screens we'd planned on using. But the people of that refugee camp were elated. They made sure their children were neatly dressed, with combed hair. These Timorese kids had been born into troubled times and seen things that most Australians will never see in a lifetime. They were the most well mannered, polite and enthusiastic kids I've ever encountered. The sight of crocodiles, manta rays, lions, snakes, spiders and so many other animals seemed to fill them with joy. If ever I need reminding of why I'm a wildlife presenter and filmmaker, I need only think of those kids.

We stayed in East Timor a month. The footage we got of water buffalo, monkeys and some of the exotic marine life off a nearby reef was incredible. A particular highlight was filming a fourteen-foot reticulated python, the longest species of snake on the planet. We came onto it while doing a spot of 4x4 driving through the jungle. Out of the corner of my eye, I saw this monster snake with a head the size of a small alligator slithering through the reeds. It looked like a prop from a Disney production.

'What the fuck is that?' I shouted.

We stopped the car and pulled over. I managed to get the snake to strike at my Akubra, and took hold of him behind his huge head. It took two of us to pick him up. It must've weighed 120 pounds and, boy, was that snake strong. Little wonder these things can eat monkeys and even small children.

The scene of me handling the python was the perfect ending to the film. We called the final product *Treasures in Paradise*. I dedicated the film to those kids in the camps outside Dili, a very small gesture to some of the bravest people I've met.

27

Great White Sharks

My first brush with a great white shark was diving off Jibbon Bombora. It happened during the heyday of Cronulla Dive School. I'd taken out four students to complete their training. The sea was oily smooth, the gentlest westerly barely raising a cat's paw on the surface. Visibility underwater, however, was poor. You couldn't see more than ten feet in any direction.

Towards the end of the dive, I heard outboard engines roaring above us. It seemed like the boat above was going round in circles. Whoever was driving was either being an idiot or trying to warn us. I did a head count – everyone was present and accounted for. I narrowed my eyes, peering into the murky water. I sensed something was terribly wrong.

Throughout this book I've made reference to getting a bad feeling or sensing danger. I'm not a superstitious man. Nor do I go in for any of the claptrap peddled by mediums, mystics and religious types. Every conclusion I've drawn has come from experience and the evidence before my own eyes. So don't think I've gone kooky when I tell you that when I get a bad feeling, I believe I'm detecting the aura of a dangerous creature or having a premonition of catastrophe.

Let me be clear. I'm not talking about being afraid. My mind must be clear to sense danger and fear distorts reality and clouds judgement. It's a sense that has saved me more times than I can remember. The times I've ignored that feeling, I've always regretted it. I'm not saying I'm special. I believe *all* humans have this ability.

And why wouldn't we? Animals are highly perceptive of danger. I've seen wildebeest become skittish long before the arrival of a pride of lions. I've observed a wallaby skip away from a billabong seconds before a snapping crocodile lunged onto the bank. I've witnessed an entire colony of seals scamper onto a rock ledge minutes before the arrival of a great white. In each of these examples, there was no obvious forewarning of impending danger. Maybe they caught a scent in the air or felt the slightest vibration in the water or heard the far-off snapping of a twig. A life lived in the wild will do that to you.

Comparatively, humans are not nearly as perceptive. The modern world has dulled our senses, made us suspicious of our own instincts. But we are still animals. Technological advancement hasn't completely drummed our base instincts out of us. Think about it. We've all had the feeling of imminent danger, like entering a pub moments before a brawl erupts or stepping onto a train full of vicious thugs. These are obviously alarming moments. Sometimes, the warning signs are so subtle we can't pin down exactly what troubles us or locate where the threat exists. It's just a bad feeling. I'm big on people paying close attention when they get that feeling.

The feeling I was getting off Jibbon was worse than bad. Something massive was out there. We were being hunted. My procedure for surfacing is to use the anchor rope as a guide. We were about fifty yards east of the anchor. The current was running out, most likely bringing the boat directly over our position. I signalled to each of the divers that it was time to head up.

We were in eighty feet of water, far too deep for a rapid ascent.

I acted as calmly as possible, desperate not to unnerve my students. After what seemed a lifetime of slow, controlled ascent, we finally broke the surface. I scanned the water, clapping eyes on the police boat pulling up alongside us. The skipper of the boat, a mate of mine named Robert Rowan, was reaching over and dragging my students over the gunwales. I was enraged. Pulling someone into a boat in that manner will hurt the diver. Rob was ignoring my students' protests.

'What the hell are you doing?' I shouted, pulling myself onto the police boat's backboard.

'Get in the boat, Dave,' Rob shouted.

'What's going on?'

'There's a huge white shark here.'

Rob had seen my boat anchored off Jibbon and come over to say hello. Normally, I leave someone in the boat to help the divers back on board, particularly in a heavy swell. It was so calm that day there was no need to leave someone up top. On his approach to my boat, he'd powered down his motors, when from nowhere a huge canonical head broke the surface and started mouthing the stern of his boat.

'The shark went down when your bubbles broke the surface,' Rob said. 'We thought he'd get one of you for sure.'

The only way to warn us was to rev his engines. Rob's quick thinking probably scared the shark off and saved our lives.

The next day, Rob called me up at the shop. 'Come down to the Royal Motor Yacht Club,' he said. 'There's something I want to show you.'

I arrived to find Rob's 21-foot Trojan pulled up the slipway. The stern of the boat was scarred with huge bite marks. The great white shark responsible was at least seventeen feet in length. Yeah, we'd been lucky.

Five years later I was on a film shoot off Dangerous Reef, east of Port Lincoln in South Australia's Spencer Gulf. I'd chartered a boat and crew from a cage-diving company with a view to filming great whites. In those days, before the Spencer Gulf was full of whites, you'd spend several days 'chumming' up the water to lure the sharks. Chumming involves throwing fish guts, bone and blood overboard.

We headed out the day before shooting to chum. Every crewman aboard was allocated a four-hour chumming shift. The current took hold of the fish bits, leaving a slick several miles long. I took the graveyard shift between midnight and four o'clock. After two days of chumming, we hadn't seen a single great white. Going into the third day, around halfway through my shift, I went for a piss. I stepped onto the backboard, grasping hold of a handrail at the stern while doing my business.

It was a beautiful night. No wind, no clouds. The smooth skin of the ocean mirrored a galaxy of stars with such clarity it was hard to distinguish between sky and sea. It almost felt like I was floating in the Milky Way. Despite the breathless conditions, a long and languid swell dunked the backboard in the water. When the boat entered the trough of each wave, the water came up to my knees.

I wasn't concerned. If I toppled into the sea the current wouldn't be strong enough to prevent me from getting back on board. I soon discovered the current was the least of my worries. About a boat's length from where I was pissing, the head of an enormous white shark was sticking two feet out of the water. I leapt back onto the boat, splashing my leg with piss, as his big black eye stared at me. I'd heard of whites sticking their heads out of the water to observe seals that are sunning themselves on rocks or platforms. But I never knew they could hold their heads above water for so long. I realised that I was looking into the eye of something very intelligent and very lethal.

That shark hung around our cage the next day. I baited up a

large chunk of tuna and threw it into the sea. Each time the shark lunged towards the bait, I'd pull it out of the water. After the fourth attempt, the shark positioned itself horizontally from the boat with its head out of the water. The shark eyed me off as it had the night before. This time it decided to attack.

The shark took hold of the tractor tyre that was positioned between the cage and the boat to act as a fender. The shark shook its head with fury, foaming up the water and causing the boat to shudder. It was as if it was saying, *Don't fuck around with me.* I unhooked the tuna and threw it into the water. The shark heard the splash, released the tyre and swallowed the fish whole. I spent the day filming the shark from the cage. All the while I became increasingly uneasy about what we were doing. It felt wrong.

Shark attacks – fatal and non-fatal – have been trending upwards worldwide since records were first taken. Having worked, lived and holidayed around the sea my whole life, I don't need statistics to know this to be true. It's important not to be alarmist. Your chances of being taken by a shark are still low. But thirty years ago, shark attacks seldom occurred in Australia. Even seeing a shark swim near a beach was a rare event. Nowadays shark sightings are commonplace.

Some experts point to an increase in the human population. Simply put, there are more people in the water these days. I'm not saying this isn't a factor contributing to the problem. But it can't be a coincidence that the increase in attacks has matched the increase in shark cage businesses.

If you create an industry whose sole purpose is to attract sharks to boats and people, then naturally these animals are going to be less wary of people. By chumming the water, you're also creating an association between people and food. Government legislation that protects the great white is compounding the problem. We either protect all shark species, or we protect none. Again, it's no coincidence that whites are responsible for most attacks in Australian waters. There are more of them in the water.

And yet, the resistance to change is incredible. I put forward my views on shark cages after being invited to address a group of marine biologists, government officials and stakeholders in the fisheries department in Albany, Western Australia. There'd been a spate of shark attacks in Western Australia the previous year and everyone was searching for reasons.

'The big whites that feed off the cages off Port Lincoln migrate just south of Albany,' I said. 'They're following the whale herds up the coast of Western Australia. These are sharks that have been conditioned to approach boats and humans for food.'

'There's no evidence to support that theory,' said one marine biologist.

I shouldn't have been surprised that my views would be met with resistance. Some marine biologists were using a similar method of luring sharks to boats to tag them for research purposes. They'd hang blood-soaked hessian bags over the side of a boat to attract sharks. When a shark approached and mouthed the bag, someone would reach over and bolt a GPS locater to its dorsal fin. I told the marine biologist that this practice was equally to blame for the increase in attacks. You can imagine how well that went down.

It's understandable why shark cage operators dismiss the link between their businesses and the increase in shark attacks. After all, their livelihoods are at stake. But the government is being wilfully naïve about the problem. We are mired in an outdated belief that sharks are mindless monsters, blithely roaming the seas for food. Nothing could be further from the truth.

Sharks are equipped with *ampullae of Lorenzini*, highly sensitive electroreceptors that look like jelly spores, located in the head. These spores pick up the electrical impulses of all living things. As the apex predator of the sea, the white's electroreceptors are superior among all shark species. In addition to sensing life, these creatures have incredible intuitive memory. They will travel thousands of miles to arrive at seal colonies exactly the day before the seals start pupping. Why wouldn't they start adjusting their behaviour towards boats and humans if they know that in certain places they'll get a feed?

It's a serious issue. The shark cage industry shows no sign of being rolled back or disbanded. Operations in South Africa and South Australia continue to do excellent business. With shark cage diving becoming a big attraction in New Zealand, my prediction is an increase in shark attacks along Australia's eastern seaboard.

Maybe the reason I'm such an advocate for banning shark cage diving is because I've come within a foot of a great white shark. What I saw terrified me. It happened off the New South Wales port town of Eden. I was shooting *Ancient Predators*, a film showcasing an assortment of exotic marine animals – moray eels, giant stingrays, cuttlefish, wobbegong sharks and many more. I decided to shoot in the vicinity of the wreck of the *Tasman Hauler*, a bulky tugboat scuttled in Twofold Bay in 1988. I brought Abraham Joffe along as my cameraman.

Diving a wreck with a heavy camera and casing poses some challenges. If the current is strong, gear can easily become entangled. These days, Abe is a confident diver, but back then, he was still a novice and I should've known that this was not a job for a beginner. In my defence, I couldn't have anticipated how bad the conditions were going to be.

Once again, we chartered a boat through a local dive school and had some hired hands to help. We tied off to a buoy that ran down to the wreck. A squally westerly was lifting a confused swell that brought my stomach up to my mouth. It was far worse below the waves. Before suiting up I could see that eddies were forming in the lee of our boat. There was a strong current running.

'When you jump in, grab the rope that leads down to the wreck,' I said to Abe. 'For God's sake, don't let it go. If you do, you'll be gone in the current.'

We dived off the boat and swam hard for the line. The waves and the current beat us back, but we eventually made it. Before slipping under, I reminded Abe to hang on tight during the descent. He nodded and down we went. It was incredibly hard work. We were like flags clinging to a pole in a gale.

At one point early in the dive, I became increasingly concerned that something wasn't right. My internal alarm was blaring out a warning. This was one of those times where I ignored the bad feeling. I guess I was just desperate for the footage. On we went.

In a matter of seconds, the sea was a mess of gelatinous streaks of white. We'd strayed into a minefield of jellyfish. They were big ones too, at least one yard across. Abe shot me a look, waiting for direction. I gave him the 'A-OK' sign. These were *Pelagia noctiluca*, jellies capable of delivering a nasty sting but nothing lethal.

We continued the descent, carefully avoiding the jellies' long tentacles. Once we were down to seventy feet, the current subsided. It was like the feeling you get on a plane, climbing through heavy turbulence before suddenly entering the stable air of the jet stream. It was now safe enough to let go of the rope.

The visibility at this depth was decent. I could see maybe twenty feet. The old tug emerged magically out of the depths. She was a big boat and in good condition. Her large hull and wheelhouse were covered in colourful sponges and anemones. At the bow of the boat, a huge octopus had wrapped himself around the handrail. It was exactly the sort of thing I was looking to shoot for the film.

I signalled for Abe to button on. Once I was next to the octopus, I very gently prised his tentacles off the handrail. There was no great resistance. The octopus allowed his freed tentacles to harmlessly drift about his head. Once I'd removed three tentacles, he became more responsive, releasing his grip on the handrail and circling around me. Very languidly, the octopus extended his eight arms towards my face before surging forward and wrapping his entire body around my head.

There was no cause for concern. I still had the regulator in my mouth and was breathing evenly. Although strong, his tentacles wouldn't have been able to strangle me, nor was there any risk of being bitten. In fact, I was delighted. The footage was going to be incredible.

The problem was the suckers on the octopus's tentacles. The octopus had a firm hold on my regulator and mask. I wasn't worried. If the octopus pulled them off, I could use my back-up regulator – ironically known to divers as the octopus reg or 'ockie'. But when I reached down for my ockie, the octopus had taken hold of that, too. In fact, every piece of my equipment was in the animal's grasp.

Now it was time to exert some strength. I ripped the ockie out of the tentacles and the octopus darted backwards, inking as he went. The sea around me turned black. When it cleared up, the octopus had disappeared. It was like a magic act.

It must've looked awesome on camera. But my elation was short-lived. Abe's free hand was flattened out and 'cutting' across his throat. It was the sign for *I'm out of air*. At a hundred feet, we were too deep to break for the surface. I could tell from the urgency in his hand motion and his football-sized eyes that he was not far from blacking out.

I swam across to assess the situation, motioning for him to stay calm. Everything appeared to be normal. There was no problem that I could see with his tank, hose and regulator. It wasn't until I looked at his mouth that I came upon the problem. The area around his lips was bright red and slightly swollen. My guess was that on the descent, a jellyfish had whipped its stinger across Abe's lips. His lips were numb and incapable of holding the regulator in place.

I pushed the regulator firmly into his mouth and bunched his lips up with my fingers. Abe took a breath. He gave me the thumbs up signal, indicating he wanted to ascend fast. I kept signalling for him to calm down. It took a while, but he managed to relax. I guided him towards the shot rope and started our ascent. It wasn't an easy decompression with the powerful current and the absolute plague of jellyfish. But we got to the surface eventually, pulling ourselves up onto the boat.

Through the entirety of that dive, the feeling of impending danger never left me. It had been a challenging dive, complete with a powerful current, a lot of jellies, an aggressive octopus and a near-fatal mishap with my cameraman. But those things weren't the cause of my worry. Something far deadlier was lurking in the vicinity of the ship.

The dramas with Abe meant I hadn't got nearly enough footage. We had to return the next day. We tied off on the shot rope and got ready. Abe was edgy.

'If we run into those jellies again,' I said to Abe, 'we'll abort.'

As soon as I was underwater, I was gripped with a feeling of dread. The conditions were worse than the previous day. The current was surging stronger than ever and the visibility was down to ten feet. I tried to convince myself that this was the source of my worry. God knows why I was trying to kid myself. In my heart of hearts I knew that something worse than the current was upsetting me. I guess I let my ambition overrule my instinct.

A few feet down, I clamped Abe's fingers around the rope, reminding him not to let go. I then signalled to descend. Slowly we went down, the internal alarm thundering in my head. My determination to get the footage was overriding my own instinctive awareness of danger.

Once again, the current became weaker the deeper we got. It was a relief when the wreck came into sight. I wanted to wrap this shoot up fast. We swam to the wheelhouse and peered inside. Groper and blue-headed wrasse were casually swimming within. Visibility was limited to the motes of light that came through the empty spaces where the wheelhouse windows were once located. Deeper inside the boat was nothing but hollow darkness.

Abe swam to the other side of the wheelhouse. The idea was that he would start shooting through the opposite porthole when I came swimming inside with my lights. When Abe was in place, he buttoned on and away I went. It wasn't easy to get through the porthole with my lights and camera housing. I was trying to work the camera through sideways when a horrible feeling enveloped me.

Maybe Abe was in danger. I looked up at him and signalled 'A-OK'. He responded in kind. I tried shaking it off. But I couldn't escape the feeling that death was very near. I was in the process of giving Abe the signal to abort the dive when a pressure wave rolled across me from behind. I turned around and stared right into the eye of an enormous great white shark.

The shark's head must've been four feet across at its widest point and the gills alone were probably three feet in length. It stared straight at me with its cold, dead eyes. I ripped the camera through the window, striking my funny bone on a steel porthole frame, and groaned. Here I was, two foot away from a great white shark, and I was more worried about the pain in my elbow.

I managed to get the camera through and lifted it up as the white turned around. I captured the *whoomp* of the tail, the pressure wave knocking me back hard against the bulkhead. I don't know why that white chose not to devour me at that moment. I may have scared it off when I struck the side of the wheelhouse. Whatever the reason, the shark's disappearance would only be temporary.

I wormed my way out of the wheelhouse and grabbed Abe by the wrist, swimming hard for the shot line. I could tell from the confused look in his eye that he hadn't seen that shark. Probably just as well. The last thing I needed was a panicked cameraman bolting for the surface. I wanted to convey a sense of urgency without causing him alarm, so I took Abe's hands and squeezed his fingers tight around the shot line. With my eyes I communicated a single message – *Don't you fucking let go of this line.*

Slowly, we worked our way up. It was the most torturous decompression I've ever done. Nothing could test a diver's nerve better than an ascent in a hundred feet of surging water with a great white shark in the vicinity. The visibility was atrocious and got worse with each passing minute. That big white might not have been able to see us but with its battery of senses it knew exactly where we were.

As we neared the surface, the current became more intense. Abe and I were like kites dancing in a cyclone, hanging on with every ounce of strength. We ascended to our safety stop at fifteen feet and waited for eight terrible minutes. We were at a depth where you can normally see the surface. But the water was so cloudy it was like diving at night. My fear was spiking. The urge to break for the surface was nearly impossible to resist.

Finally, we completed our decompression and made it to the buoy. Abe took hold of the ladder at the back of the boat while I grabbed hold of the backboard. Abe handed up his camera to one of the crewman while another reached down and took hold of mine.

At this point, Abe should've scurried up the ladder with his fins on. Instead, he took them off and handed them to the crewman. Not a second after he took off his second fin, a wave smashed into the side of the boat. Abe lost his grip on the ladder. In seconds, he was swept away ten feet. I couldn't fucking believe it!

Consider, for a moment, the great white shark's preferred delicacy: the seal. As air-breathing animals, the seal must regularly surface. A great white shark is a counter-shaded animal – white beneath, dark on top. It is virtually impossible to see from the surface. Using this camouflage to its advantage, the great white will circle below. Once it has fixed on the seal's position, the shark will perform a bounce dive – a sharp descent before a rapid ascent. The white strikes with tremendous speed, often launching the seal into the air before the hapless prey lands directly in the shark's jaws. The surface is the most dangerous place to be when a great white shark is lurking. Floundering about on the surface in our black wetsuits, guess what animal Abe and I both resembled?

I swam after Abe and managed to grab hold of him about forty feet from the boat. I swung around and screamed at him to start kicking. I gave everything I had, working my flippers like crazy. We went nowhere. It was like swimming upriver after a storm. By splashing around, all we were doing was giving away our position to the shark. I could almost sense the predator lining us up from below, winding up for a lightning attack.

The skipper of the boat threw us out a lifebuoy. We took hold and Abe and I were pulled to safety. Once we were aboard I gave Abe a frightful spray for letting go of the ladder. He looked at me completely dumbfounded. When I told him what I'd seen in the wreck, his face went grey.

That brush with the great white shark had given me a huge respect for these powerful predators. I was determined to feature sharks in the film, but not the white. They were too powerful, too unpredictable. The only way to film a great white shark with any degree of safety was in a cage. As an active campaigner against shark cages, that was obviously not an option. There was, however, another species of dangerous shark that could be filmed at close range in the wild: bull sharks.

28

The Sea God

I've been having brushes with bull sharks since the late seventies. My first run-in happened while spearfishing in New Caledonia, during the early days of Cronulla Dive. As was my custom back then, I'd take a couple of weeks off to spearfish some exotic locale in the South Pacific. I arrived in Nouméa and brokered a sweet deal with one of the resorts. I'd spearfish every morning and hand over my daily catch of fish – which they'd cook up for their guests – in exchange for a free room.

Waking up every day to beautiful weather and diving some of the most pristine waters in the world was my idea of paradise. I found a ledge that dropped down about 300 feet into an underwater gully just 400 yards out from a beach. This place was a magnet for marine life. There was no boat available so I'd have to swim out with spear gun, float and a bag, and drag my catch all the way back. Even in top physical condition, I'd still be exhausted once I made it ashore.

A few days into my working holiday, I headed out to the gully. I was out there in about fifteen minutes and immediately went to work. The wall of the ledge was the habitat for thousands of beautiful fish. Their scales reflected every colour of the rainbow. I didn't have great knowledge of fish beyond Australian waters. I was about to learn a valuable lesson about tropical fish – looks can be deceiving.

The first fish I lined up was a striking beauty with horizontal blue and white stripes about one foot in length. I speared it just behind the gills. I came up to the surface with the fish impaled on my pranger head and grabbed hold of it behind the tail. I winced as a sharp pain shot through my hand.

I'd caught a surgeonfish, named for the two scalpel-like blades protruding from the base of the body. One of the blades must've lacerated a small artery in my palm, because the wound was pumping out blood. The water around me turned red. While trying to stem the flow, I noticed a dark shadow pass beneath me.

There are two interesting points about a shark's sense of smell. First, it can detect one drop of blood in many litres of water. Second, they can pick up the scent of blood from 400 yards away. Considering I was completely immersed in my own blood, I was lucky that only one shark had picked up the scent.

Unluckily, I'd gotten the attention of a heavyset, blunt-nosed nine-foot bull shark. I abandoned the float bag, reloaded the gun and swam backwards towards the beach. The first attack came near the edge of the ledge in about ten feet of water. He came straight at me. I fended him off with the five-barbed pranger head. He swam away, obviously startled by the sharpness off the barbs. I knew he'd be back. They don't call them bull sharks for nothing. This species is famous for its aggression.

I'd barely swum twenty feet when he launched the second attack, this time from a steeper angle. Visibility in the water was excellent and I'd seen him coming from well off. I dug the pranger head hard into his nose. He retreated, circled around and then came back at me.

My heart rate was spiking, blood was spewing into the water and stirring up the bull shark even more. It didn't matter how hard

I stabbed him. This shark wanted me. When he came the seventh time, I tried to blind him. I launched the pranger head at the pupil of his right eye. An inch before I hit him, the shark's nictitating membrane – the translucent third eyelid – flicked up. The pranger head harmlessly bounced off his eye and my momentum threw me over the shark. He came within inches of taking a chunk out of my torso. I managed to fend him off with my other fist.

I can't tell you how many times that bull shark attacked me. The attacks kept coming right up to when I was standing in three feet of water. I crawled up the beach, completely spent. My hand was still bleeding and staining the white sand red. A local fisherman came down to help and provided first aid, New Caledonia style. He bathed my hand in methylated spirits and then stitched up the wound with two-pound fishing line. It was the most painful part of the day.

The incident in New Caledonia began my long association with bull sharks. Whenever I encountered them in the wild, I'd observe them closely, eventually becoming adept at reading their body language. I'd been keen to do a film on them for years. With the success of the Wildlife Man series, I now had the perfect platform. I also knew exactly where to find them.

For years, I'd heard divers talk about Beqa Lagoon in Fiji. Beqa Island is the quintessential South Pacific island paradise. Separated from the main island by ten miles of sea, Beqa is a mountainous little jungle paradise full of palm trees, white sandy beaches and clear pools. The lagoon is Beqa's centrepiece attraction. Home to an incredible array of marine life, the lagoon is also the playground of Fiji's famous shark men.

The shark is venerated in Fiji. On Beqa, the local inhabitants believe their ancestors were sharks that came out of the water. They also believe that when they die they are reborn as sharks. The faith in these beliefs is so strong that the young men of the island regularly dive down and feed the bull sharks frequenting the lagoon. The feeding has become a tourist attraction.

I needed my best cameramen for this job. You'd think it'd be hard finding a guy prepared to film man-eating sharks at close range. Well, it only took me one phone call. I guess that says something about the kind of company I keep! Mark Mountain, an old student of mine, leapt at the chance. Mark and I flew out to Beqa Lagoon, barely able to contain our excitement.

The first time I saw the shark-feeding at Beqa was as a tourist diver with no camera. The feeding takes place at the base of a hundred-foot coral wall at the edge of the lagoon. The locals have painstakingly created a four-foot high coral barrier about ten yards from the base of the wall. Tourist divers are instructed to remain behind the barrier at all times. Three shark men, meanwhile, swim beyond the barrier to a large bin that has been lowered from the boat. The bin is full of tuna and barracuda heads. One shark man, the designated feeder of the day, pulls the lid off the bin while the other two guys take up position either side with four-foot long metal rods. These two men serve as defenders.

The moment the lid was off, the sleek-lined bodies of tawny nurse sharks appeared. They were great entertainment, darting in at the food with lightning speed, even trying to get into the bins to feed. Although you wouldn't want to get your arm stuck in the jaws of a tawny nurse shark, they're not particularly dangerous to humans.

The bull shark is a different story. The sea felt as if it had been charged with electricity when the first bull shark muscled his way through the pack of tawnies for the food. There were dozens of them. They'd come in for the food one at a time. For an aggressive animal, the sharks were incredibly well behaved. They practically lined up in an orderly queue, took their food from the feeder and disappeared into the deep blue. Feeding was pretty gutsy stuff, considering the shark men had nothing but steel mesh gloves and metal rods to defend themselves.

You might think the shark men were being recklessly stupid. After all, bull sharks are extremely dangerous, responsible for many human fatalities. But what I was witnessing was actually quite safe.

It's no fluke that not one shark man has been killed while feeding bull sharks in the Beqa Lagoon. Part of the reason is the poise of the feeder. His relaxed demeanour projects an aura of calm that placates the normally aggressive animals. The shark men either side of the feeder are also vitally important, not simply in defending the feeder, but also in conditioning the sharks' behaviour. If a shark approaches too quickly, becomes aggressive or tries to jump the queue by coming in on the side, the defenders give it a stiff prod in the nose. Unless the sharks approach the feeder calmly and from head on, they won't be fed.

When we returned to the beach, the shark men offered me the chance to film them doing a feed from behind the four-foot wall. I had something else in mind. I wanted to position myself in front of the shark men so that the bull sharks would have to swim past me to get the food. The shark men didn't like it at all.

'It isn't wise to stand between the bull shark and his food,' they said. 'You will make him angry.'

That's exactly what I was hoping to do. Despite the fact that the sharks could easily get around me, I was creating an obstacle. The idea was to stimulate territorial attacks. I'd effectively be challenging them for their own bait. If a shark perceives a living thing as a threat, it will try to kill it.

The shark men reluctantly agreed. Mark sat back behind the four-foot barrier so he could film everything from afar. The shark men then swam out to the bin after it was lowered. Before the lid was taken off, I swam beyond them holding my camera with lights. I gave the signal to start the feeding and then buttoned on.

There must've been thirty-five bull sharks that came into the lagoon that day. Every single one of them wanted a piece of me. I was going to stand my ground no matter what. I wanted to exert an aura of indestructibility and dominance. I'd use my camera as a shield, bumping them off when they came too close or lunged for me.

The sharks were not deterred. They'd come at me two or three at a time from every angle. One second, the attack came from my left, the next from my right. Sometimes they looped around me and came in from behind. The shark men were gobsmacked. They couldn't understand how I knew where the attacks were coming from.

By now, I'd learnt to tap into those deep feelings, to obey my instincts. I was so calm, so in tune with my senses, that I knew exactly where the sharks were at any given moment. It wouldn't matter if a shark attacked from a blind spot. I'd always turn around and meet the attack before it was too late. And the camera captured it all.

It was the purest demonstration in my film career of the fact that we've been gifted with a primal instinct for danger. I *knew* when those sharks were coming. It was just a matter of focus and concentration. I became so accomplished at bumping them away that I felt like I was operating in slow motion. Watching the footage each night was staggering. I couldn't believe how fast everything happened.

It was as exhilarating as it was exhausting. We filmed twice a day for two weeks, accumulating more than enough footage to make a film. I was becoming seriously fatigued. Mark was getting worried that I was pushing my luck. But I just didn't feel like we had the big climax.

Sure enough, on day fifteen, the biggest bull shark I've ever seen turned up. It was a big female, at least twelve feet in length, two foot longer than the average adult. The locals believed that this shark was the incarnation of Dakuwanga, the Fijian shark god.

It was like being back in the blood drain when Fergus turned up. The lesser creatures disappeared. I signalled to the crew to keep close watch. Something big was about to happen. The beast swept in low from my left, hitting my raised camera with incredible force. It was the first of several quickfire attacks. I managed to parry her away, but her bulk knocked me backwards. Not only was she strong, she was incredibly fast.

She also proved to be cunning. After a couple of minutes of relentless attacking, Dakuwanga disappeared. I could feel myself beginning to panic. There's no way she'd leave so quickly, not without having something to eat. I scanned the seabed, but there was nothing. Then it came to me, the instinctive voice in my head screaming out two words: *Look up!* I raised the camera above my head milliseconds before the big shark was on me. Not once in the past two weeks had a bull shark pulled a vertical dive. I never even knew it was possible. She hit my camera casing harder than ever, causing my knees to buckle in the seabed. But I managed to keep her at bay.

It was the final attack. Convinced that she couldn't beat me, Dakuwanga turned her mind to food. The footage I got of her feeding would rank among some of my greatest professional achievements. In the narration, I described Dakuwanga as a masterpiece of evolution, an animal deserving of our respect and protection. She was almost certainly the largest bull shark ever caught on camera.

I named the film *Sea God* and it was a huge ratings success. Mark became my number one cameraman from then on. We went on countless film expeditions together; his skills and courage allowing me to capture some of my most action-packed and dangerous animal encounters.

Life was better than good. It was fantastic! I was at the top of my game. At home, life couldn't have been better. The boys were all doing well, forging their identities and excelling as they created their own paths. Our finances were back on track too. Sue and I were looking for a new house to rent. Everything was humming along nicely. Until it all came to a screaming halt . . .

29

The Next Challenge

Life, just like the tide, ebbs and flows.

One minute, you're summiting the peaks of professional success and great happiness; the next, you're shattered on the jagged rocks of failure, tragedy and despair. What defines us as people is how we respond when the tide turns against us. Do you crumble in the face of adversity and hardship or do you dig deep and hang tough? It's a question you can only answer in the moment, when life deals you a lousy hand. But there's no escaping the fact that at some point along the journey, you will be tested.

I was tested on a day that began full of promise. It was a gorgeous summer's morning, hardly a breath of wind – perfect weather to set the motorbike loose. I was meeting a group of mates on the Cronulla foreshore from where we'd set off on a ride down the coast. I showered, got dressed and then cooked up a hot breakfast. Before setting off, I went to the toilet. Suddenly, my world turned on its head. The toilet bowl was splattered with blood.

I went to the computer and entered 'passing blood' into a Google search. A number of ailments that present this symptom were listed. The number one result was bowel cancer. Let's not sugarcoat it – bowel cancer is a horrible way to die. An associate of mine was diagnosed with bowel cancer shortly after turning sixty-two. One minute he was fighting fit, the next he had sections of his intestine and stomach removed. The last time I saw him he'd been fitted with a stoma bag to catch his excreta. Four months later he was dead.

I'll admit it: I was bloody terrified. I didn't want to scare Sue, so I drove straight to Sutherland Hospital emergency alone. A doctor was sent down. He was very concerned that whatever was bleeding might rupture and haemorrhage. I could bleed to death.

I was sent upstairs and handed a hospital gown. They put me on a drip and started doing tests – blood tests, heart rate, an ECG and God knows what else. Everything checked out fine. For now, the bleeding had stopped. But the doctor wanted to have a look around inside.

I was wheeled into another room, knocked out and a camera was sent down my mouth. When I woke up, the doctor delivered the first positive news of the day – he'd seen nothing. But I wasn't out of the woods yet. He'd booked me in for a colonoscopy two days hence. This, he told me, would reveal what to do next. I felt like the accused being sent off by the judge as the jury deliberated on the verdict.

I drove home barely comprehending what was happening. A day earlier, I had been as healthy as a person can be for my age group. If I wasn't in the gym doing weights, I was outside running, rowing or diving. I ate well and I'd never smoked. If I had a vice, it was a beer or two after a gym session. Now I was facing the real prospect of being told my days were numbered.

I got no sleep the night before the colonoscopy. The dreadful concoction I'd been instructed to drink had brought on diarrhoea to flush everything out. My guts felt like they were on fire. I spent the night staring up at the ceiling, just like I did when I was experiencing an asthma attack in my youth. There was no constriction in my chest, but the storm clouds were gathering.

Memories of my father's death resurfaced. I'd seen how cancer had eaten him away, made his last years agony. The prospect of pain and death was scary. But my greatest fear was for my family. Sue, Nat, Jason and I had only just settled into our new rented house in Cronulla, a beautiful two-storey home with a view of the Pacific. As always, the rent needed to be paid. I knew from firsthand experience how tough it is on those left behind when the breadwinner checks out.

It was at that horrible moment when a familiar voice spoke to me. The voice belonged to the person who'd guided me through my darkest days since primary school bullies had tormented me: Don Athaldo. He was instructing me to slow my breathing, to believe in myself and to be brave. I calmed down, found my reserve of courage and mastered my fear. No matter what happened tomorrow, this was how I planned to meet my fate. If the prognosis was grim, I'd carry on doing what I'd been doing pretty much my whole life – I'd dig deep and fight.

I arrived at the hospital for the procedure with my emotions in check. I felt completely at ease. The anaesthetist took my heart rate and couldn't believe the result.

'You've got a resting pulse of forty-six beats per minute,' she said. 'You're either very fit or very sick.'

She did an ECG and concluded that I had a very strong heart.

'You know, I can slow it down more,' I said. I shut my eyes and dropped my heart rate to forty-two beats per minute. The anaesthetist smiled in disbelief.

'Are you some sort of crocodile?' she asked.

I was wheeled into the theatre. The anaesthetist, the doctor and nurses were all gathered around. As the anaesthetic was delivered, the doctor started asking me questions.

'What's your name?'

'David Ireland.'

'What suburb do you live in?'

'Caringbah.'

'Why are you here?'

'Penis reduction.'

That's the last thing I remember. I woke into that strange daze that happens after being anaesthetised. Otherwise I was fine. No wires hanging off me. I felt good. There was another guy in my room who'd just had the same procedure. He seemed okay too. Eventually the doctor walked in with a serious look on his face. He drew the curtain around my bed.

'David,' he said. 'We found nothing. No polyps. Nothing. You look to be in 100 per cent health.'

The doctor concluded that the blood was probably from a burst vessel. There was nothing to worry about at all. I sighed, utterly relieved. Once in the car, I got on the phone, rang my family and told them to come around for dinner. I was in the mood for celebration.

It was one of the greatest nights of my life. From the head of the table, I cast my eyes around the room. My four sons were all laughing along with their beautiful partners. Luke and Brooke had brought my grandkids, Oscar and Harvey, along. They call me Poppy Croc and they were absolutely stealing the show, as they always do. Adam was with his beautiful new wife, Megan, laughing along with Nathan as he cracked jokes. Jason, meanwhile, was being cheeky as always! My dear old mum, fighting fit at ninety-three years of age, was smiling quietly in the corner keeping watch over proceedings.

Then I locked eyes with Sue. Damn, I owe so much to this wonderful woman! I marvel at how she has tolerated all my crazy adventures over the years. She knew she was marrying a free-spirited bloke, but I wonder if she knew how wild that spirit would get? Her support and love for me has defied belief at times and she has done it while bringing up four boys and turning them into the kind of young men that make fathers flush with pride. My greatest achievement was gathered together in that room. It's an achievement that's far from my own, but shared with the woman sitting at the other end of the table.

Something happened to me in that moment; a new challenge was forming in my mind. I'd heard this is what occurs when a person thinks the end is near. The things that *really* matter in life are brought sharply into focus. I had a new lease on life and felt an incredible sense of gratitude. And not only because my health scare had proven to be a false alarm.

I realised just how lucky I'd been to have so many positive influences throughout my life. I wouldn't be half the man I am today without the strength of my old man, the courage of my mother, the unconditional love of my wife, the support of countless friends and family, and the inspiration of a circus strongman. I'm not saying that I haven't worked hard towards my dreams. But I'm the first to acknowledge that I've had help along the way.

I was taken by a sudden desire to help other people overcome their challenges. I've always tried to give something back, making myself available to speak to all manner of groups – schoolkids, people with special needs, the blind, the elderly and many more. Now I wanted to do something bigger. Much bigger . . .

It seems to me that the world is in the grip of an epidemic. Bullying has infiltrated every part of our lives. Whether it happens at school, in the workplace or at home, these are all variations on the same thing: the strong prey on the weak. You could say that I know a few things about bullies. I know how they instil fear and crush your spirit. I also know that bullies can be beaten by self-belief and courage. I learnt this from a long-dead circus strongman whose lessons came to underpin my personal philosophy.

My plan is to take Don Athaldo's message through schools and universities. It'll be more than just a self-help lecture. It'll be a fully-fledged Wildlife Man show, a live presentation with a focus on how to overcome bullies and how to achieve your dreams. I want people to hear the message that I was told when I was a scared and tormented little boy. I want them to know that each of us has incredible reserves of courage, that nobody can stop us from being who we want to be, that when you work hard and dream big, anything is possible.

There are a lot of people struggling out there: people with confidence issues, people who are tormented by others, people scared of their own voice and people who've given up on their dreams. If you're one of those people, then listen up.

About a month after getting the all clear from the hospital, I received an email from a major feature film producer in the US. The email went as follows –

Hi David,

I've been a fan of your films on Discovery Channel America
for years. If you can get your life story published, I believe it
would make for a wonderful movie. If you ever do, send me a
copy.

Cast your mind back to that little kid in bed, wrapped up in the sheets, his face turning blue as he struggled to breathe; the kid who was bullied and caned at school, and told he'd never acheive anything. If you'd told that kid that his life story would one day be worthy of a book – and maybe even a feature film – he'd have said you were insane.

Like I said, if you believe in the courage that is within us all, anything is possible!

Acknowledgements

My thanks and acknowledgements go to the following people:

Tom Trumble, whose passion and way with words allowed my story to be told. Tom gave up a lot of his time to write my story, he is one of Australia's best. I have great respect for him. My wife Susan for her devotion, love and support. She is my rock and I love her deeply. My sons, Luke, Adam, Nathan and Jason. My boys are my best friends, they enrich my life in so many ways. I love them and am so proud of their achievements. My mother Lotus, such a wise, courageous and wonderful mother, she has been a totally devoted mum, I love her with all my heart. Don Athaldo, the circus strongman who changed my body and mind. Without Don Athaldo I would never have become The Wildlife Man.

My film crews, who have had to work in some of the most remote regions of Australia, Asia, the Pacific and Africa. They have had to film me working with some extremely dangerous animals, often only a few feet from the action. We work in a diversity of environments, from steaming hot jungles and deserts to underwater shipwrecks and shark habitats without a cage. The following people have been part of my film crew: Fred Harris, Mark Mountain, Neil Thomas, Grant Hassall, Jason Turl, Mark Oldfield and Sue Ireland, my wonderful wife.

My sponsors, who contribute greatly to the funding of my Wildlife Man films. Without this funding any film production would be impossible. My principal sponsor is David Auger, the owner of the Australian company Pro-Tactical. Pro-Tactical not only supply financial funding for my films, but also a range of products, everything from camo clothing to spotlights. I have a huge amount of respect for David and highly recommend the quality of his products. Other sponsors include Apex Hunting, Australia's leading archery supply company, Ikelite, Canon, Panasonic, Akubra, KMart Tyres, Kakadu Clothing, Riffe, Big Blue Dive Lights, Mala Mala Game Reserve, Sabi Sabi Game Reserve, Strathburn Station, Lady Elliott Island, Merluna Station and Lorella Springs.

Wildlife Man films are available on DVD from:
www.wildlifeman.myshopify.com and www.davidireland.com